Retired Numbers

Retired Numbers

A Celebration of NHL Excellence

ANDREW PODNIEKS

Fenn Publishing Company Ltd.

Fenn Publishing Company Ltd.

A Fenn Publishing Book / First Published in 2010

Fenn Publishing Company Ltd.
Bolton, Ontario, Canada
www.hbfenn.com

The publisher gratefully acknowledges the support of the Canada Council for the Arts and the Ontario Arts Council for its publishing program. We acknowledge the support of the Government of Ontario through the Ontario Media Development Corporation's Ontario Book Initiative.

**ONTARIO ARTS COUNCIL
CONSEIL DES ARTS DE L'ONTARIO**

We acknowledge the financial support of the Government of Canada through the Canada Book Fund (CBF) for our publishing activities. Care has been taken to trace ownership of copyright material in this book and to secure permissions. The publishers will gladly receive any information that will enable them to rectify errors or omissions.

Text design: Marijke Friesen
Printed and bound in Canada

Library and Archives Canada Cataloguing in Publication

Podnieks, Andrew
    Retired numbers / Andrew Podnieks.

ISBN 978-1-55168-347-8

    1. National Hockey League—Biography. 2. National Hockey League—History. 3. Hockey players—Biography. I. Title.

GV848.5.A1P64 2010   796.962092'2   C2010-902031-6

Printed and bound in Canada
10 11 12 13 14 5 4 3 2 1

FSC
Mixed Sources
Cert no. SW-COC-001271
© 1996 FSC

CONTENTS

INTRODUCTION

RETIRING SWEATER NUMBERS became an important and common practice as the 20th century unfolded, and continues to be so today. Teams want to honour their greatest players in a way that does justice to the past and ensures the present and future are treated with the same respect, and so they give a player and his family a special night of recognition at centre ice and then raise to the rafters a banner with his name and number on it.

The tradition of retiring numbers has undergone significant changes from the early days to the more recent epic ceremony for Steve Yzerman. In the early days, many players were given a special night instead of having their number retired. This consisted of a ceremony before a game or often during the first intermission when he'd be feted, given some presents, and then watched the game.

Over time, these nights went out of fashion and teams felt if a player were deserving of such an honour he would, indeed, have his number retired. The retiring of the number originally took the form of the player being given his actual playing sweater as a way of saying, "Here—take this. It's the only one in existence and we won't make a new one for anyone else."

Today, of course, the "game-worn sweater" is big business, and players wear many sweaters every season in the name of charity, collectors, and personal archives. Perhaps partly because of this the tradition evolved to having a banner raised to the rafters and having the player's family and friends attend the increasingly lavish on-ice ceremony.

With the advent of video screens with the scoreboard above centre ice, video tributes and messages often led off the evening. And when the Detroit Red Wings retired Yzerman's number 19, they went to such an extreme that the NHL imposed a rule whereby the start of games could no longer be delayed by retired-numbers ceremonies. The Wings brought out many red carpets, a dais for speeches, many members of the organization, many family and friends. In all, the game was delayed by some 90 minutes.

Retired Numbers looks at the history of these players and ceremonies. It celebrates the careers of the NHL's greatest players but also examines the history of the ceremonies. And there have been many a strange one along the way. Of course, we all know Bobby Orr's number 4 was retired, but how many people know (or remember) that the ceremony occurred prior to an exhibition game against a touring Soviet team?

Thomas Steen's number was retired in Winnipeg after the team left for Phoenix, so once the ceremony was over, everyone went home—there was no game to cap off the evening. Peter Stastny was in a similar position in Quebec City, but the city at least held an alumni game in his honour to beef up the evening. Some teams retired two numbers on the same night. Some retired a number and had a ceremony years or even decades later.

And then there's the question of how many or who should receive the honour. Terry O'Reilly's number 24 is retired by Boston, yet he is nowhere to be seen on the Honour Roll of the Hockey Hall of Fame. His number was retired in honour of his contributions to the team and in recognition of his place in the sporting history of that city, not the league or the game in general. A few numbers are retired (formally or informally) because the player died in mid-career. In these cases the honour is given partly out of respect, partly superstition. (No player would ever assume the number of a dead person for fear of succumbing to the same fate.)

The Montreal problem is also worth considering. The Canadiens have won more Stanley Cups than any other team and have arguably more great players in its team history than any other NHL team, but it has now retired some 16 numbers. There is an aesthetic consideration here. Players who wear the traditional great numbers like 4 or 7 or 9 simply look better. Today Montreal has players wearing numbers including 46, 61, and 75, truly "ugly" numbers without the historical assocations of the classic digits, and which one could never envision in the rafters alongside le Rocket, le Roadrunner, and le Gros Bill.

In short, if this evermore popular trend to retire numbers continues, all the "good" numbers will be out of circulation. The Toronto Maple Leafs have inadvertently stumbled on a compromise, "honouring" their numbers with ceremony and banner but keeping the number in circulation. This came about because long-time owner Harold Ballard hated honouring the past and never gave due respect to former players, so over time so many players later wore a great one's number it seemed ridiculous to take it out of circulation after he died. Some say this is sacrilegious; others call it a practical and commonsense solution.

To date, NHL teams have retired more than 100 numbers officially and many others unofficially. The history is fascinating and the players themselves form the very core of the game's greatness from 1917 to the present.

Andrew Podnieks
August 2010

6

IRVINE "ACE" BAILEY

TORONTO MAPLE LEAFS
FEBRUARY 14, 1934

Born: Bracebridge, Ontario, July 3, 1903
Died: Toronto, Ontario, April 7, 1992
Position: Right wing
Shoots: Right
Height: 5'10"
Weight: 160 lbs.

HONOURS
- **Stanley Cup** 1932
- **Paul Whiteman High Scoring Trophy** (most goals) 1929
- **Hockey Hall of Fame** 1975

NHL CAREER STATS

	Regular Season					Playoffs				
Years	GP	G	A	P	Pim	GP	G	A	P	Pim
1926–34	313	111	82	193	472	21	3	4	7	12

CAREER

Ace Bailey's number 6 was the first number to be retired in the NHL, the result of both his fantastic career with the Maple Leafs and the fact that it was cut short in his prime after a near-fatal accident on ice.

The night of December 12, 1933, literally changed the history of hockey. In a Toronto-Boston game at the Garden, Eddie Shore was given a rough ride by Red Horner. But when Shore turned around to see who had hit him, he spotted Bailey first and went after him. Shore flipped Bailey from behind, and the Leafs forward landed hard on his head. Horner then knocked Shore unconscious with one punch, and in a heartbeat two great players lay on the ice bleeding from their heads.

Shore recovered quickly, but Bailey did not. He was rushed to hospital and underwent emergency surgery to take pressure off his brain. It was weeks before he could be sent home, months before he recovered with metal plates inserted into his

skull for support. His career was unquestionably over.

Bailey played seven and a half seasons in the NHL, all with the Leafs. A winger, he had great speed and a terrific shot. From the 1928–29 season through to 1930–31, he scored 22, 22, and 23 goals, which were remarkable numbers for the era. In fact, he was awarded the 1929 Paul Whiteman Trophy as the league's top goal scorer. But the true crowning moment of Bailey's career came in 1932 when the Leafs, playing their first season at the palatial Maple Leaf Gardens, won the Stanley Cup.

Oddly, Bailey's is the only number 6 that has been retired by an NHL team. Later in life, in the 1960s, he took a liking to rookie Ron Ellis and approved of Ellis wearing the number. As it turned out, Ellis enjoyed a two-part, 16-year career with the Leafs, so it wasn't until he retired for good in late 1980 that the number was taken out of circulation once and for all.

CEREMONY

Bailey's number was retired prior to a benefit game held in his honour at Maple Leaf Gardens on February 14, 1934. The Leafs arranged to play a charity game featuring an all-star team of the best players from the other teams with profits going to Bailey and his family. Thus began the annual All-Star Game. Prior to the match, the all-stars skated onto the ice in their club sweaters and had a group photo taken.

Then, league president Frank Calder, along with Lester Patrick and Leafs officials, handed each player his all-star sweater as he was introduced by Foster Hewitt. During the player introductions, Bailey shook Shore's hand, and the crowd erupted in a frenzy of celebration for the gesture of forgiveness. The ceremonies concluded with Leafs owner Conn Smythe presenting Bailey with his number 6 sweater, saying, "Allow me to present this sweater to you that you have worn so long and nobly for the Maple Leafs. No other player will ever use this number on the Maple Leaf hockey team." And so it was that the first number in NHL history was retired.

NOTE: Although this marked the retiring of the number 6, it wasn't actually raised to the rafters of Maple Leaf Gardens until October 17, 1992, alongside Bill Barilko's number 5.

THE GAME: Toronto Maple Leafs 7–NHL All-Stars 3

It was this inaugural All-Star Game that established the unwritten no-hitting rule for all future matches. Over the course of the evening, not a single infraction was whistled by referees Bobby Hewitson and Mike Rodden, but there were 10 goals scored. The Leafs jumped out into a quick 2–0 lead, but by the midway point in the game the All-Stars had tied it, 3–3. It was all Leafs after that. Hap Day made it 4–3 at 11:13 of the second period, and then Hec Kilrea, Ken Doraty, and Andy Blair scored unanswered goals in the third to make it a 7–3 win for the club team.

The All-Stars represented a who's who of future Hall of Famers, from Shore to goalie Charlie Gardiner, Howie Morenz, Aurèle Joliat, Lionel Conacher, and Hooley Smith, to name but a few. Such was the success of this format that when the league and players strove to establish a pension fund for the players, they chose an All-Star Game format as the means to generate revenue for the cause (starting in 1947).

Ace Bailey shakes hands with Eddie Shore.

3 LIONEL HITCHMAN

BOSTON BRUINS
FEBRUARY 22, 1934

Born: Toronto, Ontario, November 3, 1901
Died: Glen Falls, New York, December 19, 1968
Position: Defence
Shoots: Left
Height: 6'1"
Weight: 170 lbs.

HONOURS
- Stanley Cup 1923, 1929
- Played all but 39 career games with Boston

NHL CAREER STATS

	Regular Season					Playoffs				
Years	GP	G	A	P	Pim	GP	G	A	P	Pim
1922–34	417	28	34	62	523	35	3	1	4	73

CAREER

In his 10 years with Boston during the team's earliest days, Lionel Hitchman paired with Eddie Shore on the blue line to form one of the most effective tandems in league history. Both were tough as nails in their own end, and as play moved forward it was Shore who followed and Hitchman who hung back.

Hitchman had been an RCMP officer in Ottawa before being recruited by Senators general manager Tommy Gorman. It was a fortuitous signing, for Hitchman helped the Senators win the Stanley Cup in his first season, 1922–23. Less than two years later, though, the cash-poor team had to sell Hitchman to Boston, and it was with the Bruins he played the remaining years of his NHL career.

The Bruins won the Cup in 1929, and Hitchman and partner Shore were front and centre. Hitchman had been named captain in 1927, the first Bruins player so

honoured (it had no captain from its inaugural season in 1924), a title he held for four years. By the time he retired in 1934, his 523 career penalty minutes ranked him number one on the all-time list.

CEREMONY

The honours were emceed by Frankie Ryan and began with a moment that the Edmonton Oilers—surely unintentionally—mimicked decades later. Hitchman took a faceoff at centre ice and went in alone and scored a goal. In fact, this was a set up, but he also played this game, the final of his NHL career.

After the fancy play, Hitchman received plenty of gifts, starting with a plaque engraved with all his pertinent statistical and biographical information. He got two $500 cheques: one from the Bruins' fans and another from team president Charles Adams. Art Ross gave him a small chest full of silver, and then it was down to the business of playing the game.

The ceremony wasn't so much about formally retiring Hitchman's number 3 as it was a celebration of his career. But after this game, no Bruins player ever wore number 3 again. Hitchman's father, Edward, was at his son's side for the ceremony.

THE GAME: Ottawa Senators 3–Boston Bruins 1
Some 8,000 fans were on hand for the special night, only to see the Bruins extend their winless streak to six games. They were the last of four teams in the American Division standings with only 29 points, well behind the Rangers and Black Hawks with 45 points each and first place Detroit at 48 points.

Nick Wasnie got the opening goal at 6:41 when he stole the puck from Eddie Shore and beat Cecil "Tiny" Thompson before the goalie could get set for the shot. The next 45 minutes or so were goalless, and it wasn't until 11:44 of the third period that Dit Clapper tied the game for the Bruins.

In this era, a mandatory 10-minute overtime followed a tie game after 60 minutes, and in the extra session the Senators scored twice, Syd Howe and Bill "Flash" Hollett scoring the goals to provide the visitors with a victory.

7 HOWIE **MORENZ**

MONTREAL CANADIENS
NOVEMBER 3, 1937

Born: Mitchell, Ontario, June 21, 1902
Died: Montreal, Quebec, March 8, 1937
Position: Centre
Shoots: Left
Height: 5'9"
Weight: 165 lbs.

HONOURS
- **Stanley Cup** 1924, 1930, 1931
- **Hart Trophy** 1928, 1931, 1932
- **Led league in scoring** 1928, 1931
- **Hockey Hall of Fame** 1945

NHL CAREER STATS

	Regular Season					Playoffs				
Years	GP	G	A	P	Pim	GP	G	A	P	Pim
1923–37	550	271	201	472	546	39	13	9	22	58

CAREER

Even though he played two seasons with other teams, Howie Morenz was, is, and always will be considered a Montreal Canadiens forward. The most exciting skater of his era, he brought the crowds to their feet every time he rushed the puck up ice. Morenz began with the Habs in 1923–24, winning a Cup at the end of his rookie season. He played his last game in early 1937. His shocking death just two months later left the city in mourning, but his memory continues to live on decades later.

Morenz first played serious hockey in Stratford with a local team named the Midgets, and such was his skating that he quickly earned the nickname "Stratford Streak." He was only 21 when he entered the NHL, but in his second season he scored 28 goals, a fantastically high number for this time. In 1927–28, he led the league in both goals (33) and points (51), and he helped the Habs win the Cup twice more, in 1930 and 1931.

Playing on a line with Aurèle Joliat and Billy Boucher, Morenz was riveting to watch. He skated with abandon, blazing by opponents through sheer speed. In his first decade in the NHL he was among the top-10 scorers every year. But when the Habs had the chance to acquire Lionel Conacher from Chicago, they traded Morenz to the Black Hawks. The deal stunned fans and teammates, and no player wore the number 7 during his absence; indeed, the sweater hung at his stall, untouched. When Cecil Hart became Montreal's new general manager in 1936, he vowed to bring Morenz "home," which he did, in time for the 1936–37 season.

It was a short-lived resurrection, however. On January 28, 1937, in a game against Chicago, he lost his balance and his skate got caught in a gap in the wood boards. His leg was shattered in several places, ending his career.

Morenz never left the hospital to which he was carried after the accident. His room became a giant reception for friends and well-wishers, but the atmosphere was hardly conducive to recuperation. He suffered a heart attack and died two months later, his hospital room excesses having masked the extreme depression he felt from the injury and the end of his playing days.

CEREMONY

Prior to the Howie Morenz Memorial Game, an NHL official presented trophy winners from the previous season with their wares. However, the Honourable E. L. Patenaude, Quebec's lieutenant-governor, and Montreal mayor Adhemar Raynault, joined NHL president Frank Calder in the proceedings for Morenz. At the same ceremony, Detroit Red Wing Normie Smith won the Vezina Trophy; his teammate Marty Barry won the Lady Byng; and, the Canadiens' Babe Siebert was awarded the Hart Trophy.

During the first intermission all of Morenz's equipment, including sweater, were auctioned off, but former Canadiens owner Joe Cattarinich bought everything for $500 and then presented the purchase to Howie Morenz, Jr. And so it was that the number 7 went into retirement, never to be seen or worn again by a Canadiens player.

THE GAME: NHL All-Stars 6–Montreal All-Stars 5

The memorial game pitted the best players from the two Montreal teams—Maroons and Canadiens—against the best from the rest of the league. Not surprisingly, it was a high-scoring game with the NHLers coming out on top by a single goal.

Johnny Gagnon of the Canadiens got the opening goal, but the NHLers came back with two of their own before the end of the first, the Bruins' Dit Clapper and the Black Hawks' Johnny Gottselig beating Montreal goalie Wilf Cude.

In the second period, the Rangers' Cecil Dillon got the lone goal of the second to open a two-goal cushion, and the NHLers blew the game open in the third, running their lead to 6–2. It was only three late goals from Montreal that made the score closer, Babe Siebert, Johnny Gagnon, and Paul Haynes all scoring in the final four minutes. The Montrealers continued a furious rally in the dying moments but couldn't beat Tiny Thompson for the tying goal.

5 AUBREY "DIT" CLAPPER

BOSTON BRUINS
FEBRUARY 12, 1947

Born: Newmarket, Ontario, February 9, 1907
Died: Peterborough, Ontario, January 21, 1978
Position: Forward/Defence
Shoots: Right
Height: 6'2"
Weight: 195 lbs.

HONOURS
- **Stanley Cup** 1929, 1939, 1941
- **NHL All-Star Game** 1937, 1939
- **NHL First All-Star Team** 1939, 1940, 1941
- **Hockey Hall of Fame** 1947

NHL CAREER STATS

Years	Regular Season					Playoffs				
	GP	G	A	P	Pim	GP	G	A	P	Pim
1927–47	833	228	246	474	462	82	13	17	30	50

CAREER

One of the greatest players from the early years of the Boston Bruins, Dit Clapper was a top goal scorer in the league who later converted to defence to extend his career. He was only 20 years old when he started to play with the Bruins, and he starred with the team for the next two decades, becoming, in fact, the first player to play for 20 years in the NHL. And all with the Bruins.

Clapper was the right winger on the Dynamite Line, so called because of their scoring exploits. His line mates included Cooney Weiland and Dutch Gainor, and together they led the Bruins to a Stanley Cup in 1929. The next year, Clapper recorded 41 goals in just 44 games, second in the league to Weiland's 43.

Clapper was named captain in 1932 and remained so until 1947 (with one exception—1938–39, when Weiland assumed the duties). Starting in 1937, however, his scoring production dropped by half. The team was particularly thin on

defence, so Clapper moved back and paired with the great Eddie Shore. The move paid nearly immediate dividends as the Bruins won the Cup in 1939 and 1941.

In 1945, the team called on Clapper to assume double duty of player and coach, and for the next season and a bit he did just that. In all, he coached for four years, but the greatest night of his life came on February 12, 1947, when he was honoured by the team and inducted into the Hockey Hall of Fame at the same time.

CEREMONY

In the days when there was no set ceremony to retire a number, each team did its own thing. For Boston, on this night, they honoured Dit Clapper without actually raising his number to the rafters. Even more incredible by today's standards, the night held in his honour was also in part for Clapper's induction into the Hockey Hall of Fame mere months after he had played his final game.

Clapper was honoured at centre ice and given many presents, the most noteworthy of which was $2,000 in treasury bonds from the Bruins' fans. He wore his number 5 sweater for the ceremony and was given a hearty ovation by the capacity crowd of 13,900.

NOTE: Forty years later, Boston lured Guy Lapointe from Montreal and created controversy by allowing him to wear Clapper's number for a brief period. Reactions were so fiercely negative, however, that Lapointe didn't use it for long.

THE GAME:

Boston Bruins 10–New York Rangers 1

In the most one-sided number retirement game ever played, the Bruins scored early, regularly, and often, cruising to an easy win over the Rangers in Clapper's honour. The top story of the game was Bill Cowley, who had a goal and an assist to give him 574 points making him the all-time leading scorer in NHL history. He had been tied with Syd Howe at 572 (regular season and playoffs combined).

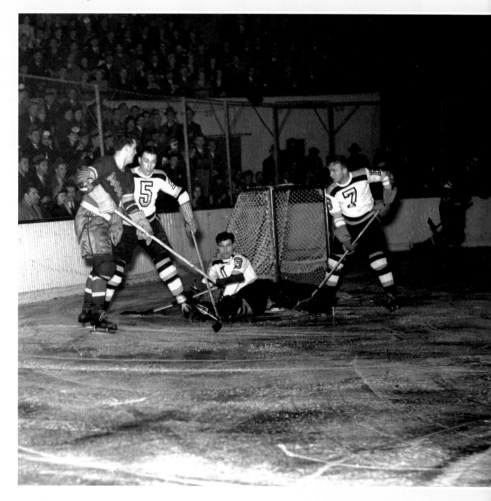

The Bruins scored three times in the first period thanks to Ken Reardon, Don Gallinger, and Kenny Smith, and it was 5–0 halfway through the game before Ab DeMarco got the lone Rangers goal to spoil Frank Brimsek's shutout.

The Kraut Line led the attack: Woody Dumart had two goals and an assist; Milt Schmidt had two goals; and Bobby Bauer had two assists.

After the game, Cowley announced that this would be his final season. "I'll play the rest of the season if they want me, but then I'm definitely through," he declared.

2

EDDIE
SHORE

BOSTON BRUINS
APRIL 1, 1947

Born: Fort Qu'Appelle, Saskatchewan, November 25, 1902
Died: Springfield, Massachusetts, March 16, 1985
Position: Defence
Shoots: Right
Height: 5'11"
Weight: 190 lbs.

HONOURS
- **Stanley Cup** 1929, 1939
- **Hart Trophy** 1933, 1935, 1936, 1938
- **Lester Patrick Trophy** 1970
- **NHL First All-Star Team** 1931, 1932, 1933, 1935, 1936, 1938, 1939
- **Hockey Hall of Fame** 1947

NHL CAREER STATS

	Regular Season					Playoffs				
Years	GP	G	A	P	Pim	GP	G	A	P	Pim
1926–40	550	105	179	284	1,047	55	6	13	19	181

CAREER

A rough-and-tumble player in the historic landscape of the NHL, Eddie Shore was both brilliant and brutal, talented and physical, feared and intimidating. When he joined the Boston Bruins as a rookie in 1926–27 he made an immediate impact, scoring 12 goals and accruing 130 penalty minutes, unheard of numbers for a defenceman of this era.

Indeed, Shore could hurt you with his talent or his fists; it made no matter to him. In his first five seasons, he scored an incredible 62 goals and averaged more than 100 penalty minutes a season. In 1928–29, he led the Bruins to the franchise's first Stanley Cup, and throughout the 1930s he was among the best players in the league. Shore won the Hart Trophy four times, something no other defenceman has done since.

Throughout the decade he alone ensured the Bruins thrived at the box office.

After he was suspended for 16 games for a vicious attack on Toronto's Ace Bailey attendance plummeted, and when he returned to the lineup the Boston Garden was once again packed. True to form, he was every bit a showman, taking the pre-game skate in a black cape or gesticulating and hollering wildly at referees as the fans went wild. Little did they know he was merely asking, "How are you?" all the while.

Shore, who was frequently partnered with Lionel Hitchman on the blue line, won his second Cup with the Bruins a decade after the first, and this proved to be his last full season. In 1939–40, he split his time between the Bruins and New York Americans, being traded to the latter so that he could also play for the AHL's Springfield Indians, the team he owned. But once he had hung up the blades for good there was no doubting the names Eddie Shore and Boston Bruins were virtually synonymous.

CEREMONY

Likely the only player to have his number retired prior to a playoff game, Eddie Shore had the double honour of being inducted into the Hockey Hall of Fame on this night as well. In this era, honoured members were presented with a scroll declaring their induction.

Joining Shore were J. Stewart Crawford, the mayor of Kingston, Ontario—Shore's hometown; Captain James Sutherland, one of the founders of the Hockey Hall of Fame in Kingston; Charles Adams, the first president of the Boston Bruins Hockey Club; Frank Selke, general manager of the visiting Montreal Canadiens; Lester Patrick, representing the NHL; Weston Adams, president of the Bruins; and writer Baz O'Meara.

"I sure thank you all so much," Shore told the crowd. At that point, referee King Clancy shook his hand, followed by all the players from both teams. He was presented with his old number 2 sweater in honour of it being retired, but Crawford and Sutherland took it from him immediately for the Hockey Hall of Fame.

THE GAME: Montreal Canadiens 5–Boston Bruins 1

This was game four of the semi-finals, and it was a game Boston needed to win. Going back to Montreal trailing 3–1 in games was a pretty much hopeless situation for the Bruins, but that's what happened by the end of the night.

The Canadiens broke open the game in the second period after a scoreless opening 20 minutes, going up 3–0 by the midway point on 2 goals from Billy Reay sandwiched around a singleton from Johnny Quilty.

The crowd was so disgusted by the turn of events that fans in the balcony started to hurl tomatoes and eggs towards the Montreal players' bench. The announcer quelled the riotous behaviour through clever means, asking the fans to be more respectful because "patients from the Veterans' Hospital were sitting in the vicinity" of the Habs' bench!

Kenny Smith beat Bill Durnan with a screen shot during a four-on-four to make it 3–1, but two more goals from Reay in the final period sealed the rout.

Montreal advanced to the Final, but the team lost the Stanley Cup to the Maple Leafs in six games, 4–2.

15 MILT SCHMIDT

BOSTON BRUINS
DECEMBER 25, 1954

Born: Kitchener, Ontario, March 5, 1918
Position: Centre
Shoots: Left
Height: 6'
Weight: 185 lbs.

HONOURS
- **Stanley Cup** 1939, 1941
- **Hart Trophy** 1951
- **Lester Patrick Trophy** 1996
- **NHL points leader** 1940
- **NHL All-Star Game** 1947, 1948, 1951, 1952
- **Hockey Hall of Fame** 1961

NHL CAREER STATS

| Years | Regular Season | | | | | Playoffs | | | | |
	GP	G	A	P	Pim	GP	G	A	P	Pim
1936–55	776	229	346	575	466	86	24	25	49	60

CAREER

One of the most exciting lines in NHL history is undoubtedly the Kraut Line of Milt Schmidt, Woody Dumart, and Bobby Bauer. The troika got its nickname because they all grew up in Kitchener (formerly Berlin), Ontario, and all wound up playing together in Boston where they were the most potent line of their era.

Bauer was the one initially invited to try out with the Bruins, but he brought his friends with him and all three were assigned to the Providence Bruins to start the 1936–37 season. Schmidt was recalled halfway through the year, but it wasn't until the final night of the season all played on a line together. They scored, and the next season began with the three amigos skating as a unit as they would the rest of their careers.

Schmidt was the biggest and most physical of the three, and although he was a centreman, he liked to carry the puck along the boards and burrow his way into

enemy territory before making a pass. The Kraut Line led the Bruins to two Stanley Cup wins, in 1939 and 1941, and in between, 1939–40, the line finished 1-2-3 in scoring, the first time in NHL history this had happened. Schmidt led the way with 52 points.

The game and lives of the three men changed on the night of February 10, 1942. That night, at home, they helped beat Montreal before heading off to war. It was their last game as a group for almost four years. After the game, players from both teams heaved the men on their shoulders and skated around the rink.

Once the war was over and the players returned safe and sound, they picked up as if they'd never left. Bauer retired in 1947, and Schmidt was named captain in 1950. He won the Hart Trophy at season's end. On March 18, 1952, the team wanted to honour the three men, so Bauer came out of retirement for a night and scored a goal. Schmidt also scored, the 200th of his career, and he moved back to defence to extend his playing days. He retired early in the 1954–55 season to take over immediately as coach, a position he held most of the next dozen years.

Although the Bruins retired his number 15, he wanted it back in circulation, and in 1957 Larry Regan wore the sacred number. Once Regan left the team, the number returned to the rafters where it has been ever since, honouring one of the greatest players in NHL history.

CEREMONY

The 36-year-old Schmidt retired on December 22, 1954, and immediately assumed the position of head coach for the Bruins. He had been injured for two weeks, during which time he acted as coach in place of Lynn Patrick. It was a strange setup. Indeed, Schmidt signed a two-year contract at the start of the season to be the team's coach, but then he decided he still had some games left in him as a player.

The team, which had been struggling, rallied for an impressive 4–2–1 record, but sagged again when Schmidt came back to play, losing three in a row. He decided to retire as a player and coach full-time, and the team immediately retired his number 15. His was the fourth number so honoured, after Eddie Shore's 2, Fred Hitchman's 3, and Dit Clapper's 5.

THE GAME: Boston Bruins 3–Chicago Black Hawks 3

In the old days, NHL teams often played on Christmas night, and for Schmidt, in 1954, this special day marked his first game as a coach, and the first game the Bruins played with the number 15 retired.

It started off poorly, and finished with a bang courtesy of Doug Mohns. The visiting Chicago Black Hawks built an impressive 2–0 lead through two periods, big Harry Watson scoring both goals for the Hawks.

Cal Gardner got the Bruins going early in the third thanks to a determined effort around Hank Bassen's goal, and Fern Flaman brought the Bruins even a few minutes later. Cheers turned to jeers, however, when Nick Mickoski gave the visitors another lead, and that goal looked as though it would hold up.

Boston, however, refused to give up, and in the final minute Doug Mohns converted a pass from René Chevrefils to tie the game again at 19:07.

Boston's Kraut Line.

9

MAURICE
RICHARD

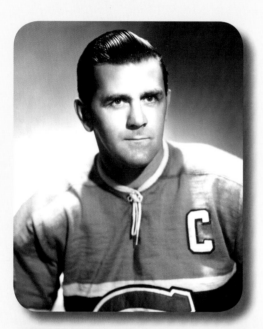

Born: Montreal, Quebec, August 4, 1921
Died: Montreal, Quebec, May 27, 2000
Position: Right wing
Shoots: Left
Height: 5'10"
Weight: 170 lbs.

HONOURS
- **Stanley Cup** 1944, 1946, 1953, 1956, 1957, 1958, 1959, 1960
- **Hart Trophy** 1947
- **NHL All-Star Game** 1947, 1948, 1949, 1950, 1951, 1952, 1953, 1954, 1955, 1956, 1957, 1958, 1959
- **NHL First Team All-Star** 1945, 1946, 1947, 1948, 1949, 1950, 1955, 1956
- **Hockey Hall of Fame** 1961

NHL CAREER STATS

	Regular Season					Playoffs				
Years	GP	G	A	P	Pim	GP	G	A	P	Pim
1942–60	978	544	421	965	1,285	133	82	44	126	188

CAREER

Although he retired in 1960 as the all-time highest goal scorer in NHL history, Maurice "The Rocket" Richard had a rocky start to his career. One year he broke his arm, the next year his leg, and anxious Montreal Canadiens fans were wondering if this highly touted prospect was made of glass. But everything turned around in 1943—Richard was healthy, his wife had a baby, and he had switched to number 9. It was all glory after that.

In his first full season, Richard scored 32 goals in the regular season and 12 more in the playoffs to lead the Canadiens to the Stanley Cup. The next year, he scored 50 goals in 50 games, a feat never before accomplished and one which became the benchmark to which all future goal scorers aspired. Although he himself never reached 50 again, he set scoring records that took many years to equal.

In all, Richard led the league in goals five times, and such was his skill with the puck he almost always had more goals than assists, with a career total of 544 goals and only 421 assists. When he was on the ice, the goal was to get him the puck, not expect a pass back. The best example of his ability to put the puck in the net occurred on November 8, 1952. Only in the middle of his career, he scored his 325th career goal, passing Nels Stewart as the league's all-time scorer.

Richard's importance to the Canadiens, the city of Montreal, and the province of Quebec came to the fore on March 15, 1955, when NHL president Clarence Campbell suspended the player for the rest of the season after he hit a linesman over the head with a stick. At the next game at the Forum, fans rioted and forced the forfeit of the game. The rioting continued all night through the streets of Montreal, and Richard was forced to go on radio to ask the people for peace.

He played the last five years of his career with brother, Henri, nicknamed the "Pocket Rocket," and together they won five Stanley Cups in a row (1956–60). Although Maurice attended training camp in September 1960 he knew he had lost that leg strength and scoring touch, and retired. His number, of course, was immediately taken out of circulation by the team.

CEREMONY

There is virtually no evidence to suggest there was a ceremony to retire the Rocket's number 9. Indeed, the Canadiens and several other sources cite the home opener

of the 1960–61 season as the date the number was raised to the rafters, but the only account of this is a fleeting reference in a book called *Maurice Richard: Reluctant Hero* by Frank Orr and Chris Goyens in which they write: "Jacques Plante recorded his forty-eighth career shutout in the Canadiens 5–0 win over Toronto in Montreal. Before the game, Maurice Richard's uniform No. 9 was retired in a special ceremony."

Yet, the day after the game, there wasn't a single reference to any special ceremony in the local papers. Indeed, Dink Carroll's game report in the *Montreal Gazette* makes no reference to the name Maurice Richard at all. Nor does the *Montreal Star* or *Le Devoir*. As for eye witnesses, *Gazette* writer Red Fisher, broadcaster Dick Irvin, and Frank Selke Jr., son of Canadiens general manager, all said the same thing—they remember no ceremony.

Indeed, only *La Presse* uses the name Maurice Richard—and it does so frequently, just not to mention any pre-game ceremonies. Writes Gerard Champagne in his game story: "In truth, coach Toe Blake has always looked for someone to wear number 9 again . . . Tonight Maurice Richard was above the ice, clapping with appreciation among the fans as his old team won, 5–0."

Perhaps part of the dilemma came from the fact that Richard had retired only days earlier. Common wisdom today has it that he won his fifth Cup in a row in the spring of 1960 and retired after an historic career. But, in fact, Richard attended training camp for the 1960–61 season and only then decided that the legs couldn't keep up with the heart. He retired on September 15, 1960, just three weeks before the team played its first game of the new season. The date of his

sweater retirement is likely given, therefore, as a way of saying that as of that day, no player ever wore number 9 again.

THE GAME: Montreal Canadiens 5–Toronto Maple Leafs 0
Although there were only 13,746 fans at the Forum on this night, they were treated to a great game by the home side thanks to some timely scoring and great defence. Jacques Plante had to stop only 19 mostly routine shots to earn the shutout, and Henri Richard had two goals for the winners. Johnny Bower surrendered all five goals in the Leafs' net.

Bernie "Boom Boom" Geoffrion got the only goal of a physical first period, just 66 seconds after the drop of the puck, but this turned out to be the game winner. Marcel Bonin made it 2–0 just 15 seconds into the middle period, and Richard and Billy Hicke made it 4–0 by the midway point of the game. Richard got his second goal early in the third.

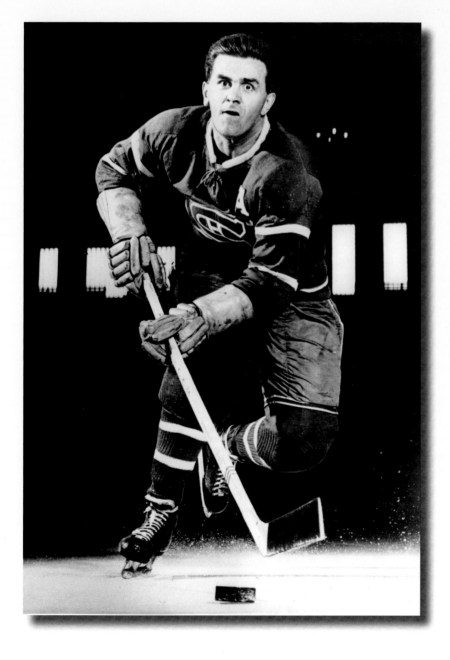

4 JEAN BÉLIVEAU

MONTREAL CANADIENS
OCTOBER 9, 1971

Born: Trois-Rivières, Quebec, August 31, 1931
Position: Centre
Shoots: Left
Height: 6'3"
Weight: 205 lbs.

HONOURS
- **Stanley Cup** 1956, 1957, 1958, 1959, 1960, 1965, 1966, 1968, 1969, 1971
- **Hart Trophy** 1956, 1964
- **Art Ross Trophy** 1956
- **Conn Smythe Trophy** 1965
- **NHL All-Star Game** 1953, 1954, 1955, 1956, 1957, 1958, 1959, 1960, 1963, 1964, 1965, 1968, 1969
- **Hockey Hall of Fame** 1972

NHL CAREER STATS

	Regular Season					Playoffs				
Years	GP	G	A	P	Pim	GP	G	A	P	Pim
1950–71	1,125	507	712	1,219	1,029	162	79	97	176	211

CAREER

Mere numbers cannot quantify the contribution Jean Béliveau made to the NHL and the Montreal Canadiens, and mere words cannot do his skills justice. A great player and a greater man, he embodied all that is good about hockey and inspired a generation of kids to aspire to the NHL. In 20 seasons he won the Stanley Cup 10 times. He was the team's captain, a pillar of the community, and an ambassador for the sport.

Béliveau was playing for the Quebec Aces in both junior and senior hockey in Quebec City. He loved it there, and the people loved him back. The Canadiens, of course, wanted him to play for them in the NHL, but he politely demurred. He was called up to play two games in 1950–51 and had a goal and an assist. Two years later, he was called up for three games and scored five goals.

The Habs did the only thing they could think of to get him to play for their team—they bought the entire Quebec senior league, making Béliveau their

property. They then signed him to the richest contract in league history—five years and $100,000. This was 1953, and Béliveau never played another game for a team other than the Club de Hockey.

His first three years saw wild improvements as he went from 13 to 37 to 47 goals and 34 to 73 to 88 points, the last of these tops in the league. That was 1955–56, the season the Habs won their first of five straight Stanley Cup titles, an historic achievement yet to be equalled. Of course, Béliveau was surrounded by some of the best players in the league: Jacques Plante, Maurice and Henri Richard, and Doug Harvey. Béliveau was a gentleman and an impressive force. Tall and graceful, he was also incredibly strong and a fierce competitor.

At the end of this championship run, Maurice Richard retired. Doug Harvey took over as captain and Beliveau took over a year later from Harvey. a position he held the rest of his career. He took the job seriously, on ice and off, believing he was the voice of reason between players and management. Under his leadership, the team won the Cup five more times, starting with the "silent dynasty" of the 1960s when they won in 1965, 1966, 1968, and 1969 despite being overshadowed by the four wins by the Maple Leafs between 1962 and 1967.

At the end, Béliveau was as remarkable as ever. His final season was 1970–71, but he did not go out a battered old man. Instead, he led the team in scoring during the regular season, finished third in playoff scoring, and took the team to its 10th Cup during his career. And, when NHL president Clarence Campbell presented the trophy to him on ice, Béliveau made history by being the first Montreal player to skate around the ice with the trophy, a custom that has become an important part of the celebrations ever since.

CEREMONY

Béliveau shared the spotlight on this night with Aurèle Joliat, another number 4 from a much earlier era. The two men were co-feted by the Canadiens. In the tradition of the day, the two were given their sweaters to take home. Toe Blake presented Béliveau with his number 4 while Joliat received his from Gerard Dandurand, grandson of former owner Leo.

Much of the day's discussion revolved around Henri Richard, who was named the team's new captain on this day, taking over for the just-retired Béliveau. Nevertheless, Béliveau got the greatest applause when he accepted the number 4 sweater and then put it on over his jacket and tie with the help of Blake.

THE GAME: Montreal Canadiens 4–New York Rangers 4

The Rangers spoiled the fun a bit by scoring the first and last goals of the game and limiting the Canadiens to a 4–4 tie on this special night. Dave Balon got the only goal of the first period, beating Montreal goalie Ken Dryden. Bobby Rousseau got the fans worried when he made it a 2–0 game early in the second.

Frank Mahovlich got one back for the home side at 5:05, but less than two minutes later Vic Hadfield restored the two-goal lead. "The Roadrunner," Yvan Cournoyer, scored on Ed Giacomin before the end of the second to cut the Rangers' lead to 3–2.

The Habs took control in the third on second goals each from Cournoyer and Mahovlich, but the Forum faithful were given a rude jolt when Pete Stemkowski scored with just 1:29 remaining to salvage a 4–4 tie for the Blueshirts.

9 GORDIE HOWE

DETROIT RED WINGS
MARCH 12, 1972

Born: Floral, Saskatchewan, March 31, 1928
Position: Right wing
Shoots: Right
Height: 6'
Weight: 205 lbs.

HONOURS
- **Stanley Cup** 1950, 1952, 1954, 1955
- **Hart Trophy** 1952, 1953, 1957, 1958, 1960, 1963
- **Art Ross Trophy** 1951, 1952, 1953, 1954, 1957, 1963
- **Lester Patrick Trophy** 1967
- **NHL All-Star Game** 1948, 1949, 1950, 1951, 1952, 1953, 1954, 1955, 1957, 1958, 1959, 1960, 1961, 1962, 1963, 1964, 1965, 1967, 1968, 1969, 1970, 1971, 1980
- **Hockey Hall of Fame** 1972

NHL CAREER STATS

Years	Regular Season					Playoffs				
	GP	G	A	P	Pim	GP	G	A	P	Pim
1946–80	1,767	801	1,049	1,850	1,685	157	68	92	160	220

DETROIT CAREER

To celebrate the career of Gordie Howe by pointing to his longevity is like saying the pope is religious. In truth, what was most extraordinary about Howe was that he was among the best players in the league for every year he played. To wit, he finished in the top-10 scoring for 21 consecutive seasons. He scored at least 23 goals in a season for 22 straight seasons. In his 26 NHL seasons, he played the full schedule a preposterous 17 times.

As he got older, he didn't hang around or rest on his laurels. He had only one season of 100 points or more—in 1968–69 when he had 103. He was 41 years old, by far the oldest player in league history to surpass the century mark for points. By the time he retired in 1971, his records included 1,767 games played, 801 goals, 1,049 assists, and 1,850 total points.

Howe's first season was 1946–47, when the 18-year-old started a quarter of a

century of play with the Detroit Red Wings. He was quickly put on a line with friend and youngster Ted Lindsay and veteran Sid Abel, and together the three became the highest-scoring line in the league. Known as the Production Line, they took the Wings to the Stanley Cup in 1950 after finishing 1-2-3 in regular-season scoring.

Howe possessed unique skills. Although he was a natural right-handed shot, he could switch easily to left if that produced a favourable scoring chance or pass. Nicknamed "Elbows," he was tough as nails in an era when every player had to carve out his own respect one game at a time, one fight at a time. In truth, Howe rarely fought—he didn't have to.

Howe and Lindsay led the Red Wings to the Cup in 1952, 1954, and 1955, and Howe was named winner of the Hart Trophy four times in that decade. He continued to play at the highest level throughout the 1960s, but after the 1970–71 season—his 25th—arthritis in his wrists forced him to retire.

CEREMONY

How prescient were Howe's words at the ceremony at the Olympia to retire his number when he said to owner Bruce A. Norris at centre ice: "Don't wrinkle this [sweater]. I've got a couple of boys . . . who might wear it someday." He said this while standing beside his father, his wife, Colleen, and three of his children—Cathy, Murray, and Mark, who would, indeed, play for the Red Wings (though he didn't wear number 9). They stood at centre ice on a large red carpet with the number 9 appropriately emblazoned on it. Howe's other son, Marty, was back in Toronto playing hockey with the junior Marlboros and unable to attend.

Norris announced that he was contributing $1,500 to establish a scholarship in Howe's name, which would be awarded to a high school student who played hockey. Howe also received a sketch of the Production Line.

U.S. vice president Spiro Agnew attended and read a tribute from President Richard Nixon: "When most men retire, they are put on ice. But in your case, there isn't a hockey fan in America who wouldn't want to put you on the ice again to enjoy and savour the wizardry of your incredible hockey skills."

"If there was anything else I wish now, it would be to have another Howe here with me," Gordie said with poignancy, referring to his mother who had passed away only a few months earlier after falling at the family cottage.

THE GAME: Chicago Black Hawks 3–Detroit Red Wings 2

This was a big game for the Red Wings. As the playoff race was heating up, the loss put the team five points behind Toronto for the final spot with only eight games left to play (the Leafs had nine left). The loss was particularly bitter because the Wings fought back from 2–0 down to tie the game, only to lose on a late goal by Pit Martin with just 2:13 left to play.

Martin also opened the scoring in the first minute of the game, and Dennis Hull added a goal late in the period to make it 2–0. But Mickey Redmond with his 40th of the year in the second and veteran Alex Delvecchio with his 17th in the third at 0:53 made it a 2–2 game.

That set the stage for Martin's heroics later on. The game featured a relative newcomer in goal for Detroit—Andy Brown. Playing in only his second NHL game, he was the last bare-faced goalie in pro hockey.

4

BARRY ASHBEE

PHILADELPHIA FLYERS
APRIL 3, 1975

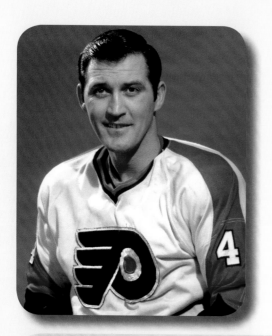

Born: Weston, Ontario, July 28, 1939
Died: Philadelphia, Pennsylvania, May 12, 1977
Position: Defence
Shoots: Right
Height: 5'10"
Weight: 180 lbs.

HONOURS
- **Stanley Cup** 1974
- **NHL Second All-Star Team** 1974

NHL CAREER STATS

	Regular Season					Playoffs				
Years	GP	G	A	P	Pim	GP	G	A	P	Pim
1965–74	284	15	70	85	291	17	0	4	4	22

CAREER

Barry Ashbee didn't live long, but he was loved by everyone in Philadelphia during his brief time with the Flyers. He made his NHL debut with the Boston Bruins during the 1965–66 season. The Original Six was a tough league to crack, so after 14 games with the Bruins he was sent back to Hershey in the American Hockey League (AHL) to resume his career in anonymity.

The next year, though, he suffered a back injury at the Bears' training camp and missed the entire season after surgery. He returned to play for two more years and then Hershey traded him to the Flyers. He made the team at training camp in 1970 and was a rock on the blue line for four years. He was one of the Broad Street Bullies in both spirit and deed, but he wasn't around the night the team won its first Stanley Cup in 1974.

On April 28, 1974, in a semi-finals playoff game against the New York Rangers,

Ashbee was struck flush in the eye by a shot off the stick of Dale Rolfe. In one second, Ashbee's career was over. Days earlier, he had been named to the league's end-of-season Second All-Star Team.

Ashbee became an assistant coach with the team in 1975, and near the end of that season the Flyers retired his number 4. Tragedy struck two years later, though, when he was diagnosed with leukemia. A month later, he was dead at age 37. The Flyers established a trophy in his name for the team's best defenceman, and when they started a hall of fame, he was in the first group of inductees. He may have been skating with the Flyers for only four years, but Barry Ashbee has been spiritually connected to the team from the day he arrived in 1970 right up to the present.

CEREMONY

Now an assistant coach with the team, this was Ashbee's night to be honoured by a team to which he gave so much and which loved him right back. Captain Bobby Clarke gave Ashbee a 22-foot motorhome and a cheque, which Ashbee donated to the Wills Eye Hospital Retina Research Unit. Ashbee also received a copper etching of himself and his children; a diamond-studded silver puck to honour his selection to the 1974 Second All-Star Team; a diamond bracelet; luggage for his wife, Donna; and, from the visiting New York Rangers, a dedicatory plaque.

THE GAME: Philadelphia Flyers 1–New York Rangers 1

As the season's end was in sight and the playoffs on everyone's mind, this was an important game. Buffalo led the division with 111 points, with Philly and Montreal right behind with 109 each. The key was to finish in first place and avoid playing the mighty Bruins in the first round of the playoffs.

"I would be crazy if I said we wanted to play a team with Orr and Esposito," coach Fred Shero said unabashedly.

If that was the case, the start of the game was befuddling, for Jean Ratelle gave the Rangers a 1–0 lead only 15 seconds after the drop of the puck to start the game. The Flyers settled down and tied the game, though, on a lucky play at 11:27 when a Ted Harris shot hit Bobby Clarke's skate and beat goalie Ed Giacomin.

The goal extended Clarke's point streak to 18 games and ensured the Flyers were now unbeaten in their last 12 games (10–0–2), and the game became a tough, hard-fought one full of fights and penalties. By the third period, both teams were too tired to slug it out and seemed happy and willing to leave with a point each.

Bernie Parent, celebrating his 30th birthday, saved the point for the Flyers by making a huge glove save off Ratelle in the final minute of play.

16

HENRI RICHARD

MONTREAL CANADIENS
DECEMBER 10, 1975

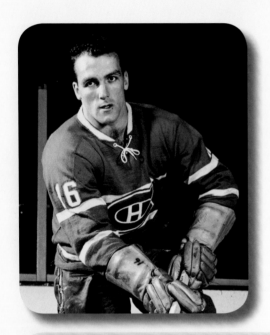

Born: Montreal, Quebec, February 29, 1936
Position: Centre
Shoots: Right
Height: 5'7"
Weight: 160 lbs.

HONOURS

- **Stanley Cup** 1956, 1957, 1958, 1959, 1960, 1965, 1966, 1968, 1969, 1971, 1973
- **Bill Masterton Trophy** 1974
- **NHL First All-Star Team** 1958
- **Hockey Hall of Fame** 1979

NHL CAREER STATS

	Regular Season					Playoffs				
Years	GP	G	A	P	Pim	GP	G	A	P	Pim
1955–75	1,256	358	688	1,046	928	180	49	80	129	181

CAREER

Even though Henri Richard won 11 Stanley Cups as a player—more than any other in NHL history—and had more than 1,000 points in his career, he is considered the second-best member of his family. It just isn't fair, but when your older brother is Maurice Richard, it's also true.

Henri entered the NHL in 1955 at the height of the Canadiens' powers, winning the Stanley Cup the first five years of his career. He often played on a line with his brother, and he had to do more than his fair share of fighting with opponents who trash-talked him for being Maurice's younger brother. Sometimes he stood up to the much bigger opponents; sometimes his brother stepped in and gave the foe a good pummeling.

Nicknamed the "Pocket Rocket," he was 15 years younger than Maurice and so saw him more like a fan than a sibling. They didn't play in the driveway or

backyard together, exchange tips or make great passes to each other—at least not until they were both wearing the vaunted C H of Montreal.

Maurice retired in 1960, but Henri still had many years ahead of him. In the 1960s, he won the Cup four more times, most memorably in 1966. He came down the left wing, as Dave Balon drove a shot on Detroit Red Wings goalie Roger Crozier. Richard fell into the goalie and the puck bounced off his glove and into the net. The goal stood and the Habs won the Cup on this controversial play. In 1971, Henri again scored the Cup winner, one of only a few players with two Cup-winning goals to his credit.

That summer he was named captain of the Canadiens, and he retired early in the 1974–75 season when he felt he had slowed too much. Incredibly, he was never named to a First All-Star Team. His forte was quietly consistent play rather than a few spectacular seasons at the height of his career. In all, he played 1,256 games and had 1,046 points. In 20 seasons, he missed the playoffs once, and in an era when there were only two rounds needed for the Cup, he played an amazing 180 playoff games. He was a star and a record setter, a dynamic little centreman with skills in all areas of the game. He just wasn't his brother.

CEREMONY

Henri Richard shared the spotlight on this night with Elmer Lach, but Lach was part of a more lavish ceremony for his number 16 many years later.

Both men came out to centre ice accompanied by teammate Butch Bouchard and Toe Blake, who had played with Lach and coached Richard. The honourees were given number 16 sweaters. There was no banner raising on this night or any other at the Forum. Indeed, the first time the Canadiens actually hoisted a banner to the rafters was on the opening of their new arena, the Molson Centre, on March 16, 1996.

In fact, the ceremony on this night was as much for the retiring of the number as paying tribute to the two men. Blake had even worn number 16 for one season, as had 18 other players including Art Alexandre, Paul Bibeault, George Brown, Tony Demers, Art Giroux, Sam Godin, Cliff Goupille, Gizzy Hart, Art Lesieur, Ron McCartney, Johnny Quilty, Paul Raymond, Gus Rivers, Don Wilson, and Jimmy Ward.

THE GAME: Montreal Canadiens 3–Toronto Maple Leafs 3

The Maple Leafs were the better team this night but came out of the game with only a tie. They were held in the game by goalie Wayne Thomas, who was traded by the Canadiens the previous summer. He was sensational, but the Leafs also created plenty of scoring chances against Ken Dryden at the other end.

Toronto defenceman Jim McKenny got the only goal of the opening period, but Yvan Cournoyer tied the game at 2:30 of the second period. The Leafs were relentless, though, and two goals by Lanny McDonald put the visitors in the driver's seat for the final 20 minutes.

They failed to hold the lead, though. Jacques Lemaire made it a 3–2 game early in the final period and then Guy Lapointe tipped in a shot from John van Boxmeer with just 3:52 left in the game to tie the score.

"We started to get really careless, and we gave up the big play," Dryden said. "You just can't be successful if you give up the big play."

3 BOB GASSOFF

ST. LOUIS BLUES
OCTOBER 1, 1977

Born: Quesnel, British Columbia, April 17, 1953
Died: Villa Ridge, Missouri, May 29, 1977
Position: Defence
Shoots: Left
Height: 5'10"
Weight: 195 lbs.

HONOURS
• Selected 48th overall by St. Louis in 1973 Amateur Draft

NHL CAREER STATS

	Regular Season					Playoffs				
Years	GP	G	A	P	Pim	GP	G	A	P	Pim
1973–77	245	11	47	58	866	9	0	1	1	16

CAREER

Bob Gassoff didn't have much opportunity to make an impact in the NHL, but that was because his life was cut tragically short as a result of a motorcycle accident. One of four hockey-playing brothers, Bob was selected 48th overall by St. Louis in the 1973 Amateur Draft at the end of his second season in the Western Hockey League (WHL) with Medicine Hat Tigers.

He split his rookie year between the Blues and their WHL affiliate and the year after played only a bit in the minors before becoming a full-time member of the team. A defensive defenceman, he was well respected for dropping his gloves more than scoring big goals.

The tragic accident occurred in 1977 when teammate Gary Unger had a barbeque at his ranch, and after some food and too much drink, Gassoff headed out for a quick ride on a motorcycle. He came over a hill and didn't see an oncoming car, colliding head on. He wasn't wearing a helmet and died instantly.

The Blues immediately took his number 3 out of circulation and donated a trophy to the CHL to be given annually to the league's most improved defenceman.

CEREMONY

Gassoff's number was retired prior to an exhibition game between the St. Louis Blues and the Atlanta Flames. Proceeds from the Bob Gassoff Memorial Game were directed to the St. Louis Children's Hospital, which Gassoff visited regularly.

This was also the first game under the ownership of Ralston Purina, which also changed the building's name from The Arena to the Checkerdome.

Prior to the opening faceoff, Gassoff's wife, Diane, came out to centre ice with their son, Bob Jr. Diane was six months pregnant when Gassoff was killed and Bob Jr. never got to see his father. Joining them were Gassoff's parents and brothers. They were joined by hundreds of young amateur players to recognize Gassoff's love of children.

Gassoff's last sweater was put on display in the lobby of the St. Louis Checkerdome. The evening was further enlivened by the announcement that fan favourite Bob Plager was going to retire to take on the job of special assignment scout effective immediately.

THE GAME: St. Louis Blues 4–Atlanta Flames 2

The crowd of 7,909 got its money's worth as the Blues rallied for a pre-season win over the Flames. Guy Chouinard scored for the visitors at 7:06 before Bernie Federko tied it late in the period. Both teams exchanged goals in the second as well, with the Blues scoring first.

The third period was all St. Louis. Gary Unger and Claude Larose scored the only goals. Yves Belanger and Ed Staniowski shared the goaltending equally, but the third was enlivened by some physical play typical of an exhibition game where rookies and newcomers try to impress.

The two teams had played earlier in the exhibition season, St. Louis winning more handily, 10–3. Coach Leo Boivin was particularly impressed by two youngsters, Jamie Masters and Jack Brownschidle.

4 BOBBY ORR

BOSTON BRUINS
JANUARY 9, 1979

Born: Parry Sound, Ontario, March 20, 1948
Position: Defence
Shoots: Left
Height: 6'
Weight: 198 lbs.

HONOURS
- **Stanley Cup** 1970, 1972
- **Calder Trophy** 1967
- **Conn Smythe Trophy** 1970, 1972
- **Norris Trophy** 1968, 1969, 1970, 1971, 1972, 1973, 1974, 1975
- **Art Ross Trophy** 1970, 1975
- **Lester B. Pearson Award** 1975
- **Canada Cup MVP** 1976
- **Lester Patrick Trophy** 1979
- **Hockey Hall of Fame** 1979

NHL CAREER STATS

	Regular Season					Playoffs				
Years	GP	G	A	P	Pim	GP	G	A	P	Pim
1966–79	657	270	645	915	953	74	26	66	92	107

CAREER

He revolutionized the game. He set records for defencemen that stand to this day. He was arguably the greatest player hockey has ever known, despite being forced to retire because of bad knees at age 30. His name was Bobby Orr.

From the time he was a child he seemed destined for greatness. At age 14, he was already playing junior hockey, in Oshawa, and in 1966, age 18, he joined the Boston Bruins and only got better and better. Orr won the Calder Trophy his first year, and by his third year he had already set his first major record, most goals by a defenceman (21).

In 1969–70, he obliterated that and almost every other record. He had 33 goals, 87 assists, and 120 points—tops in the league. This marked the first time a defenceman had ever won the Art Ross Trophy. To this day this feat has been accomplished only one other time—by Orr again, five years later.

Over the course of his 10 years with the Bruins, he increased his records to include 46 goals by a defenceman in a season (1974–75), 102 assists (1970–71), and 139 points (1970–71). He also had a plus-minus record of +124 in 1970–71. What made Orr so magical? He was the first defenceman who could take the puck from behind his own goal, survey the landscape in front, and skate the length of the ice to score a goal. He had speed, great stickhandling ability, daring nerve to go to the net, a blazing shot, and finesse around the opposition's goal.

But, of course, the puck carrier is the one who gets hit the most, and the more Orr had the puck, the more he got hit. His knees took the brunt of the force, and as a result he missed many games during his career, often spending the off-season in surgery and rehabilitation until training camp.

In his prime, he led the Bruins to the Stanley Cup in 1970 and 1972, the first wins since 1941. Orr scored the game-winning goal both times and was named the Conn Smythe Trophy winner on each occasion. His swan song came during the 1976 Canada Cup when he led Canada to victory and was named tournament MVP playing virtually on one knee. In fact, he had missed the Summit Series in 1972 because of his knees, and after leaving Boston to sign with Chicago in 1976, he played just 26 games over three seasons. In essence, 1974–75 was his last complete season. He was 27 years old.

Orr retired as the leading scorer for a defenceman in NHL history despite playing just 657 regular-season games, and he was inducted that same year into

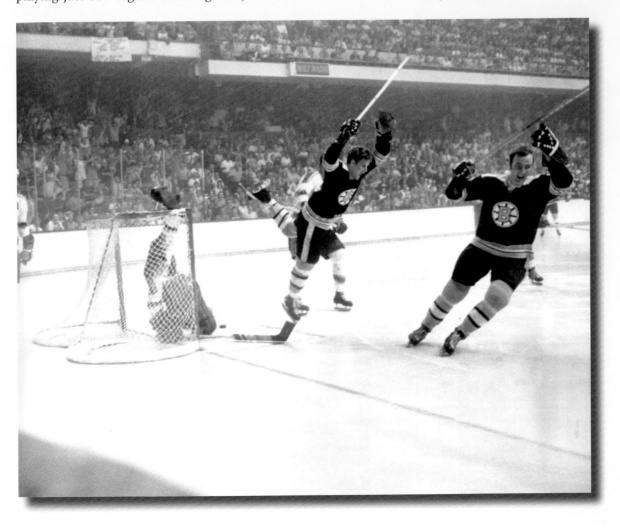

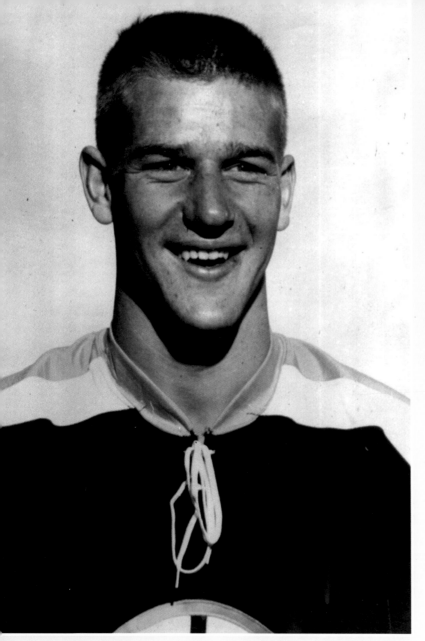

the Hockey Hall of Fame, the three-year waiting period deservedly waived for the great Number Four.

CEREMONY

In what was surely the strangest retiring of a number—and for a player of this magnitude—Bobby Orr's number 4 send off took place midway through the 1978–79 season prior to an exhibition game against the travelling Soviet Wings.

Nevertheless, it was also one of the most memorable evenings in hockey history, thanks in large part to a standing ovation that lasted six minutes and five seconds, an unofficial world record.

The gifts were many. Orr was invited to Beacon Hill for an afternoon presentation during the joint session of the Massachusetts legislature. He was given a gavel engraved with "To Boston's No. 4, hockey's No. 1" while Boston city council gave him a Paul Revere bowl, a bean pot, and a clock.

With his wife, Peggy, by his side, Orr stood at centre ice with other Bruins' legends and officials, but nothing quite equalled the moment when Johnny Bucyk handed him a number 4 sweater and egged him to put it on. The crowd joined in, shouting, "Put it on! Put it on!"

Orr took off his jacket, and the crowd roared. He put the sweater on one last time, and the walls of the Garden shook. "I spent a long time trying to figure out what to say to you," he began, breaking down. "And you know what . . . I love you all so much. I spent 10 years here, and they were the best 10 years of my life."

His wife was crying, and then he started. "I shouldn't have looked at you, Peggy," he said, wiping away the tears.

THE GAME: Soviet Wings 4–Boston Bruins 1

The Bruins were a top team in the middle of the season, and the last thing they wanted to do was upset their rhythm by playing an exhibition game that meant nothing in the standings. "We had no injuries, and that's the main thing," Boston coach Don Cherry said later. "I couldn't care less about this game."

Still, they had to play it, grudgingly if necessary, and for half a game they played it well. Rick Middleton scored midway through the opening period, a goal that stood up until 6:22 of the second when Mikhail Varnakov beat backup goalie Jim Pettie while short-handed. After that, it was all Wings.

They went ahead for good two minutes later and added two more goals in the third, Boston garnering only 10 shots over the final 40 minutes of play. The score was there for all to see, but the night belonged to Bobby Orr.

1

BERNIE
PARENT

PHILADELPHIA FLYERS
OCTOBER 11, 1979

Born: Montreal, Quebec, April 3, 1945
Position: Goalie
Catches: Left
Height: 5'10"
Weight: 180 lbs.

HONOURS
- **Stanley Cup** 1974, 1975
- **Conn Smythe Trophy** 1974, 1975
- **Vezina Trophy** 1974 (with Tony Esposito), 1975
- **NHL All-Star Game** 1969, 1970, 1974, 1975, 1977
- **Hockey Hall of Fame** 1984

NHL CAREER STATS

Regular Season

Years	GP	W-L-T	Mins	GA	SO	GAA
1965–79	608	271-198-121	35,136	1,493	54	2.55

Playoffs

Years	GP	W-L-T	Mins	GA	SO	GAA
1965–79	71	38-33-0	4,302	174	6	2.43

CAREER

Perhaps no goalie is more associated with his team's Stanley Cup victories than Bernie Parent and the playoff fortunes of the Philadelphia Flyers. And, although he played parts of two seasons for both Boston and Toronto during his career, he is much more closely connected to the Flyers in the late 1960s and '70s when the team won the Cup twice—in 1974 and 1975—than any other team.

Parent won the Memorial Cup with the Niagara Falls Flyers in 1965 while playing in the Bruins' organization, but when the Philadelphia Flyers joined the NHL in 1967 as part of the league's massive expansion, the Bruins left him exposed in the draft and Philadelphia happily claimed the 22-year-old goalie.

His first tour of duty with the team lasted just three and a half years before he was traded to the Maple Leafs, but he was unhappy in Toronto and decided to test the new WHA in the summer of 1972, signing, ironically, with the Philadelphia Blazers.

After one year, Parent wanted to return to the NHL and stay in the city he had come to love, but he was still Toronto property. The Leafs cashed in their chips and traded their prized asset to the Flyers in return for a first-round draft choice in 1973 (Bob Neely) and future considerations (another goalie, Doug Favell).

It was at this point that Parent, now a mature goalie, was ready to take control of the team. In 1973–74, Parent led the league in just about every significant category for goalies: most games played (73), most wins (47), most minutes played (4,314), most shutouts (12), and best goals against average (1.89). Parent replicated his efforts in the playoffs, and the Flyers eliminated the favoured Bruins en route to an historic Stanley Cup, the first by a 1967 expansion franchise.

The 1974–75 season was virtually identical for both goalie and team. Parent played brilliantly in the regular season, played even better in the playoffs, and brought the Flyers their second straight Cup victory. He won the Conn Smythe Trophy both years, the only goalie to win in consecutive years. In fact, the only other player to win back-to-back Smythe trophies was Mario Lemieux, with Pittsburgh, in 1991 and 1992.

Parent's career ended suddenly on February 17, 1979, when he was poked in the eye by a stick. The horrible injury caused a quick shift in goalie masks from the style Parent wore, which was made of Plexiglas and fit tight to the face, to a cage style, which protected the eyes more completely.

CEREMONY

Incredibly, Bernie Parent's number 1 was the first number 1 to be retired by an NHL team even though so many great goalies of the Original Six era and earlier had donned the hallowed number.

This night of honour marked the home and season opener for the Flyers, and once the banner was in the rafters it held a special place down the line from the several banners for division and conference championships.

When he was asked about his brilliant career, Parent answered, "What I'll remember most is the Cup. I guess that's obvious. But not winning the first one. The second one is the one I remember the most. The first time, there was too much excitement. I didn't realize what was going on."

THE GAME: Philadelphia Flyers 5–New York Islanders 2
They may have been on the cusp of a Stanley Cup dynasty, but on this night the visiting Islanders were no match for an inspired Flyers team led by goalie Phil Myre, who said afterwards: "Bernie's always going to be Bernie. And I'm just here to be Phil Myre, that's all."

Indeed, he would prove not to be Parent's capable replacement over time—who could be?—but on this night Myre stopped 32 of 34 shots and was key to the win. The Flyers got the only goal of the opening period, courtesy of Rick MacLeish halfway through, and in the second they stormed out of the dressing room and made it 4–0 by 3:15 of the period, rattling the entire Islanders team and goalie Billy Smith in particular.

Mike Bossy and Bryan Trottier scored in the third to make the score a bit closer, and Tom Gorence for Philadelphia closed out the scoring.

7

ROD GILBERT

NEW YORK RANGERS
OCTOBER 14, 1979

Born: Montreal, Quebec, July 1, 1941
Position: Right wing
Shoots: Right
Height: 5'9"
Weight: 180 lbs.

HONOURS
• Bill Masterton Trophy 1976
• Lester Patrick Trophy 1991
• NHL All-Star Game 1964, 1965, 1967, 1969, 1970, 1972, 1975, 1977
• Played for Canada in 1972 Summit Series
• Hockey Hall of Fame 1982

NHL CAREER STATS

	Regular Season					Playoffs				
Years	GP	G	A	P	Pim	GP	G	A	P	Pim
1960–78	1,065	406	615	1,021	508	79	34	33	67	43

CAREER

After playing 18 years in the NHL, all with the New York Rangers, Rod Gilbert can look back and think one thing—it's a miracle. While in junior, he slipped on debris on the ice, suffered a serious back injury, then complications, and came within a couple of days of losing his leg. But doctors fused three vertebrae, loosened the blood clot that had resulted from the operation, and got him back on his feet. Gilbert did the rest.

The injury occurred early in 1961, shortly after Gilbert had played his one and only NHL game of the season. He played once more the next year, but by the start of the 1962–63 season he was in excellent health and made the Rangers roster full-time. He was a solid player, relentless and physical, who could dig the puck out of any corner to make a play. Unfortunately, he began during an era when the Rangers were the worst (or second worst) team in the Original Six and saw precious little

playoff action in the 1960s.

But the team built steadily and developed a core of excellent young players, Gilbert among them. Although they missed the playoffs for four straight years (1962–66), they qualified in 1967 and made it for the next nine years in a row. It was during this time that Gilbert shone brightest, but not before he underwent another painful surgery to correct problems with his back resultant from the original injury. Gilbert played on a line with Jean Ratelle and Vic Hadfield, and the threesome was so effective they earned a nickname—the GAG Line (Goal-a-Game Line).

Their best year was 1971–72, when each member of the line scored at least 40 goals, and the team went all the way to the Stanley Cup Final before losing to Bobby Orr and the Boston Bruins. That fall, Gilbert, Ratelle, and Hadfield were invited to play for Canada at the historic Summit Series.

By the time he retired, early in the 1977–78 season, Gilbert had played 1,065 games and recorded 1,021 points, still a club record (as are his 406 career goals).

CEREMONY

Precious little is known about the ceremony for Gilbert on this night. Neither the *New York Times* nor the *New York Post* mentioned it; indeed, the only journalistic record comes at the very end of the game recap provided by the *New York Daily News* the day after the game: "Rangers retired No. 7 in pre-game ceremonies and honored six players, including Rod Gilbert, who wore it."

Other players who wore number 7 include Frank Boucher, Don Raleigh, Red Sullivan, and Phil Watson.

The main thing is, of course, that the number, bearing Gilbert's name, was hoisted to the rafters. His was the first Rangers' number so honoured.

THE GAME: Washington Capitals 5–New York Rangers 3

The Rangers opened the season with a convincing win over the Leafs a few nights earlier at Maple Leaf Gardens, but they mailed in a dud for their own opener at Madison Square Garden. The 5–3 loss was largely courtesy of the four goals produced by Dennis Maruk—three in the second period and the last into an empty net at 19:56.

Equally important was the play of Capitals goalie Gary Inness, who stopped 19 of 20 shots in the first period alone and 43 of 46 on the evening. "You've got to give credit to their goaltender," Rangers coach Don Murdoch said after.

The first period not only featured sensational work from Inness, it also produced 70 minutes in penalties thanks to a series of fights and three game-misconduct penalties. The Rangers squandered a 1–0 lead after the first, but were tied 2–2 early in the second before the Caps pulled away.

Anders Hedberg scored for the Blueshirts early in the third to make it a 4–3 game, but despite a ferocious attack from the home side Inness held the fort and Maruk sealed the win with a late goal into the empty net when Wayne Thomas was on the bench.

3

J. C.
TREMBLAY

QUEBEC NORDIQUES
OCTOBER 28, 1979

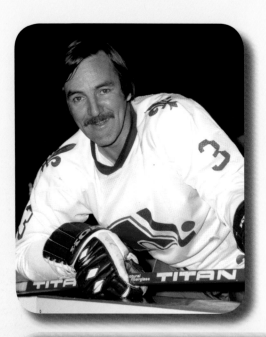

Born: Bagotville, Quebec, January 22, 1939
Died: Montreal, Quebec, December 7, 1994
Position: Defence
Shoots: Left
Height: 5'11"
Weight: 170 lbs.

HONOURS
- **Stanley Cup** 1965, 1966, 1968, 1969, 1971
- **NHL First All-Star Team** 1971
- **NHL All-Star Game** 1959, 1965, 1967, 1968, 1969, 1971, 1972
- **Played for WHA Team Canada at 1974 Summit**
- **WHA First All-Star Team** 1973, 1975, 1976
- **Best defenceman in WHA** 1973, 1975

NHL CAREER STATS

	Regular Season					Playoffs				
Years	GP	G	A	P	Pim	GP	G	A	P	Pim
1959–72	794	57	306	363	204	108	14	51	65	58

CAREER

Sometimes circumstance decides a player's fate, and such was the case for a teen-aged J. C. Tremblay. In junior he was a left winger in the Montreal organization, but this was the late 1950s when the Habs were stocked with offensive power. He moved back to defence, got called up for two extensive visits, and never looked back.

Tremblay was by no means an offensive force from the blue line, but he was an excellent skater who could move the puck up ice and out of harm's way. He became a player recognized league-wide after his performance during the 1965 play-offs. The Canadiens had lost Jacques Laperriere to injury in the semi-finals against Toronto, and Tremblay filled the void with remarkable skill during the finals against Chicago. He was runner-up for the Conn Smythe Trophy and was instrumental in the team winning its first Stanley Cup since 1960.

With league expansion and personal maturity, Tremblay became more confident with the puck and did, indeed, become more successful on offence. In 1970–71, he set a team record with 63 points by a defenceman and was second to Bobby Orr in voting for the Norris Trophy. But by 1972, he had won the Cup five times with Montreal and wanted a new challenge.

The WHA offered him that and more. For starters, he was wooed by the Quebec Nordiques, so he could remain in his home province. The team's offer was also far more lucrative than anything the Habs were willing to offer. To cap it off, the league, being a new outfit, promised Tremblay an opportunity to extend his career beyond what he could have hoped for in the NHL.

He left Montreal, his home of 13 years, where he'd played every year of the WHA's existence—from 1972 to 1979—leaving only to retire. Such was his success and popularity in the provincial capital that the Nordiques retired his number 3 sweater—fitting tribute to a beloved local hero.

CEREMONY

The retiring of J. C. Tremblay's number 3 took a back seat to the arrival of the hated Montreal Canadiens and their star forward, Guy Lafleur, who was revered in Quebec City for his years as a junior. Also in attendance was Jean Béliveau, who also received a tremendous ovation in remembrance of his years with the Quebec Aces in the early 1950s. Nonetheless, Tremblay received his due and was humble in accepting his sweater. "I've played many big games in my life, but I've never been as nervous as I am tonight. I'm honoured the Nordiques considered having this presentation for me."

The energetic Tremblay was no longer playing in the NHL (or the WHA), but that didn't prevent him from thinking big. "My projects for the future do not change," he told everyone. "I still intend to play in Europe next year. I might stay there 10 years. Or, I might come home and begin a new career as an assistant coach."

THE GAME:

Quebec Nordiques 5–Montreal Canadiens 4

It was Quebec's fourth game since joining the NHL, but this was the one everyone had been waiting for—the first showdown against provincial nemesis, les Canadiens. Le Colisée was sold out, and fans spilled into the streets in anticipation The roaring reached deafening levels in the first period when Richard Leduc scored to give the Nordiques a 1–0 lead.

That lead held up until the first minute of the second period when Pierre Mondou tied the game on a power play, and the crowd grew quiet when Steve Shutt put the visitors up 2–1 at the halfway point. But the Nordiques tied the game and the teams exchanged goals later in the period to make it 3–3 after 40 minutes, setting up a wild and raucous finish.

When Pierre Plante scored at 10:48 of the third on a shot from in close to put Quebec up 4–3, the crowd went crazy. And they went crazy again when Jamie Hislop gave the team a two-goal cushion. The Habs rallied for one late goal but couldn't tie the score, and the first great game in the NHL history of the Nordiques went into the books as a victory.

19

JOHN
MCKENZIE

HARTFORD WHALERS (WHA)
FEBRUARY 27, 1980

Born: High River, Alberta, December 12, 1937
Position: Right wing
Shoots: Right
Height: 5'9"
Weight: 175 lbs.

HONOURS
- **Stanley Cup** 1970, 1972
- **NHL All-Star Game** 1970, 1972
- **NHL Second All-Star Team** 1970
- **Played for WHA Team Canada at 1974 Summit**
- **Played 1976–79 with New England Whalers (WHA)**

NHL CAREER STATS

	Regular Season					Playoffs				
Years	GP	G	A	P	Pim	GP	G	A	P	Pim
1958–72	691	206	268	474	917	69	15	32	47	133

CAREER

During the first part of McKenzie's career, prior to expansion, he was a part-time player at best with Chicago, Detroit, and New York. He played more in the minors than the NHL, but midway through the 1965–66 season he was traded to Boston by the Rangers and everything fell into place. McKenzie was joining a team that was destined for greatness thanks to Bobby Orr, and he had a more defined role with the "Big Bad Bruins." That is, McKenzie was a first-class agitator and disturber, but one who could also put the puck in the net.

During his six and a half seasons with the Bruins, McKenzie averaged about 25 goals and 100 penalty minutes: testament to his two finest qualities. The Bruins won the Stanley Cup in 1970 and 1972, but after the latter victory he up and moved to the WHA, signing with Philadelphia Blazers as its playing-coach. McKenzie had been left unprotected by the Bruins in the 1972 Expansion Draft,

and although he wasn't selected he still felt slighted. He spent the rest of his career in the pirate league, retiring in the summer of 1979 after 21 seasons of pro hockey just as four more teams joined the NHL.

One of those was the New England Whalers, the team for which McKenzie played the final two and a half seasons in the WHA. Although he was a popular player with the fans, his is perhaps the most curious of all retired numbers. He never played in the NHL with the Hartford Whalers (they changed their name in the summer of '79), had a short career with New England in the WHA, and enjoyed only moderate success while there. The number, however, was taken out of retirement when the Whalers left Hartford to become the Carolina Hurricanes.

CEREMONY

McKenzie came to his retirement honestly. He attended the Hartford Whalers' training camp in Bolton, Ontario, in September 1979, and saw 51-year-old Gordie Howe and 39-year-old Dave Keon skating like crazy to keep up. McKenzie got in his car, drove home to Boston, and never played again.

He saw two games in Boston during the season, but this night of honour was his first trip to another arena since he'd retired. He was joined by his wife, Joyce, and three teenaged daughters—Betty, Jackie, and Laurie—while their infant daughter stayed at home with a babysitter.

The Whalers gave him a Volkswagen Rabbit with the number 19 painted on the hood and the visiting Bruins gave him a cowboy hat. His night was somewhat overshadowed by the late-evening announcement by the team that it had acquired another future Hall of Famer, Bobby Hull, from the Winnipeg Jets. "We weren't going to make this announcement until today," Jack Kelley, Hartford's director of hockey operations said later, "but word leaked out in Canada."

Further distraction came in several forms. First, the entire United States was still buzzing from the "Miracle on Ice" victory at the Lake Placid Olympics just five days earlier, and local rivals Boston and Hartford were active in recruiting players from that team. The Bruins were on the verge of announcing that they had signed goalie Jim Craig, while the Whalers were pursuing captain Mike Eruzione.

THE GAME: Boston Bruins 6–Hartford Whalers 3

The Whalers played some of their home games in Springfield and some at the Civic Center in Hartford, but on this night the ice was so bad it probably should have been played in the parking lot. "It was the worst ice I've ever seen," said the Bruins' Terry O'Reilly, no ballerina on blades by any means.

In fact, the game was nearly halted by referee Wally Harris at the end of the first period, but after conferring with both teams he decided to play the remaining two periods. Boston jumped into an early 3–1 lead, starting with a Rick Smith goal just 4:23 into the game.

Blaine Stoughton got his team-best 38th of the year to tie the score, but the Bruins pushed ahead with two more. The teams alternated in the second period, each scoring twice and the Bruins unable to pull away while the Whalers were unable to tie the game.

In the third, the puck bouncing like a tennis ball, Peter McNab got his third goal of the game to put away an easy 6–3 win. John Garrett gave up the first five Boston goals before giving way to Al Smith early in the second period when Craig MacTavish made it a 5–3 game for Boston.

9

JOHNNY
BUCYK

BOSTON BRUINS
MARCH 13, 1980

Born: Edmonton, Alberta, May 12, 1935
Position: Left wing
Shoots: Left
Height: 6'
Weight: 215 lbs.

HONOURS
- **Stanley Cup** 1970, 1972
- **Lady Byng Trophy** 1971, 1974
- **Lester Patrick Trophy** 1977
- **NHL All-Star Game** 1955, 1963, 1964, 1965, 1968, 1970, 1971
- **Hockey Hall of Fame** 1981

NHL CAREER STATS

Years	Regular Season					Playoffs				
	GP	G	A	P	Pim	GP	G	A	P	Pim
1955–78	1,540	556	813	1,369	497	124	41	62	103	42

CAREER

When you play 21 years for the same team you are bound to experience the full range of devastating lows and exultant highs, and Johnny Bucyk certainly did. In the pre–Bobby Orr days, Bucyk and the Bruins made the playoffs twice in 10 years. During Orr's career, they made it each and every year. Be that as it may, the resilient Bucyk started his Bruins life after being traded from the Red Wings in the summer of 1957, a young prospect going to Boston so Detroit could re-acquire goalie Terry Sawchuk. Bucyk has been with the Bruins ever since—50 years and counting.

As a youngster, Bucyk played junior with his hometown Edmonton Oil Kings before signing with the Detroit Red Wings for the 1955–56 season. But he played only 104 games with the team before it gave up on him and sold him to Boston. Bucyk developed into a high-scoring left winger. Tall, strong, and husky, he was no

lightning bolt on the port side, but he had great instincts and could pass the puck through whatever opposition traffic tried to block him. In the 1950s he played on a line with Bronco Horvath and Vic Stasiuk and they called themselves the Uke Line (because all three were of Ukrainian heritage), the team's top line and the only bright spot during some dismal seasons.

In all, Bucyk had 16 years of 20 goals or more, climaxing in 1970–71 when he had career highs for goals (51) and total points (116). Even when he was 37 years old, he still managed a 40-goal season in 1972–73, a rare achievement indeed. Bucyk was also a gentlemanly player who rarely fought during his 23 years in the NHL, and by the time he retired he had gone well past Hall of Fame plateaus for goals (556) and points (1,369). His 1,540 games played was also among the most all-time.

Despite the great players who were his teammates in the Orr era, it was Bucyk who was the de facto team captain, especially from 1967 to 1973 when there was no official captain. He had worn the "C" in 1966–67 and wore it the last five years of his NHL career (1973–78), but it was also he who received the Cup after each victory.

CEREMONY

His mother was there. So were his wife and three children. So were Bruins general manager, Harry Sinden, and 14,024 fans. All gathered at the Garden to say good-bye to one of the team's greatest players.

Bucyk admitted to conflicting feelings as he watched his number 9 rise to the rafters. "I was thinking that I'd never be wearing that number again," he said. "That's the thing when you see that number go up there. It's final. You're not going to play again."

On the other hand, he wasn't selfish or possessive about the number itself. "If Mr. Mooney [Paul, the team's president] were to call me at some time in the future and say, 'We've got a kid we think is good enough to wear number 9,' then I'd say sure, let him have it. Why not? That banner with my name and number is up there in the rafters. It will always stay up there."

That kind of selfless remark was one of the reasons why it was up there in the first place.

THE GAME: Boston Bruins 4–Detroit Red Wings 2

The Bruins left no doubt this was Bucyk's night and would not be spoiled by the Red Wings. They scored three goals in the opening period and rolled to an impressive 4–2 win over one of their Original Six rivals.

Jean Ratelle got the first goal, lifting a puck over Jim Rutherford as he was falling down. The point was the 1,230th of his career, moving him into sixth place on the all-time list. Bob Miller and Peter McNab made it 3–0 before the first intermission, and the Bruins got the only goal of the second to make it a four-goal cushion.

"The fourth goal finished us," Detroit coach Bobby Kromm admitted after.

The Red Wings scored twice in the final period when the game was out of reach, and they had only 16 shots all night at Gerry Cheevers. "We won this game for the Chief," Dick Redmond declared in the jubilant Boston dressing room afterwards.

21

STAN MIKITA

CHICAGO BLACK HAWKS
OCTOBER 19, 1980

Born: Sokolnice, Czechoslovakia, May 20, 1940
Position: Forward
Shoots: Right
Height: 5'9"
Weight: 170 lbs.

HONOURS
- **Stanley Cup** 1961
- **Hart Trophy** 1967, 1968
- **Art Ross Trophy** 1964, 1965, 1967, 1968
- **Lady Byng Trophy** 1967, 1968
- **Lester Patrick Trophy** 1976
- **NHL All-Star Game** 1964, 1967, 1968, 1969, 1971, 1972, 1973, 1974, 1975
- **Hockey Hall of Fame** 1983

NHL CAREER STATS

	Regular Season					Playoffs				
Years	GP	G	A	P	Pim	GP	G	A	P	Pim
1958–80	1,394	541	926	1,467	1,270	155	59	91	150	169

CAREER

Stan Mikita played all of his 22 seasons and 1,394 regular-season games with Chicago—winning the Stanley Cup in 1961, appearing in four decades, and making history at several points along the way. He had a three-game tryout with the team in 1958–59 before joining the Black Hawks full time the next year, and his goal production increased each of his first five years until 1963–64 when he had 39 goals and led the league with 89 points to capture his first of four Art Ross Trophies.

Mikita made history in 1967 when he won the Art Ross, Hart, and Lady Byng trophies all in the same year—the first player to do so. He repeated the feat the next year, but what was most incredible was the turnaround in his style of play that allowed him to be considered for the Byng.

In his first several years in the league, Mikita wasted a great deal of time and effort fighting, trying to prove himself as a tough guy. Coach Billy Reay took him

aside and told him to focus on his skills and not waste time in the penalty box. Mikita listened and went from being one of the most penalized players to one of the least penalized.

Mikita put together a string of 14 successive seasons with at least 24 goals, an accomplishment attributable to two factors. First, he played on the Scooter Line with Ken Wharram and Ab McDonald, the highest-scoring threesome in Hawks history. Second, Mikita discovered that a sharply hooked blade created shots that caused the puck to dip and dance unpredictably. Thus was born the banana blade.

Although his longevity was remarkable, Mikita suffered two injuries in the 1970s that had long-term effects. First, he suffered a bad concussion and became an advocate of mandatory helmets. Then, early in the 1979–80 season he suffered a serious back injury that forced him to retire. He was 39 and had enjoyed a superb career that included 541 goals and 1,467 points.

CEREMONY

For the first time in the great history of the Chicago Black Hawks, a number was retired to the rafters. And what a moving ceremony it was, in part because of Mikita's contribution to the team, in part because of the man Mikita was.

He was joined on ice by his uncle Joe; his wife, Jill; and their four children—Meg, Scott, Jane, and Christopher. Joe, who was like a father to Stan, had gotten the boy out of Communist Czechoslovakia and given him a life of freedom in Canada; Stan owed virtually everything to him.

"I can say this is not the happiest night of my life," Mikita started, wistfully. "I think it's the greatest, but not the happiest."

He continued by thanking the three coaches he'd played under—Rudy Pilous, Tommy Ivan, and Billy Reay. Then he thanked his teammates. "Over the 21 years I skated on this pond, I played with 170 of them, but I really only had five linemates—Kenny Wharram, Ab McDonald, and Doug Mohns, from the days of the Scooter Line. And, I'm extremely proud to say that I also played with a couple of plough-horses—Cliff Korroll and John Marks."

In finishing, he added: "I have one more duty and that comes from the heart. I'd like to pay tribute to someone who besides giving me love and affection gave me the greatest commodity in life. He took me out of a Communist country and gave me something I think we're all striving for. He gave me freedom. I'd like to pay tribute to the greatest guy I know—my pop."

THE GAME: Chicago Black Hawks 8–Washington Capitals 4

The Black Hawks stepped onto the Stadium ice after the ceremonies and delivered a performance worthy of the history attached to the evening, scoring the first goal just 1:15 into the game courtesy of Rich Preston and not letting up. The entertaining first period saw the Capitals rally for a 2–1 lead, but Tom Lysiak scored two goals later in the period to make it a 3–2 Hawks lead after 20 minutes of play.

Chicago pulled away in the second, scoring three unanswered goals. In the third, Lysiak completed his hat trick with a goal at 1:24, and only two late goals from Washington brought the score a bit closer. The Hawks improved to 6–1–1 on the young season to stay in first place of the Smythe Division. Tony Esposito was in goal for the Hawks while Mike Palmateer allowed all eight goals on 40 shots for the Caps.

9

GORDIE
HOWE

HARTFORD WHALERS (NHL)
FEBRUARY 18, 1981

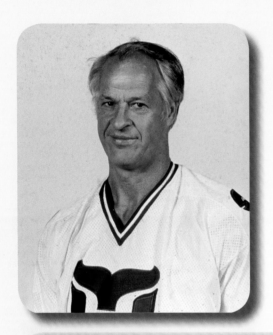

Born: Floral, Saskatchewan, March 31, 1928
Position: Right wing
Shoots: Right
Height: 6'
Weight: 205 lbs.

HONOURS
- **Stanley Cup** 1950, 1952, 1954, 1955
- **Hart Trophy** 1952, 1953, 1957, 1958, 1960, 1963
- **Art Ross Trophy** 1951, 1952, 1953, 1954, 1957, 1963
- **Lester Patrick Trophy** 1967
- **NHL All-Star Game** 1948, 1949, 1950, 1951, 1952, 1953, 1954, 1955, 1957, 1958, 1959, 1960, 1961, 1962, 1963, 1964, 1965, 1967, 1968, 1969, 1970, 1971, 1980
- **Hockey Hall of Fame** 1972

NHL CAREER STATS

	Regular Season					Playoffs				
Years	GP	G	A	P	Pim	GP	G	A	P	Pim
1946–80	1,767	801	1,049	1,850	1,685	157	68	92	160	220

HARTFORD CAREER

Gordie Howe's life changed again, forever, in February 1971. After playing a charity game with his two teenaged sons, Marty and Mark, and at the end of this NHL season, he retired and had surgery on both his arthritic wrists. For two years Gordie worked a desk job with the Red Wings, a happily contented alumnus whose number 9 had been immortalized by the team and wafted slowly in the rafters of the old Olympia.

But in the summer of 1973, Houston Aeros management approached the Howe clan. They wanted Marty and Mark to forget about waiting until they turned 20 to play in the NHL and instead sign right away with the Aeros in the WHA. Oh, and they wanted Gordie to come out of retirement and play with the kids, something that had never been done at such a high level of the game.

They all said yes, and one year turned into two and three and so on. Incredibly,

Gordie scored as if he were 25 years old, not 45. In all, he played six years in the WHA, averaging about 70 games and 30 goals a season. In the summer of 1979, the unthinkable happened. The Whalers became one of four teams to join the NHL. More amazing, Gordie and the kids signed on for another season.

By this time Gordie was 51 years old and worried about making a fool of himself. No need. He played the full season, scored 15 goals, and his plus-minus stat was, appropriately enough, +9. By the time he retired he had played in his fifth decade, passed 800 career goals, and appeared in his 23rd All-Star Game. His first came in 1948, his last in 1980 with Detroit, where he was given the most emotional ovation in that game's history. When the Whalers retired his number 9, they did it to honour not only the team's greatest player, but also the game's.

CEREMONY

Any tribute to Gordie Howe cannot be a simple one, and this day was hardly limited to the pre-game retiring of his number 9; indeed, the celebrations began at a dinner the day before at the Grand Ballroom of the Sheraton Hartford Hotel. The sumptuous dinner was attended by an impressive array of guests such as Phil Esposito, Tommy Ivan, NHL president John Ziegler, and Whalers owner Howard Baldwin.

At the pre-game event, Gordie was flanked as always by his wife, Colleen; their daughter, Cathy; and their three sons, Marty, Murray, and Mark, who was accompanied by his own young family.

Gordie was given a golf bag and custom irons from the Hartford media. Winnipeg coach Bill Sutherland gave Howe a mounted bison, and Ziegler offered a framed portrait of "Mr. Hockey." Connecticut governor William O'Neil gave a framed citation that declared this to be Gordie Howe Week, and current team captain, Mike Rogers, presented Gordie and Colleen with a four-day trip to Bermuda.

To top off the evening, Bobby Orr appeared in the passenger seat of a new golf cart with the Whalers' logo and Howe's number 9 on the sides. "Being here this evening, taking part in the retirement of number 9, is right up there on the top of the highlights of my career," Orr told the cheering crowd.

And then the team raised the number 9 to the rafters of the Civic Arena, where it would hang in perpetuity.

THE GAME: Hartford Whalers 3–Winnipeg Jets 3
A late goal by the tired visitors spoiled an otherwise excellent night for the Whalers, who now had run their winless streak to 10 games. The Jets were running on adrenaline for this game. They were stranded in Detroit before busing to Toronto and getting a charter to Hartford, arriving after the scheduled 8 p.m. start. The game was delayed by Howe's tribute, but teams had only a five-minute warm-up before the game began. As well, the Jets were the worst team in the league, having gone a record 35 games without a win earlier in the year.

Whalers defenceman Norm Barnes was proud to see his wife, Cid, sing the national anthem, and then the game started. In a radical experiment to improve telecast quality, the match was played on blue ice. The first period was without a goal, and Ron Wilson of the Jets scored the only goal of the second.

Don Nachbaur got the Whalers on the scoreboard early in the third, and Rick Dudley put the Jets up, 2–1. The Whalers then scored twice, but Barry Long tied the game with just 2:34 left to make it a 3–3 final.

8 BARCLAY PLAGER

ST. LOUIS BLUES
MARCH 24, 1981

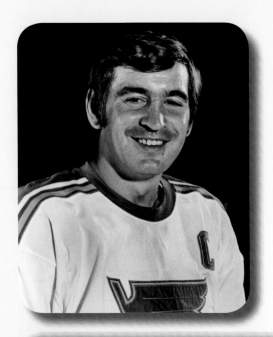

Born: Kirkland Lake, Ontario, March 26, 1941
Died: Creve Coeur, Missouri, February 6, 1988
Position: Defence
Shoots: Left
Height: 5'11"
Weight: 175 lbs.

HONOURS
- **NHL All-Star Game** 1970, 1971, 1973, 1974
- **Played entire career with St. Louis Blues**
- **St. Louis captain** 1970–76
- **Central Hockey League MVP** 1977

NHL CAREER STATS

	Regular Season					Playoffs				
Years	GP	G	A	P	Pim	GP	G	A	P	Pim
1967–77	614	44	187	231	1,115	68	3	20	23	182

CAREER

Number 8 in your program; number one in your hearts. So they said about Barclay Plager whose life was cut short by a brain tumour at age 46. Yet while he was alive, he gave 10 years of his life playing for the St. Louis Blues and the rest of it in the organization in a coaching capacity.

Plager was the eldest of three brothers—Bill and Bob were the others—who came out of Northern Ontario, but like so many aspirants of his day he couldn't crack the Original Six. He played in the minor pros for several years, but the doors opened in 1967 when expansion doubled the NHL from six to 12 teams. He found himself with the Blues in 1967–68, and they soon called him up to bolster the blue line.

Big and tough, Plager was just the type of player coach Scotty Bowman needed. He had experience and, of course, the desire not to return to the minors, and

he delivered the goods every night. Only once during his playing career did the Blues team fail to make the playoffs; indeed, the first three years were the most special because the team went to the Cup Final each year. Granted they lost all 12 games, but this was when the expansion teams played the Original Six in the mismatched Final.

Barclay was always a fan favourite, and although he played for several years with his brothers in St. Louis, he was the most cherished of the three. The team retired his number just a few years after his retirement, knowing full well his value to the players, the team, and the city that had become his home.

CEREMONY

As the ceremonies began at 7:45 p.m. prior to a big game at the Checkerdome, Plager came onto the ice with his wife, Helen, and their daughters, Karen and Kerri. Emcee Dan Kelly then introduced Emile Francis, the Blues' president and general manager. "We feel that Barc, more than anyone else, exemplifies what it means to be a member of the Blues," Francis declared to a thunderous roar of approval.

Joining Plager on ice for the honour were many teammates and friends in the game, including Gary Sabourin, Claude Larose, Jimmy Roberts, Noel Picard, Ab McDonald, former coach Scotty Bowman, current Islanders coach Al Arbour, Cliff Fletcher, and Bud Poile.

Gifts for Plager this night included golf clubs, a television, watches for him and his wife, a trip to Hawaii, a case of wine, patio furniture, and a stereo. Denis Potvin, on behalf of the opposition Islanders, gave Plager an old photo of Arbour and Plager from their playing days together, and Brian Sutter gave him a ring engraved with the number 8.

Then came the topper as Francis presented Plager with a 1981 Buick Century that was driven out to centre ice. Of course it was blue, and it bore the license plate "BARC-8." Once the car came to a halt, out stepped his brothers, Bill and Bob, and his parents, who'd made the trek from Kapuskasing, Ontario.

Finally, Plager addressed the crowd. "I like speaking about as much as these two teams like losing," he began. "It's something to be honoured by a team I was proud to play for and by fans I was happy to play in front of. I feel grateful and humble."

THE GAME: New York Islanders 5–St. Louis Blues 3

The Blues may have been first overall in the standings at this point in the season, but they were playing the defending Stanley Cup champions and on this night they couldn't keep pace for a full 60 minutes. In fact, the Blues built an impressive 3–1 lead by the midway point of the game only to see the Islanders rally in impressive fashion.

Wayne Babych opened the scoring with his 53rd goal of the season for St. Louis at 4:36 of the first, but Bryan Trottier got the first goal of his hat trick to answer back. In the second, St. Louis got a pair from Blake Dunlop, but then New York took control.

Trottier got a late one to make it a 3–2 game after two periods and then the visitors scored the only three goals of the final period, the last one, by Trottier, into an empty net. Said St. Louis coach Red Berenson "It was a great game between two great teams and both played well. All it took was a couple of breaks either way to win it."

7

YVON LABRE

WASHINGTON CAPITALS
NOVEMBER 7, 1981

Born: Sudbury, Ontario, November 29, 1949
Position: Defence
Shoots: Left
Height: 5'11"
Weight: 190 lbs.

HONOURS
- Drafted by Pittsburgh 38th overall 1969
- Played for the Toronto Marlies in OHA 1967–69
- Played all but 37 games of his career with Washington

NHL CAREER STATS

	Regular Season					Playoffs				
Years	GP	G	A	P	Pim	GP	G	A	P	Pim
1970–81	371	14	87	101	788	—	—	—	—	—

CAREER

Yvon Labre might well have the fewest career goals by any player whose number is retired—14. That's because, of course, scoring wasn't his forte. He was a defenceman first, an enforcer second, but above all he was the most beloved member of the Washington Capitals during an era when they were just about the worst sports team on the planet.

Drafted by Pittsburgh in 1969, Labre played only 21 games with the Penguins a year later and 16 games three years thereafter while spending most of his time in the minors. When the Capitals entered the league in 1974, they claimed him in the Expansion Draft and his career was given a major boost.

Labre was the heart and soul of the team at a time when it gave up more goals than any other in NHL history. His plus-minus was nothing to boast about, but his dedication to the team and his competitive fire every night in the face of defeat en-

deared him to teammates and fans alike.

He was named captain in 1976, but suffered two serious knee injuries that cost him most of the 1977–78 and 1979–80 seasons. Try as he might, he couldn't return to his former playing shape and was forced to retire midway through the 1980–81 season.

Although he and the Caps never appeared in the playoffs during these years, Labre made such an impact in the community that early the next season the team retired his number 7 sweater. It remained the only number in the rafters for 16 years until Rod Langway's number 5 joined his, in 1997.

CEREMONY

Yvon Labre had his number 7 sweater retired twice. The first time came informally, and the second time was a far grander occasion. Never the most talented player, Labre was always worried about making the team at training camp every year, but every year he made the grade. His knee injury in 1979–80 was so bad that no one thought he could recover, so owner Abe Pollin, on the occasion of the team's 500th game in franchise history, on November 22, 1980, presented Labre with the sweater and vowed no one else would ever wear it.

But Labre was proud, even though he was on the injured list. He trained hard, and came back to the ice until a final hit in a game on February 14, 1981, left no doubt his career was over. Only then did he accept the formal retiring of his number 7.

A more official ceremony was held for him on November 7, 1981, but this time Pollin wasn't present. It was a tough time for a sweater retirement given that the team had just fired general manager Max McNab and coach Gary Green the previous day, in a forceful reaction to the team's 11-game winless streak.

Still, the 15-minute ceremony was put into perspective by Labre, who told the 12,719 fans: "I'd like to dedicate this night to the Clydesdales of the game, the muckers, because they won't have the opportunity to have a night like this." Broadcaster Ron Weber was the host for the ceremony.

THE GAME: New York Rangers 3–Washington Capitals 1
The struggles continued for the Capitals as they lost their 12th straight game, a first for incoming coach Roger Crozier, who saw up close what the team's many troubles were.

The Caps got the only goal of the opening period, by Gaetan Duchesne, but after that the Rangers took over. They got two goals in the second and one in the third to pull away, despite a fine night from Washington goalie Dave Parro. "I wish we could have played the whole game like we did the first period," lamented Crozier, honing in on one of the team's troubles.

Mike Rogers, Eddie Johnstone, and Ron Duguay got the Rangers' goals.

2

RICK LEY

HARTFORD WHALERS (WHA AND NHL)
DECEMBER 26, 1982

Born: Orillia, Ontario, November 2, 1948
Position: Defence
Shoots: Left
Height: 5'9"
Weight: 190 lbs.

HONOURS
- WHA best defenceman 1979
- Captain of Hartford in WHA & NHL 1975–81
- Played for WHA Team Canada in 1974 Summit
- Won Memorial Cup with Niagara Falls Flyers 1968
- Later became head coach for Hartford and Vancouver, NHL

NHL CAREER STATS

	Regular Season					Playoffs				
Years	GP	G	A	P	Pim	GP	G	A	P	Pim
1968–81	310	12	72	84	528	14	0	2	2	20

CAREER

One of the charming aspects about a team retiring a player's number is that the honour is reserved for players special to that particular team. In Rick Ley's case, he was no Hall of Famer, no pioneering defenceman or record setter. He was merely a very important part of the Hartford Whalers for a decade—and that's what retired numbers are all about. He also, interestingly, played in every All-Star Game hosted by the WHA.

Ley was drafted by the Toronto Maple Leafs in 1966, but he played only four seasons with the team (1968–72). A classic stay-at-home defenceman, he was neither big nor physical, but he was effective in his own end and could move the puck out with efficiency. He was one of dozens of players to leave the NHL in 1972, however, and sign with the WHA, in his case with the New England Whalers.

Although his style of play never changed, the size of his paycheque certainly

acceleration even at the NHL level. The banana hook was soon outlawed by the league because it not only added velocity to the puck, it also added unpredictability to its direction, making it dangerous for goalies. Hull liked to shoot high on one shift, to make the goalie nervous, and then low the next, when he often scored.

From the time he entered the league in 1957 as a fresh-faced 18-year-old until 1972, Hull played exclusively for the Chicago Black Hawks, becoming the highest-scoring left winger in the game's history. Those 604 goals also put him behind only Gordie Howe on the career list, although Phil Esposito soon passed him. Only twice in 15 years did his Hawks fail to qualify for the playoffs, and in 1961 they won the team's most recent Cup until 2010, beating Detroit in six games, the first time the Hawks had been in the Final in 17 years.

CEREMONY

"The biggest mistake I ever made in my life was leaving this city," Bobby Hull told the 17,697 fans at the Chicago Stadium from centre ice. "I'm so proud to have my jersey hoisted beside that of my great friend and a wonderful athlete, Stan Mikita." Indeed, Mikita and Hull's were the only numbers retired by the Hawks at that time.

Hull was surrounded by former teammates as he spoke, notably Pat Stapleton, Bill White, Pierre Pilote, Keith Magnuson, "Pit" Martin, Dale Tallon, Reggie Fleming, Jim Pappin, Glen Skov, "Chiko" Maki, Fred Stanfield, Gerry Desjardins, Elmer "Moose" Vasko, coach Billy Reay, and, of course, Bobby's brother, Dennis.

Most important, Bill Wirtz was front and centre, the man who righted a wrong done by his father, Arthur Wirtz, who never forgave Hull for leaving the Hawks to sign with the upstart WHA. The symbolism was not lost on anyone.

THE GAME:

Boston Bruins 5–Chicago Black Hawks 1
Coach Orval Tessier had been battling with 40-year-old goalie Tony Esposito in recent weeks as Murray Bannerman's play was excellent and the veteran's not so impressive. Bannerman had started the last nine games since Esposito was shelled in a 9–3 loss to the Islanders three weeks before. But the coach had long ago decided that with so many alumni from Esposito's early days in house to honour Hull, "Tony O" should get the start this night. Although the score was unflattering, he did face 19 shots in the first period alone.

Steve Ludzik, in fact, got the game's first goal at 7:24, but it wasn't long before Boston's Mike Krushelnyski tied the score. In the middle period, though, the Bruins struck for four unanswered goals, three coming on set-ups from Mike O'Connell who, three years to the day earlier, had been traded by Chicago to Boston for Al Secord.

16

BOBBY CLARKE

PHILADELPHIA FLYERS
NOVEMBER 15, 1984

Born: Flin Flon, Manitoba, August 13, 1949
Position: Centre
Shoots: Left
Height: 5'10"
Weight: 185 lbs.

HONOURS
- **Stanley Cup** 1974, 1975
- **Hart Trophy** 1973, 1975, 1976
- **Lester B. Pearson Award** 1973
- **Lester Patrick Trophy** 1980
- **Bill Masterton Trophy** 1972
- **Frank Selke Trophy** 1983
- **Played for Canada in 1972 Summit Series**
- **Hockey Hall of Fame** 1987

NHL CAREER STATS

	Regular Season					Playoffs				
Years	GP	G	A	P	Pim	GP	G	A	P	Pim
1969–84	1,144	358	852	1,210	1,453	136	42	77	119	152

CAREER

Not the most gentlemanly player to skate in the NHL, Bobby Clarke was the gap-toothed leader of the Philadelphia Flyers during the reign of the "Broad Street Bullies," from 1969 to 1984, during which time the team won two Stanley Cups.

Despite Clarke's great junior career with Flin Flon, general managers were reluctant to draft him in 1969 because he was diabetic, and they feared he wouldn't be able to handle the rigours of a typical NHL season, its physical demands, the travel, and inconsistent eating habits that went with the game.

But anyone who knew Clarke knew that first and foremost he was a fighter, a persistent and dogged young man determined to make it at any price. He stuck to a plan to take his insulin and played many a full season, the diabetes having no noticeable effect on his health or play at all.

Clarke quickly put himself front and centre on an emerging team in the early

1970s, scoring more than 30 goals with regularity despite not being a pretty, one-on-one type player or one with a great shot or moves. His goals came through fighting for territory, banging home a rebound, a quick shot in tight.

Incredibly, he had three seasons of more than 100 points playing on a line with Bill Barber, and to start his third season, 1971–72, he became the youngest captain in NHL history when he had the "C" sewn onto his sweater. He won the Masterton Trophy in 1972 in recognition of his ability to play despite the diabetes, and, more telling, he won the first of three Hart Trophies the next year along with the Lester B. Pearson Award. Clarke led the Flyers to Cup wins in 1974 and 1975, taking out Boston and then Buffalo, backed by the goaltending of Bernie Parent.

After his third season, he had already acquired such a reputation for his skill and tenacity that he was named to Team Canada for the 1972 Summit Series, won in dramatic fashion by Paul Henderson in the final minute of the final game. By the time he retired in 1984 to become the team's general manager, Clarke had played in 1,144 games and recorded 1,210 points—not bad for a guy with diabetes. Clarke defined the term leadership, led by example, and willed the team to win on many nights.

CEREMONY

Clarke's celebrations began when the team hosted a black-tie dinner for 350 guests, including his Stanley Cup teammates, at a downtown hotel. Former coach Fred Shero made a speech honouring Clarke.

Two days later, the 45-minute number-retirement ceremony was held at the Spectrum. It was punctuated by a four-minute ovation after which the team played a video of Kate Smith singing "God Bless America" on the giant scoreboard above centre ice.

Clarke came out to centre ice with his mother, Yvonne; father, Cliff; wife, Sandy; children, Jakki, Jody, Wade, Lucas; and mother-in-law. It was Wade who came up to him at the appointed hour to give his father the number 16 sweater, as the banner, high in the rafters already, was unfurled to display the retired number.

Clarke was given a sterling silver hockey stick while he and his wife received Rolex watches. As well, the team commissioned two identical sculptures depicting Clarke jumping for joy after scoring the overtime winning goal in game two of the 1974 Stanley Cup Final in Boston. One was given to him and the other, called the Bobby Clarke Trophy, was to be presented annually to the team's best player. Even the opposition Whalers contributed with a new set of golf clubs, and the Flyers also gave him and Sandy gold watches.

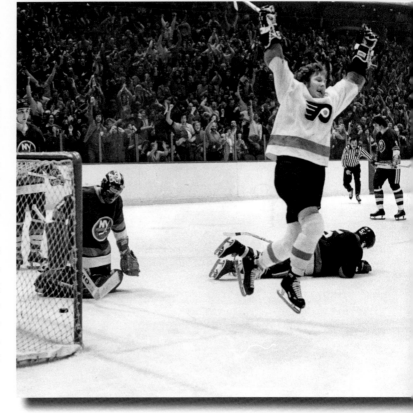

THE GAME: Philadelphia Flyers 6–Hartford Whalers 1
The Flyers stormed out to a 3–0 lead after the first period and coasted to a 6–1 win over the visiting Hartford Whalers. Derrick Smith, Dave Poulin, and Tim Kerr got the early goals, and in the second period Risto Siltanen made it 3–1 halfway through after which Kerr, with his second, brought it to 4–1.

Rich Sutter and Murray Craven scored late goals to put the game well out of reach as 17,191 fans roared their approval in honour of Bobby Clarke's special night. Goalie Pelle Lindbergh picked up the win by stopping 26 of 27 shots.

4

AURÈLE JOLIAT

MONTREAL CANADIENS
OCTOBER 9, 1971
AND JANUARY 12, 1985

Born: Ottawa, Ontario, August 29, 1901
Died: Ottawa, Ontario, June 2, 1986
Position: Left wing
Shoots: Left
Height: 5'7"
Weight: 136 lbs.

HONOURS
- **Stanley Cup** 1924, 1930, 1931
- **Hart Trophy** 1934
- **First NHL All-Star Team** 1931
- **Second NHL All-Star Team** 1932, 1934, 1935
- **Hockey Hall of Fame** 1947

NHL CAREER STATS

Years	Regular Season					Playoffs				
	GP	G	A	P	Pim	GP	G	A	P	Pim
1922–38	655	270	190	460	771	46	9	13	22	66

CAREER

By the time he retired in 1938, Aurèle Joliat was ranked third all time for goals behind only Howie Morenz and Nels Stewart. The "Little Giant" scored at least 12 goals in 15 of his 16 seasons, totals which might not sound like much today, but in the era before the centre red line was added and offense minimal, this was an impressive fact.

Joliat was sent from the Saskatoon Sheiks to the Montreal Canadiens when Habs forward "Newsy" Lalonde signed with the Saskatchewan team. It seemed like a lopsided deal at first blush, but it didn't take long for fans to see that the youthful speed of Joliat made up for the nostalgic love for the ageing Lalonde. In just his second season with the team, Joliat helped bring the Stanley Cup to the Canadiens. He won the trophy twice more with the Habs, in 1930 and again in 1931.

In his prime, Joliat skated on a line with friend Morenz and Billy Boucher, and the three proved among the most dangerous and explosive stars of their day. Joliat

was prematurely bald and wore a black cap to hide his bare head. Opponents earned his wrath when they knocked it off, something they were ill-advised to do because it made him so angry he became more motivated to play well.

CEREMONY

The Montreal Canadiens feted Aurèle Joliat with another number 4, Jean Béliveau. In keeping with tradition at the time, they were given their sweaters to take home as a symbol of the number never being worn again. Gerard Dandurand presented Joliat with his number 4 while Toe Blake presented Béliveau with his.

Joliat was honoured a second time during the Canadiens' 75th anniversary on January 12, 1985. The evening started with a dinner, during which time an 18-minute video documenting the team's history was shown. Prior to the game, elaborate ceremonies featured Prime Minister Brian Mulroney and his wife, Mila, Montreal mayor Jean Drapeau, longtime general manager Frank Selke, and Canadiens president Ronald Corey.

The team's all-time "dream team" appeared in full equipment: Joliat, goalie Jacques Plante, defencemen Doug Harvey and Larry Robinson, and forwards Maurice Richard, Jean Béliveau, and Dickie Moore. They were accompanied by coach Toe Blake. One scary moment occurred when Joliat tripped over the red carpet and fell, but the 83-year-old recovered and was uninjured.

THE GAMES:

October 9, 1971, Montreal Canadiens 4–New York Rangers 4
The Rangers spoiled the fun a bit by scoring the first and last goals of the game and limiting the Canadiens to a 4–4 tie on this special night. Dave Balon got the only goal of the first period, beating Montreal goalie Ken Dryden. Bobby Rousseau got the fans worried when he made it a 2–0 game early in the second.

Frank Mahovlich got one back for the home side at 5:05, but less than two minutes later Vic Hadfield restored the two-goal lead. The "Roadrunner," Yvan Cournoyer, scored on Ed Giacomin before the end of the second to cut the Rangers' lead to 3–2.

The Habs took control in the third on second goals each from Cournoyer and Mahovlich, but the Forum faithful were given a rude jolt when Pete Stemkowski scored with just 1:29 remaining to salvage a 4–4 tie for the Blueshirts.

January 12, 1985, Montreal Canadiens 1–Buffalo Sabres 1
Sabres goalie Tom Barrasso was the hero of the night, making several great saves and stopping 29 of 30 shots to give Buffalo a road tie. Mario Tremblay got the game's first goal at 5:58 on the power play, and Mike Foligno tied the game midway through the period. That was all the scoring to be seen this night in an entertaining game.

30

ROGIE
VACHON

LOS ANGELES KINGS
FEBRUARY 14, 1985

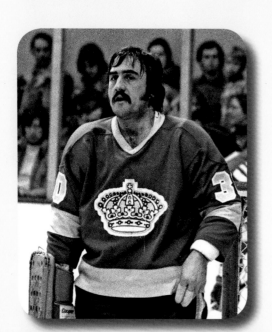

Born: Palmarolle, Quebec, September 8, 1945
Position: Goalie
Catches: Left
Height: 5'7"
Weight: 170 lbs.

HONOURS
• **Vezina Trophy** 1968 (shared with Gump Worsley)
• **NHL All-Star Game** 1973, 1975, 1978
• **Played in 1976 Canada Cup for Canada**

NHL CAREER STATS
Regular Season

Years	GP	W-L-T	Mins	GA	SO	GAA
1966–82	795	355-291-127	46,298	2,310	51	2.99

Playoffs

Years	GP	W-L-T	Mins	GA	SO	GAA
1966–82	48	23-23-0	2,876	133	2	2.77

CAREER

In the old days, goalies were small and often a little chunky, a description that fit Rogie Vachon pretty accurately. Yet the diminutive star of the crease is today possibly the best goalie (certainly of the modern era) *not* in the Hockey Hall of Fame.

Vachon first rose to prominence with the Montreal Canadiens during the last year of the Original Six, 1966–67. He got into a few games down the stretch of the regular season, as Gump Worsley's backup, and he played so well he became the starter for the playoffs. When the Habs faced the Maple Leafs in the Stanley Cup Final, Toronto coach Punch Imlach crowed that his team would not lose to a "junior B goalie." He was right, but Vachon played well enough in defeat to show the

Canadiens he was their goalie of the future.

Over the next four years, Montreal won the Cup three times with Vachon playing about half the team's games. His career was turned upside down, though, late in the 1970–71 season when Ken Dryden came in and stole the show, leaving general manager Sam Pollock little option but to trade Vachon. Early the next season he was sent to Los Angeles for four players: Denis DeJordy, Noel Price, Dale Hoganson, and Doug Robinson.

The trade proved to be a career change in the extreme. Vachon went from a hockey-mad, Cup-winning city to an expansion team on the West Coast of the U.S. Nevertheless, it was there he became the number-one goalie for the better part of six and a half years.

His crowning glory, however, came back home, at the inaugural Canada Cup in 1976. Vachon played every minute of the series for Canada and allowed just 10 goals in seven games, leading the team to victory and earning his place in the nation's international hockey history.

Although he never won an individual award and never led the NHL in any statistical category after sharing the Vezina Trophy with Worsley in 1967–68, Vachon was always respected as one of the best goalies around. Because he was small, he relied on quick limbs and solid positioning for effective play.

CEREMONY

The 20-minute pre-game ceremony marked the first time the Kings had retired a number in its 18 years of existence. The club brought in Vachon's parents from Quebec for the honour.

Gifts included a cruise from owner Jerry Buss, as well as a bronze replica of his goalie mask. He was also given the NHL's Milestone Award from league president John Ziegler. Vachon received a number 30 sweater from Marcel Dionne, and after putting it on he received a lengthy ovation. Then, a large version of that sweater was lifted into the rafters where it settled beside the jerseys of Lakers' stars Jerry West, Wilt Chamberlain, and Elgin Baylor.

"You fans are responsible for me having that sweater up there," he said in praise of the 13,122 fans who'd made their way to the game.

THE GAME: Los Angeles Kings 3–Boston Bruins 3
On this night, all fans entering the Forum were given megaphones to help cheer on Vachon, but by the end of the game they were being used for booing the Kings, who blew a two-goal lead and had to settle for a tie.

Marcel Dionne got the game's first goal at 6:19 of the second period, his 34th of the year and 1,468th career point, third on the all-time list. The Bruins tied the game three minutes later, though, thanks to Rick Middleton. The goal marked the 11th straight time "Nifty" had reached the 20-goal mark on a season.

The Kings then went ahead by two with quick goals late in the middle period from John Paul Kelly and Steve Shutt, but they weren't able to preserve the win in the final 20 minutes. In all fairness, though, both Boston goals in the third were lucky. The first was scored accidentally by Bernie Nicholls past his own goalie, Darren Eliot, and the second banked in off the skate of defenceman Mark Hardy, again past an unsuspecting Eliot.

"Those were two of the flukiest goals you'll ever see, never mind that they were back to back," a frustrated Eliot noted later.

10 GUY LAFLEUR

MONTREAL CANADIENS
FEBRUARY 16, 1985

Born: Thurso, Quebec, September 20, 1951
Position: Right wing
Shoots: Right
Height: 6'
Weight: 185 lbs.

HONOURS
- **Stanley Cup** 1973, 1976, 1977, 1978, 1979
- **Hart Trophy** 1977, 1978
- **Art Ross Trophy** 1976, 1977, 1978
- **Lester B. Pearson Award** 1976, 1977, 1978
- **Conn Smythe Trophy** 1977
- **NHL All-Star Game** 1975, 1976, 1977, 1978, 1980, 1991
- **Hockey Hall of Fame** 1988

NHL CAREER STATS

Years	Regular Season					Playoffs				
	GP	G	A	P	Pim	GP	G	A	P	Pim
1971–91	1,126	560	793	1,353	399	128	58	76	134	67

CAREER

Montreal general manager Sam Pollock had to make two ingenious trades to get Guy Lafleur into a Montreal sweater. Lafleur was the wunderkind teen in Quebec playing for the Remparts and scoring at an unheard of rate in the late 1960s (to wit, 130 goals in a 62-game season in 1969–70), and Pollock just had to have this player on his team. So, he acquired the first-round draft choice of the Oakland Seals for 1971, the year Lafleur was eligible.

Unfortunately, the Los Angeles Kings were having an even worse year than Oakland to start the 1970–71 season, so Pollock practically gave the Kings Ralph Backstrom in a trade. Backstrom helped prop up the Kings, Oakland finished dead last, and Montreal swooped in and selected Lafleur.

Jean Béliveau had just retired, and Pollock offered Lafleur the number 4. The right winger was smart enough to demur, and he went on to score 29 goals as a

rookie. This was mere child's play to what he would accomplish after a few years of experience.

The Habs won the Cup in his second season, and after a disappointing third year of just 21 goals "The Flower" erupted to score 53 times in 1974–75 and finish with 119 points. It was the first of six straight seasons he reached 50 goals and 100 points, three of these resulting in his claiming the Art Ross Trophy. And the Canadiens dominated the game, winning the Stanley Cup four years in a row.

The last of these was to be the last of Lafleur's career with the Canadiens, and his scoring prowess dropped to half what it was in his prime. He retired early in the 1984–85 season, but made a comeback with the New York Rangers and then rival Quebec Nordiques three years later. He was given a standing ovation every time he returned, fans recognizing how special and important he had been to the CH sweater.

After his rookie season, Lafleur played without a helmet. This allowed fans to see his long blond hair streaking behind him as he flew down the wing and unleashed his patented slap shot. Fans would cry, "Guy! Guy!" when he had the puck or after he scored. He was one of the team's great personalities, imperfect off ice in some ways, but brilliant on it when he had the puck.

Despite being closely checked most of his career, Lafleur was also one of the most gentlemanly players of his or any other era. Yet, despite his scoring titles and Hart Trophies, he never won the Lady Byng Trophy. Montreal had many elements to its successes, from Ken Dryden in goal to the "big three" of Larry Robinson, Serge Savard, and Guy Lapointe on defence, but it was Lafleur who drove the offense and generated the wins with his goals.

It's impossible to imagine him playing today with a helmet, his hair—his personality—hidden from view, but even more impossible is imagining him being drafted by the Oakland Seals and playing on one of the worst teams in NHL history, in California, thousands of miles from the Forum.

CEREMONY

The standing ovation Guy Lafleur received after he skated out of the corner of the Forum in full equipment to centre ice was timed at five minutes and 22 seconds, with an impossible-to-count number of chants of "Guy! Guy!" to boot. Less than three months after retiring from the game because of frustration with his diminished skills, Lafleur had his number retired by the team with which he had played every NHL game.

"After 13 years, I did not accept to be number two," he told the 18,084 fans. "I'm proud of what I did in the past, and I'm proud I played for the Canadiens, especially on five Stanley Cup winners."

Lafleur was surrounded by his wife, Lise, both his parents, one of his two sons, Martin, and Mrs. Eva Baribeau, who had been his landlady when he was a teenager playing junior for the Quebec Remparts.

Lafleur finished his speech by saying, "I'm leaving the ice, but I want everyone to know that I'll never leave the sport." And then he skated one final lap around the Forum and left the ice.

THE GAME: Buffalo Sabres 4–Montreal Canadiens 3

Steve McKenna opened the scoring for the visiting Sabres just 50 seconds after the ceremony for Lafleur had ended. It wasn't until near the midway point of the period that Mike McPhee could respond for the Canadiens, but the Habs dominated the rest of the period. Nonetheless, the pattern repeated itself when Sean McKenna put the Sabres up 2–1 and Mario Tremblay tied it again at 13:41. Normand Lacombe closed out a busy period with the go-ahead goal with just 23 seconds left.

McPhee tied the game again in the second only to have young defenceman Phil Housley put the Sabres up for a fourth time. There was still half a game to play, but the Habs couldn't beat Bob Sauve for the tying goal despite having a power play early in the third. Steve Penney was the losing goalie for the Canadiens.

"We've got to play better on the power play," Mats Naslund opined. "You don't win games unless you jump on the other team when you have the manpower advantage."

Montreal defenceman Larry Robinson rued the Sabres' fortuitous play. "We made four errors in the game, and they capitalized on every one of them," he said.

2

DOUG
HARVEY

MONTREAL CANADIENS
OCTOBER 26, 1985

Born: Montreal, Quebec, December 19, 1924
Died: Montreal, Quebec, December 26, 1989
Position: Defence
Shoots: Left
Height: 5'11"
Weight: 187 lbs.

HONOURS
- **Stanley Cup** 1953, 1956, 1957, 1958, 1959, 1960
- **Norris Trophy** 1955, 1956, 1957, 1958, 1960, 1961, 1962 (playing-coach)
- **NHL All-Star Game** 1951, 1952, 1953, 1954, 1955, 1956, 1957, 1958, 1959, 1960, 1961, 1962, 1969
- **Hockey Hall of Fame** 1973

NHL CAREER STATS

	Regular Season					Playoffs				
Years	GP	G	A	P	Pim	GP	G	A	P	Pim
1947–69	1,113	88	452	540	1,216	137	8	64	72	152

CAREER

To some people Doug Harvey was the precursor to Bobby Orr, but to compare the two players' merits is different from comparing their styles. It's true that Harvey rushed the puck. He didn't make a play in his own end, look for an open man, and make a quick pass. He enjoyed skating with the puck and creating plays, dictating pace, as did Orr.

But where Orr loved going end to end and driving to the net, Harvey had no such ambitions. As he saw it, his job was (a) to get the puck out of his own end and (b) establish possession in enemy territory. To that end, he was among the greatest of them all.

He joined the Montreal Canadiens midway through the 1947–48 season and remained on the team's blue line for 14 years. He won the Norris Trophy seven of eight years between 1955 and 1962 and played in 13 straight All-Star Games (1951–62).

Harvey was a brilliant skater—ergo the comparisons to Orr—and when he was on the ice he controlled the pace and tempo of play. The very ability to move the puck up ice was unique and made him a threat even though he rarely scored a goal himself. In fact, although he was part of the Stanley Cup teams of 1953 and the five in a row from 1956 to 1960, he scored only eight playoff goals in 137 games, his first not coming until his eighth playoff season.

Harvey's involvement in trying to form a players' union led to his being traded to the New York Rangers in 1961, where he became not only the team's best defenceman but also its playing coach. When he won the Norris Trophy that year, he became the first player to win that trophy in consecutive years with different teams, and he became the first (and only) player to win a major individual playing award while also coaching a team.

Harvey was named to the NHL's First All-Star Team a record 10 times, which indicates how good Harvey was for so long.

CEREMONY

It took 16 years after his final NHL game—and more than a quarter of a century after his last Canadiens game—but Doug Harvey's number 2 finally made it into the rafters alongside teammate Maurice Richard's.

"Taking home this sweater is the ultimate in my career," Harvey told the crowd of 16,735 after being given a standing ovation that was clocked at 80 seconds by the esteemed *Montreal Gazette* writer, the late David Johnston.

Harvey received several gifts, notably a gold watch from Emile Francis, president and general manager of the Hartford Whalers, the evening's opposition. Dickie Moore and Réjean Houle, representing the Canadiens alumni, gave him a set of golf clubs. Jean Béliveau, on behalf of the organization, presented him with a pastoral oil painting, and finally, current captain Bob Gainey, on behalf of the players, gave Harvey a silver platter signed by all members of the team.

After that, it was up to Jacques Lapèrriere, who wore number 2 after Harvey, to hand back the sweater, retiring it forever.

THE GAME: Montreal Canadiens 5–Hartford Whalers 3

These weren't the glory days of the late 1970s, but the Habs still had plenty of firepower to earn a victory against a Hartford team that was in its prime. Montreal jumped into a 3–0 lead after 20 minutes thanks to goals in the last half of the period from Stephane Richer, Ulf Dahlen, and Mike McPhee.

Mats Naslund scored in the second to make it 4–0 before Pierre Turgeon got the Whalers on the board, and he scored again early in the third to make things interesting. When Ray Neufeld cut the lead to 4–3 the Habs were in for a struggle, but they rose to the occasion. Naslund's second goal of the game gave the Habs a bit of breathing room in the last half of the period.

Steve Penney was the winning goalie for Montreal while Mike Liut allowed all five goals for Hartford in a losing cause.

7

BILL
BARBER

PHILADELPHIA FLYERS
MARCH 6, 1986

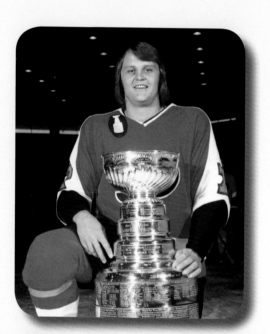

Born: Callander, Ontario, July 11, 1952
Position: Left wing
Shoots: Left
Height: 6'
Weight: 195 lbs.

HONOURS
- **Stanley Cup** 1974, 1975
- **NHL All-Star Game** 1975, 1976, 1978, 1980, 1981, 1982
- **Played for Canada in 1976 Canada Cup**
- **Hockey Hall of Fame** 1990

NHL CAREER STATS

Years	Regular Season					Playoffs				
	GP	G	A	P	Pim	GP	G	A	P	Pim
1972–84	903	420	463	883	623	129	53	55	108	109

CAREER

On a team with plenty of toughness and not much talent, Bill Barber brought an offensive threat to a physical Philadelphia Flyers team from 1972 to 1984. In each of his 12 seasons in the league, all with the "Broad Street Bullies," Barber scored at least 20 goals each and every time, leading the team to two Stanley Cup wins in 1974 and 1975.

Like many Canadians, Barber learned the game on his backyard rink, but in his case his dad created an elaborate skating area worthy of an NHL outdoor game. It had lights and was much bigger than the average backyard, and on it young Bill learned to skate and shoot. He started the 1972–73 season with the Richmond Robins in the AHL, but when the Flyers lost Bill Flett to an injury, Barber was called up and never returned.

He scored 30 goals in just 69 games as a rookie, and in each of his next two

seasons scored 34 times, both years winning the Stanley Cup. A natural centre, he moved to the left wing to play alongside Bobby Clarke, and the two were an effective pair. Barber's best statistical year was 1975–76 when he had 50 goals and 112 points, but in the playoffs the team was crushed by the Montreal Canadiens' greater skill and speed.

Barber's career started its decline in 1982 when he suffered a serious knee injury, and although he tried hard to recover he was forced to retire two years later because of pain and ineffective play. Yet in just 903 career games in the regular season he scored 420 goals and played in the All-Star Game six times. He later coached the team and won the Jack Adams Award in 2000–01, the culmination of a nearly three-decade association with the Flyers, to complement the two Stanley Cup wins in the mid-1970s.

CEREMONY

Philadelphia Flyers president Ed Snider praised Barber's determination during his speech. "No matter how well you played, no matter how many goals you scored, you never got the recognition you were due. Sometimes it takes a while to recognize brilliance, Bill. This was long overdue."

Fans cheered loudly when Bobby Clarke, general manager of the Minnesota North Stars, appeared alongside Barber and their line mate, Reggie Leach. The famed LCB line was the team's greatest and most successful.

Despite having been retired for a year and a half, "I was never overly concerned with the fact that my number hadn't been retired," Barber said. "Now that it's happened, whether it's now or whether it's three years, it's a great honour. It was worth the wait."

Although Barber's number 7 wasn't hoisted into the rafters during the half-hour ceremony, it was understood no one would ever wear it again. Barber was also given a truck and a portrait of himself that was also made into a poster and given to all fans entering the Spectrum on this night. Barber's number was raised to the rafters at a later date, making the retirement somewhat more official.

THE GAME: Philadelphia Flyers 7–Toronto Maple Leafs 4

Peter Ihnacak got the first goal of the game less than three minutes after the opening faceoff, and the teams swapped goals later in the period to make it a 2–1 game for the Leafs after the first period.

The Flyers took control in the middle 20 minutes but couldn't quite put the game out of reach. Mark Howe scored twice to give the Flyers the lead, and after a second goal by Ihnacak, Tim Kerr scored his team-leading 45th to make it a 4–3 game for Philadelphia. Dave Poulin had a great chance to make it a two-goal lead with a penalty shot, but he was bettered by goalie Don Edwards.

Walt Poddubny tied the game for Toronto at 1:30 of the final period, but Ron Sutter gave the Flyers a 5–4 lead. The home side got two late goals to ensure victory. The Flyers peppered Edwards with 53 shots and surrendered only 31.

19 BILL MASTERTON

MINNESOTA NORTH STARS
JANUARY 17, 1987

Born: Winnipeg, Manitoba, August 13, 1938
Died: Minneapolis, Minnesota, January 15, 1968
Position: Centre
Shoots: Right
Height: 6'
Weight: 190 lbs.

HONOURS
• **NCAA Championship tournament MVP** 1961 (University of Denver)

NHL CAREER STATS

	Regular Season					Playoffs				
Years	GP	G	A	P	Pim	GP	G	A	P	Pim
1967–68	38	4	8	12	4	—	—	—	—	—

CAREER

If it weren't for expansion, Bill Masterton never would have played in the NHL, never would have even considered playing in the NHL. He was a solid player, but in the days of the Original Six he knew he couldn't compete with Béliveau, Mahovlich, Howe, and Hull. He attended the University of Denver where he earned a bachelor's degree in engineering, but he also played hockey, and at the NCAA final in 1961 he played well enough to be named tournament MVP.

End of story. He graduated, earned a master's degree in finance, and supported himself by playing minor pro. After a few years, though, he was invited to play for the U.S. National Team, which he did in 1966–67, and he made a favourable impression. That summer, when the NHL went from six to 12 teams, his rights were bought by Minnesota from Montreal. The North Stars wooed him, and the chance to play in the city where he lived, in the NHL no less, was too good to pass up.

Just as juniors who come to the NHL today discard their visors, similarly Masterton abandoned his helmet when he got to the NHL. On January 13, 1968, in only his 38th big-league game, he was checked and fell awkwardly. He couldn't protect his head and didn't have time to turn in any way, and his head struck the ice with full force. He fell into a coma, and two days later died in hospital surrounded by his wife and family.

The tragedy came just two days before the All-Star Game, and although there were kind words and tears, almost all players continued to play without head protection. An award was established by the league in Masterton's honour, going to the player who best exemplified perseverance and dedication to the game. Montreal's Claude Provost was the first recipient.

Masterton is the only NHLer to have died as a direct result of an on-ice incident, and hopefully he will be the only one. Today, of course, no player would even consider—let alone be permitted—to play without a helmet, although NHL rules still permit a player to finish his shift without one if it comes off during play.

MINNESOTA NORTH STARS ™

CEREMONY

As honours go, this was as sombre as they get. Yes, Bill Masterton was being honoured with a number retirement, but it was in large measure in tribute to his death during a game as anything else. In his prime, Masterton would have likely never been a superstar player.

The ceremonies involved his widow, Carol; son, Scott; and daughter, Sally, as well as team president John Karr and teammate Bill Goldsworthy.

The banner bearing his name, number, and team logo was unfurled over the goal at the west end of the building, where the accident occurred.

THE GAME: Minnesota North Stars 3–Chicago Black Hawks 2
The North Stars were on a roll, improving their record to 4–0–1 in their last five games and helping solidify their playoff position. The hero of the night was Brian Bellows who'd had a hot hand since returning from a wrist injury the previous week. He scored two goals, including the only goal of the third period, to break a 2–2 tie and lead the team to victory. Goalie Don Beaupre was also excellent for the winners, stopping 28 of 29 shots.

Steve Larmer opened the scoring for Chicago early in the game on a power play, but Bellows tied the game at 15:34 by converting a pass from Kent Nilsson on a two-on-one.

The teams exchanged goals in the second period as well, this time the Stars scoring first when Bob Brooke took advantage of a clearing mistake by goalie Murray Bannerman. Troy Murray tied the game for the Hawks later, setting the stage for an exciting third period.

Nilsson again was the agent for Bellows's second of the night. On the power play, Nilsson took a shot that was deftly tipped by Bellows into the top corner. Beaupre then took care of things the rest of the way, making several fine saves to preserve the victory in Masterton's honour.

"We have to learn from these one-goal games," said the goalie, "and it seems like we're getting there. I don't know if it's just hard work or what, but we didn't let down in the third period."

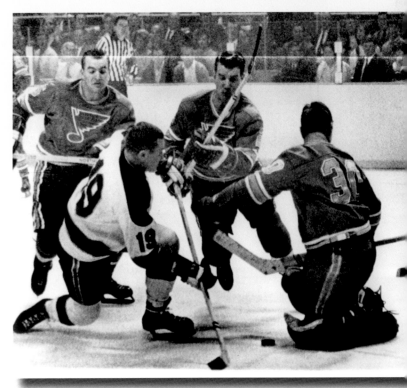

7 PHIL ESPOSITO

BOSTON BRUINS
DECEMBER 3, 1987

Born: Sault Ste. Marie, Ontario, February 20, 1942
Position: Centre
Shoots: Left
Height: 6'1"
Weight: 205 lbs.

HONOURS
- **Stanley Cup** 1970, 1972
- **Hart Trophy** 1969, 1974
- **Art Ross Trophy** 1969, 1971, 1972, 1973, 1974
- **Lester B. Pearson Award** 1971, 1974
- **Lester Patrick Trophy** 1978
- **NHL All-Star Game** 1969, 1970, 1971, 1972, 1973, 1974, 1975, 1977, 1978, 1980
- **Played for Canada in 1972 Summit Series and 1976 Canada Cup**
- **Hockey Hall of Fame** 1984

NHL CAREER STATS

	Regular Season					Playoffs				
Years	GP	G	A	P	Pim	GP	G	A	P	Pim
1963–81	1,282	717	873	1,590	910	130	61	76	137	138

CAREER

"Espo" was hockey's Ali, a man of immense size and talent and mouth and pride. He didn't look like a hockey player; he didn't even skate much like a hockey player. But put the puck on his stick in the slot, and sure as the puck was black it was going in the net.

As a young prospect in the Chicago organization, Esposito weighed too much, didn't skate well, and was cocky. But over time he trimmed down, developed an incredible, quick release to his shot—and was traded to the Boston Bruins in 1967.

Of course, with Bobby Orr on the blue line life was good, but with Esposito up front life was easier. He played on a line with Ken Hodge and Wayne Cashman, two wingers whose job it was to get the puck in the slot for Esposito to fire on goal. He led the league in goals for six straight years, obliterating records in 1970–71 for goals (76) and points (152). These numbers stood until a kid named

Gretzky came along and did unto Esposito what Esposito had done unto Bobby Hull and Bernie Geoffrion, top scorers of the previous generation.

Esposito was on Boston's two Stanley Cup-winning teams, in 1970 and 1972, but he was as well known for his leadership during the 1972 Summit Series. More specifically, he delivered a speech to the people of Canada after game four of the series, in Vancouver, chastising those fans who had booed the team. The speech galvanized the nation and rallied the players who received tremendous support for the second half of the series in Moscow. Paul Henderson was the scoring hero, but Phil Esposito was the team's inspiration.

By the time he retired, Esposito was third all-time in points with 1,590, behind only Gordie Howe and Marcel Dionne. He had scored 717 goals and was inducted into the Hockey Hall of Fame three years later. He was a sporting player who despised violence in the game, a superstitious player who wore a black turtleneck every game after playing well with a cold one time, a player who was supremely talented and vocal. He was, in short, one of a kind.

CEREMONY

One moment stands out with such historic power that the rest of the ceremony dims by comparison. There was Esposito at centre ice being honoured many years after his final game, all the current Bruins on ice taking in the moment. And then defenceman Ray Bourque, wearing the number 7 that was given to him as a rookie seven years before (1979–80), skated over to Espo and took his sweater off. He handed it to the legend and said, "It's all yours," and then did a quick spin for him and everyone else to see. Bourque was now wearing a 77 sweater. No player for Boston would ever wear number 7 again.

The gesture was planned only that day and kept secret from all except general manager Harry Sinden, coach Terry O'Reilly, and the trainer who helped Bourque smuggle the two sweaters onto the ice. It was the final moment in a reconciliation between player and team whose relationship had soured when Espo was traded to the New York Rangers. But Boston could not *not* honour Espo, the team's greatest scorer and the man who helped the Bruins to the Stanley Cup in 1970 and 1972, their only two wins between 1941 and 2010.

THE GAME: Boston Bruins 4–New York Rangers 3

Neither team managed a goal in the first period, and they exchanged goals in the second. Reed Larson got the first one for Boston and Kelly Kisio tied it a minute later for the Blueshirts.

The action started in the third period. The Rangers got two quick goals from Brian Mullen to silence the Garden crowd, but then Bourque, in his first game wearing number 77, came to the rescue. He made it a 3–2 game at 13:12 to begin the comeback, which continued with a tying goal from Rick Middleton. It was his first goal in 24 games, ending one of the longest goal-scoring slumps of his career.

Bourque then had the second assist on Steve Kasper's quick shot off a rebound with exactly two minutes left, giving the Bruins a 4–3 win. "We had played hard," Bourque explained, "and they had turned a couple of breaks into a 3–1 lead. But we kept coming back."

"Once Ray scored, the momentum switched," Middleton noted. "That got us going."

11

BRIAN SUTTER

ST. LOUIS BLUES
DECEMBER 30, 1988

Born: Viking, Alberta, October 7, 1956
Position: Left wing
Shoots: Left
Height: 5'11"
Weight: 173 lbs.

HONOURS
• **Jack Adams Award** 1991 (coaching St. Louis, the team for whom he played his entire career)
• **NHL All-Star Game** 1982, 1983, 1985

NHL CAREER STATS

	Regular Season					Playoffs				
Years	GP	G	A	P	Pim	GP	G	A	P	Pim
1976–88	779	303	333	636	1,786	65	21	21	42	249

CAREER

To paraphrase Rodney Dangerfield in a serious way, if you look "heart" up in the dictionary, you'll see a picture of Brian Sutter. One of seven children brought up on a farm in tiny Viking, Alberta, Brian was the first of six to play in the NHL. He never won a Stanley Cup, but he played all of his 12 years with the St. Louis Blues before having to retire at age 31 because his body, simply put, had nothing left to give.

Sutter led by example. He hated losing a faceoff let alone an entire game, and he expected his teammates to hate losing just as much. At the start of his fourth year, when he was just 21, he was named captain, and he maintained that leadership role until the day he retired. Sutter lacked much of the skill one typically expects from a leader. He was more Bobby Clarke, say, than Wayne Gretzky, but his tenacity and competitive fire made him effective all the same. He had seven seasons of at least 23 goals, twice eclipsing 40 and four times 30 goals.

He rarely beat a player one-on-one in open ice, but he almost always got a loose puck that had to be contested, earned his space in the enemy slot, got to rebounds, and played tenacious defence. The Blues made the playoffs nine times during his career, but they never advanced past the second round, such was the competition in the Clarence Campbell Conference. The Blues finished first or second in their division six times in 12 seasons, but simply couldn't advance deep into the playoffs.

Today Sutter remains the third-highest scorer in team history with his 636 points. Only Bernie Federko (1,073) and Brett Hull (936) have more.

CEREMONY

For Brian Sutter, coach of the Blues, the most special thing about this ceremony was that the Blues were able to get so many of his family together in one place: parents Louis and Grace, brothers Gary and Ron and their wives, brothers Brent and Duane, and wife Judy with their children Shaun and Abby. In fact, only Rich and Darryl, who both had hockey commitments, weren't there.

Brent and Duane both had games to play the next day and left right after the ceremony by police escort to the airport, but the gesture was made all the same. "I'm in and out, but it's worth it," Brent said. "This is a very special thing for Brian . . . We're not only brothers, but we're really close. I'm pretty proud of the guy."

"I know there are a couple of people who aren't here tonight, but they're up there watching me," Sutter said in his speech to the crowd, acknowledging the other men whose numbers had been retired and who died too young: Barclay Plager and Bob Gassoff.

Team captain Bernie Federko presented Sutter with a bronze sculpture of a hockey player wearing a number 11 sweater. Other gifts included two airplane tickets anywhere in the world and two other framed St. Louis sweaters with the number 11. Then country star Charlie Daniels sang the national anthem in tribute to Sutter, a huge country music fan.

THE GAME: St. Louis Blues 5–Minnesota North Stars 5

Although this was a high-scoring and entertaining game, no one could have seen the wild ending that precipitated this 5–5 tie on Sutter's special night. The first period was such a disaster it's amazing the Blues got anything positive out of the game. The North Stars scored at 4:14 thanks to Curt Giles, and added goals at 6:57, 9:51, and 11:32 to build a 4–0 lead and spell the end for goalie Greg Millen.

The thrill and honour of the pre-game ceremonies gave way to a ferocious tirade from coach Sutter in the dressing room during the first intermission, and the Blues came out with a great effort in the second, scoring the only three goals and getting right back in the game. Peter Zezel and Gino Cavallini scored power play goals around a Herb Raglan five-on-five goal that was more indicative of how the Blues could play.

Despite outshooting the Stars 11–3 in the third, however, the Blues couldn't tie the game and Marc Habscheid scored into the empty net to make it a 5–3 game with only 33 seconds left in the third period. And then the home side got a miracle finish. Just 15 seconds later Todd Ewen made it 5–4, and then with just four seconds left on the clock Brett Hull ripped a patented one-timer past Jon Casey to tie the score and give the Blues an improbable point.

9

BOBBY
HULL

Born: Pointe Anne, Ontario, January 3, 1939
Position: Left wing
Shoots: Left
Height: 5'10"
Weight: 195 lbs.

Honours
- **Stanley Cup** 1961
- **Hart Trophy** 1965, 1966
- **Art Ross Trophy** 1960, 1962, 1966
- **Lady Byng Trophy** 1965
- **Lester Patrick Trophy** 1969
- **NHL All-Star Game** 1960, 1961, 1962, 1963, 1964, 1965, 1967, 1968, 1969, 1970, 1971, 1972
- **Played in WHA** 1972–79
- **Hockey Hall of Fame** 1983

NHL CAREER STATS

| Years | Regular Season | | | | | Playoffs | | | | |
	GP	G	A	P	Pim	GP	G	A	P	Pim
1957–80	1,063	610	560	1,170	640	119	62	67	129	102

WINNIPEG CAREER

Hockey history changed forever in the summer of 1972 the day that Bobby Hull signed a $1 million contract with the Winnipeg Jets of the new World Hockey Association. Dozens of players soon migrated to the new league for inflated salaries all because Hull, the second leading scorer in NHL history and at 33 still in the prime of his career, left the league to prove NHLers were underpaid. Hull's signing, more than any other, legitimized the league and brought it instant respect, and over the course of time it raised NHL salaries more than players could have imagined.

His signing sparked outrage and disappointment in NHL circles, but it had one immediate effect. The NHL took his name off its list of players invited to training camp for the 1972 Summit Series that August. This was comeuppance in

the league's eyes, but to fans across the country, and even Prime Minister Pierre Trudeau, it was unjust punishment.

Hull played all seven years the WHA was in operation, all with the Jets, and he was a member of the first truly international line in hockey with Swedes Ulf Nilsson and Anders Hedberg (they were called the Hot Line). The threesome set every scoring record in the WHA, and Hull averaged nearly a goal a game over these years. In 1974–75, he scored 77 goals, one better than Phil Esposito's record of 76, but the NHL refused to acknowledge Hull's record because it considered the WHA an inferior league.

In 1979, the Jets and three other teams joined the NHL, and Hull, now 40, played one final season. He started with Winnipeg, but was traded mid-season to Hartford where he played alongside Gordie Howe and Dave Keon; combined, the three players had played more than 75 years of pro hockey. Hull wasn't an effective player at this stage, though, and he retired before the end of the season.

CEREMONY

It was a long and emotional day for the "Golden Jet." First, there was a gala luncheon held in his honour at which the city of Winnipeg gave him a set of gold cufflinks and the province of Manitoba presented him with the Order of the Buffalo Hunt. Hull openly wept during his brief speech. "I've had my nose broken, my shoulder separated, and my tendon cut, but I've never cried before. I've never had this kind of feeling before."

Then, it was off to the Winnipeg Arena for a formal ceremony in front of some 14,354 fans who were treated to a spectacular 35-minute pre-game ceremony. Hull skated around the rink dressed in full uniform, much to everyone's delight. Most of Hull's family shared the spotlight with him, as did Gordie Howe, who talked about Hull's singular importance to kick-starting the WHA. "Bobby helped me to fulfill one of my fondest dreams. He gave me a chance to play hockey with my two youngsters. Without Bobby, the WHA would never have been a reality."

Howe then read a message form Nilsson and Hedberg who were in Stockholm working on a cancer fundraiser and couldn't attend.

Other notables on ice for the retiring of number 9 included Jets president, Barry Shenkarow; Hull's junior coach, Rudy Pilous; Ab McDonald, the first Jets captain; brother Dennis; and sons Brett and Blake.

Finally, emcee Don Wittman read a note from Doug Smail, the team's current number 9 who changed to 12 to ensure no one wore Hull's number again. Smail was in hospital at the time, after suffering a broken cheekbone in a recent game.

THE GAME: Winnipeg Jets 7–Hartford Whalers 6

In the high-scoring days of the 1980s, there was nothing particularly unusual about this game. Winnipeg's Pat Elynuik started things off with a goal in the first minute, but the Whalers scored the only other two goals of the period to take a 2–1 lead after 20 minutes.

Hartford made it 3–1 early in the second, but Brent Ashton and Dale Hawerchuk tied the score. Two more quick goals from the Whalers, and a second from Hawerchuk, rounded out the scoring in the middle period. The Whalers restored their two-goal lead at 3:44 of the third thanks to a John Anderson goal, but Iain Duncan and Ashton tied the game to send it to overtime. Ashton completed the hat trick at 3:23 of the extra period on a nice pass from new line mate Duncan.

ED
GIACOMIN

NEW YORK RANGERS
MARCH 15, 1989

Born: Sudbury, Ontario, June 6, 1939
Position: Goalie
Catches: Left
Height: 5'11"
Weight: 180 lbs.

HONOURS
- **Vezina Trophy** 1971 (with Gilles Villemure)
- **NHL All-Star Game** 1967, 1968, 1969, 1970, 1971, 1973
- **Hockey Hall of Fame** 1987

NHL CAREER STATS

Regular Season

Years	GP	W-L-T	Mins	GA	SO	GAA
1965–78	610	289-208-97	35,693	1,675	54	2.82

Playoffs

Years	GP	W-L-T	Mins	GA	SO	GAA
1965–78	65	29-35-0	3,838	180	1	2.81

CAREER

Was there ever a more genuinely beloved member of the New York Rangers than goalie Ed Giacomin? Despite suffering serious burns in a kitchen accident when he was a teenager, he persevered in his dream to play hockey. His desire to make the NHL was so great he even turned down American football and baseball scholarships. He worked his way up from the lowest depths of pro hockey until making it with the Providence Reds in the AHL, and in 1965–66 he finally got a chance when the New York Rangers acquired him.

Despite making it to the NHL, and sharing goaltending duties with Cesare Maniago, he played poorly in his first games. A couple of weeks in, though,

Maniago pulled himself out of a game. Giacomin came in, pulled himself together, and played well, staying in net for most of the next nine seasons in New York.

He quickly helped turn the team's fortunes around and the Rangers made the playoffs every year Giacomin was their goalie. He led the league in games and minutes played for the next four years, and in wins the next three years. The team made inroads in the playoffs as well, culminating in 1972 when they advanced to the Final to play the Bruins. Bobby Orr, Phil Esposito, and the rest of the great lineup was too much even for Giacomin to contain, and this was as close as he ever got to the Cup.

Not only was he a winner, he was exciting to watch. Cut from the same cloth as Jacques Plante, Giacomin hated to stand in his crease and wait for bullets to fly his way. He wandered from the net, made passes up ice like a third defenceman, and engaged in play the way few goalies before him ever did.

Early in the 1975–76 season, Detroit claimed Giacomin after New York put him on waivers. The move incited howls of protest from the Rangers' faithful, and as fate would have it his first game in a Red Wings sweater came two nights later—in Madison Square Garden! All night long fans chanted "Eddie! Eddie!" in honour of their beloved goalie.

CEREMONY

Only the second member of the Rangers to have his number retired, after Rod Gilbert, Ed Giacomin was also part of another elite group. He became just the fourth goalie in NHL history to have his number retired, following Bernie Parent (Philadelphia), Rogie Vachon (Los Angeles), and Tony Esposito (Chicago).

Of course, Gilbert was with Giacomin for the 30-minute ceremony, as were other great Rangers netminders, namely Gump Worsley and Chuck Rayner, both of whom wore number 1. Giacomin's wife and three children were also by his side, and as the number 1 was lifted into the rafters fans chanted "Eddie! Eddie" as they had for most of the decade he played at Madison Square Garden.

"I'm not running for mayor," he said during his speech, "but you have been my motivation, my inspiration. It's the most thrilling moment of my life."

THE GAME: Winnipeg Jets 6–New York Rangers 3

Unfortunately, Giacomin's stirring tribute could not rustle up a win by the struggling Rangers who lost for the sixth time in their last seven games. Worse, the loss came to the Jets, cellar dwellers in the Smythe Division and winless in their previous 11 road games. The Jets scored four of their goals on the power play and another while short-handed.

All started out well. Michel Petit put New York up 1–0 after just 14 seconds of play. Although Thomas Steen tied the game for Winnipeg, Brian Leetch put the home side up 2–1 by the end of the period. That goal gave the rookie defenceman 22 on the season, tying Bobby Orr's record. Leetch left the game soon after, however, suffering a hip pointer injury that put him out of the lineup for a week.

The Jets took control in the middle period, scoring twice with the extra man and adding the short-handed goal. Although Carey Wilson made it 4–3 with a goal just eight seconds after the faceoff, the Jets pulled away with two more of their own to seal the rare road win.

9 LANNY McDONALD

CALGARY FLAMES
MARCH 17, 1990

Born: Hanna, Alberta, February 16, 1953
Position: Right wing
Shoots: Right
Height: 6'
Weight: 185 lbs.

HONOURS
- **Stanley Cup** 1989
- **Bill Masterton Trophy** 1983
- **King Clancy Memorial Trophy** 1988
- **NHL All-Star Game** 1977, 1978, 1983, 1984
- **Played for Canada in Canada Cup** 1976
- **Hockey Hall of Fame** 1992

NHL CAREER STATS

	Regular Season					Playoffs				
Years	GP	G	A	P	Pim	GP	G	A	P	Pim
1973–89	1,111	500	506	1,006	899	117	44	40	84	120

CAREER

One of the finest men ever to skate through the NHL ended his career in fairy-tale fashion on three fronts. In his final season, 1988–89, Lanny McDonald scored his 500th goal and his 1,000th point and won his only Stanley Cup, with Calgary, after scoring a goal in the Cup-winning game.

A westerner drafted by the Toronto Maple Leafs in 1973, McDonald spent seven seasons in Toronto where he developed into one of the best right wingers in the league. Easy to identify by his bushy moustache, he was more famous for his dynamite wrist shot that exploded off his stick as he drove down the right side.

He played on a line with centre Darryl Sittler, his best friend off ice, and left winger Errol Thompson, and the three terrorized enemy goalies with superstar consistency. When the Leafs failed to get to the Cup Final, though, owner Harold

Ballard brought in Punch Imlach as coach and general manager, and one of his first moves was to trade McDonald to the lowly Colorado Rockies.

McDonald was soon traded again to Calgary, and it was there he enjoyed his finest seven and a half years. Shortly after arriving back home in Alberta he was named captain. His greatest years were 1982–83 when he had 66 goals, and the 1986 playoffs when the Flames advanced to the Stanley Cup Final for the first time. McDonald had 11 goals in 22 games that post-season, but it wasn't enough. They were beaten by Montreal.

Three years later, however, the team was back, against Montreal, no less. McDonald was now 36 years old and not the player he had been, and he suffered the ignominy of being a healthy scratch for several games in the playoffs, including game five. Game six, however, was scheduled for the Forum, and the Cup was in the building. Playing a hunch, coach Terry Crisp inserted McDonald in the lineup. Lanny scored a goal, and after 60 agonizing minutes the Flames won the game and series, 4–2. McDonald could finally hoist the trophy high above his head.

CEREMONY

Few NHL players have been as respected, loved, and admired as Lanny McDonald, so on the night the Calgary Flames retired his number 9, you could be sure there wasn't going to be a dry eye in the house. And there wasn't.

McDonald came to centre ice with his wife and children, and he received a trove of gifts to honour his career and contributions to the game. Harley Hotchkiss, the team's owner, established a hockey scholarship in McDonald's name. Flames executives gave each member of his family a Rolex watch, and the players contributed gold bracelets. The Hockey Hall of Fame presented him with a plaque, and the opposing Hartford Whalers gave him a silver tray. Molson's not only gave McDonald a Glen Green painting, it distributed poster versions to every fan in the Saddledome.

McDonald kept his emotions in check during his speech, though he lost it when he looked up to see his number 9 float up to the rafters for permanent display. "What more can you say when you've had the time of your life?" he asked, rhetorically. "What more can you say when all of your dreams are coming true."

Looking back on his career, he cited three highlights: raising a family; winning the Stanley Cup with the Flames and his teammates; and, "having a chance to play the greatest game in the world, in front of that wonderful sea of red," he finished, referring to the colour most Calgary fans wear to the games.

THE GAME: Calgary Flames 5–Hartford Whalers 4

The Flames extended their winning streak to eight games with a determined effort almost matched goal for goal by the Whalers. Calgary scored four times after which Hartford scored each time to tie the game on four occasions, but finally a goal from Paul Ranheim at 12:53 of the final period was one the Whalers couldn't match.

Doug Gilmour scored the only goal of the first period, but Pat Verbeek tied the game at 1:12 of the second. Joe Mullen came back 36 seconds later to make it 2–1 Calgary, but Dean Evason tied it 2–2 just three minutes later. Joel Otto and Verbeek, with his 40th of the year, exchanged goals to close out the second period.

Al MacInnis put the Flames up 4–3 just 48 seconds into the third period only to see Dave Babych tie the game on the Whalers' second power-play goal of the game, and that set the stage for Ranheim's winner.

11

GILBERT
PERREAULT

BUFFALO SABRES
OCTOBER 17, 1990

Born: Victoriaville, Quebec, November 13, 1950
Position: Centre
Shoots: Left
Height: 6'1"
Weight: 180 lbs.

HONOURS
- **Drafted first overall by Buffalo** 1970
- **Lady Byng Trophy** 1973
- **Calder Trophy** 1971
- **Played for Canada in 1972 Summit Series and Canada Cup** 1976, 1981
- **Won Memorial Cup with Montreal Jr. Canadiens** 1969, 1970
- **Hockey Hall of Fame** 1990

NHL CAREER STATS

	Regular Season					Playoffs				
Years	GP	G	A	P	Pim	GP	G	A	P	Pim
1970–87	1,191	512	814	1,326	500	93	33	70	103	44

CAREER

Of course, Gilbert Perreault, like any other NHLer, dearly wanted to win the Stanley Cup, but that he didn't in no way undermined his legacy as one of the game's greats. A brilliant skater, he brought the Aud faithful to their feet whenever he started a rink-long dash. Indeed, there were hundreds such occurrences because Perreault played all of his 17 seasons with the Buffalo Sabres at the Memorial Auditorium.

Drafted first overall by the Sabres in 1970 (after winning the lottery with the other expansion team that year, Vancouver), Perreault jumped into the lineup right away and was nothing short of sensational. He scored 38 goals as a rookie to win the Calder Trophy, and he continued to flourish as a top scorer most of the rest of his career.

Playing on a line with René Robert and Rick Martin, the trio became known as the French Connection Line. They scored goals seemingly every game, and when

they didn't they still provided fans with glorious play and high-speed puck movement. Perreault had won consecutive Memorial Cups with the Montreal Jr. Canadiens in 1969 and 1970, and his transition to the NHL was seamless.

In all, he reached 40 goals in a season three times and twice exceeded 100 points, but it was 1974–75 that was perhaps his best memory. That year, he helped the Sabres reach the Stanley Cup Final, against Philadelphia, the closest he came to hoisting the sacred silverware. Perreault did play for Canada at the Canada Cup in both 1976 and 1981, the former a victory the latter a loss, although he skated on a line with Wayne Gretzky.

Perreault retired early in the 1986–87 season, unhappy with his declining play and the demise of his leg speed, which prevented those end-to-end rushes.

CEREMONY

In the years immediately after his retirement, there was unhappiness and a lack of communication that led to a four-year gap between the greatest player in team history playing his final game and his number being retired. But owner Seymour Knox, respecting the team's tradition and history, initiated a successful reconciliation with Perreault.

"Four years is a long time," number 11 agreed. When he spoke to the crowd, his wife, Carmen, and children, Marc and Sean, were by his side. He was nostalgic and elated. "I feel like I'm the luckiest person in the world," he said, paraphrasing Lou Gehrig's farewell baseball speech. "I was very fortunate, but I didn't do it alone."

Perreault thanked everyone he could think of, from Seymour and Northrup Knox to line mates Rick Martin and René Robert, to trainers Frank Christie and Rip Simonick. He thanked Mike Foligno and Bill Hajt, the players who drew assists on Perreault's 500th career goal. "This game is a wonderful sport, and I am thankful I could play it and for just one team only, the Buffalo Sabres. I am proud of this city and of the Buffalo Sabres' organization."

He received a silver stick from the Knoxes and his last game sweater framed from the alumni. Current players gave him a cruise and trip to Disney World, and the Montreal Canadiens gave him a briefcase.

Other teammates participating in the ceremony included Jim Schoenfeld, Bob Sauve, Don Edwards, Ric Seiling, Gerry Korab, Andre Savard, Wilf Paiement, and Derek Smith.

THE GAME: Montreal Canadiens 4–Buffalo Sabres 3

The ceremonies had no positive effect on a team struggling from the get-go, as the Sabres remained winless after their first six games of the new season. The Canadiens jumped into an early lead they never relinquished, and the Sabres couldn't find that spark to end their miserable start to the new season.

Brian Skrudland got the game's first goal after just 34 seconds, and Montreal made it 2–0 at 7:49 on a Mike Keane power-play goal. Dave Andreychuk brought the Sabres to within a goal, but the Habs scored again before the end of the period.

Keane made it a 4–1 game in the second and then Pierre Turgeon beat Patrick Roy on a penalty shot at 11:39, and that's how the middle period ended. Turgeon scored again late in the third.

"It's all confidence," Rick Vaive said. "It's been damn frustrating. But I'll tell you, nobody here is going to quit. We're going to keep plugging away."

16

MARCEL DIONNE

LOS ANGELES KINGS
NOVEMBER 8, 1990

Born: Drummondville, Quebec, August 3, 1951
Position: Centre
Shoots: Right
Height: 5'9"
Weight: 190 lbs.

HONOURS
- Lady Byng Trophy 1975, 1977
- Art Ross Trophy 1980
- Lester B. Pearson Award 1979, 1980
- NHL All-Star Game 1975, 1976, 1977, 1978, 1980, 1981, 1983, 1985
- Drafted by Detroit second overall 1971
- Hockey Hall of Fame 1992

NHL CAREER STATS

	Regular Season					Playoffs				
Years	GP	G	A	P	Pim	GP	G	A	P	Pim
1971–89	1,348	731	1,040	1,771	600	49	21	24	45	17

CAREER

When he retired in 1989, Marcel Dionne was the second-leading scorer in NHL history behind only Gordie Howe. Yet despite eight seasons of 100 points, and six seasons of 50 goals, despite his colossal statistics at the end of his career, Dionne never came particularly close to winning the Stanley Cup. That's because he started his career with Detroit in 1971 when the team was dreadful, continued with Los Angeles when the Kings were mediocre, and finished with the Rangers when they were rebuilding. That's how you have a player score 731 goals and finish with 1,771 career points—and no Cup engravings.

Drafted second overall by Detroit in 1971 (Guy Lafleur was first), Dionne scored 28 goals as a rookie and made it known he was a star in the making. He had great speed for a small player, and terrific stickhandling skills, but in his four years with the Red Wings he didn't play a minute in the playoffs. His final season

produced 121 points and then he signed as a free agent with Los Angeles. Dionne was going from a hockey city to an expansion team far removed from the hockey community, but he ended up being the centrepiece of the Kings for the next 11 and a half seasons.

He centred the famed Triple Crown Line with Charlie Simmer and Dave Taylor, and together they were among the league leaders in all major offensive numbers for several years. But the Kings suffered from weak defence and poor goaltending, and although the team qualified for the playoffs eight times they won only three rounds and never more than one in a season.

Dionne was remarkably content in Los Angeles despite coming from a small French-Canadian city. Year after year he reached 100 points, and he won his only Art Ross Trophy in 1980 under unique circumstance. Tied for top spot with Wayne Gretzky with 137 points, Dionne got the nod because he had 53 goals and Gretzky 51. In his 18 seasons, Dionne played the full schedule nine times, testament to his durability despite his small stature.

Supremely talented and one of the greatest offensive players in history, Dionne would have gladly traded all his points for one Stanley Cup. That he didn't get one, though, hardly diminishes such a great career.

CEREMONY

The second member of the Kings to have his number retired after goalie Rogie Vachon, Marcel Dionne was as rightful an honouree as any. By the time he retired, he was second in scoring to Gordie Howe, and he led the Kings in games played (921), goals (550), assists (757), and points (1,307).

Teammates joining him for the celebrations included Butch Goring, Gary Simmons, Mike Murphy, and Vic Venasky. Among his gifts were a clock from the NHL, a gold plate from the opposition Red Wings, a trip to Hawaii from the Kings players, and a trip to Europe from Kings owner Bruce McNall.

THE GAME: Los Angeles Kings 5–Detroit Red Wings 1

Dionne's main team faced his first team on this tribute night, and the home side won handily, scoring five goals in a row before allowing a late one to Steve Yzerman, on the power play, with just 1:44 left in the game. That goal ended Kelly Hrudey's shutout bid, although he blocked 28 of 29 shots he faced, including one that hit him square in the mask and required a couple of minutes to recover from with the trainer by his side.

The Kings outshot Detroit 13–5 in the opening period and were rewarded with two late goals, the first from Jay Miller at 15:48, and the second from Todd Elik two and a half minutes later. Wayne Gretzky made it 3–0 early in the second to increase his point-scoring streak to 14 games. The Kings scored twice more in the third before Yzerman counted the lone Detroit score.

24

BERNIE
FEDERKO

ST. LOUIS BLUES
MARCH 16, 1991

Born: Foam Lake, Saskatchewan, May 12, 1956
Position: Centre
Shoots: Left
Height: 6'
Weight: 178 lbs.

HONOURS
• **NHL All-Star Game** 1980, 1981
• **Hockey Hall of Fame** 2002

NHL CAREER STATS

	Regular Season					Playoffs				
Years	GP	G	A	P	Pim	GP	G	A	P	Pim
1976–90	1,000	369	761	1,130	487	91	35	66	101	83

CAREER

It took Bernie Federko eight years after he became eligible to be inducted into the Hockey Hall of Fame, a curiously long waiting period given that he had done everything during his playing days to be enshrined. At the very least, by 2002, when he was inducted, every other 1,000-point man had been duly honoured, but not Federko.

Drafted seventh overall by St. Louis in 1976, he played the first 13 seasons of his 14-year career with the Blues, taking them to the playoffs in each of his final 10 seasons. Federko was, if nothing else, highly skilled but unspectacular. He never went end-to-end with the puck, wasn't a fighting power forward, didn't lead the league in anything or win any individual awards, and didn't get his name on the Stanley Cup.

Yet he was a model of consistency for a long period of time. He was the first player in NHL history to record 50 assists for 10 straight seasons. In exactly 1,000

career games, he averaged more than a point a game (1,130 in all). He recorded four seasons of at least 100 points, proving for several years to be among the best players in the league.

Resilient, he was seldom out of the lineup because of injury. He weathered the franchise storm when the team was on the brink of relocating to Saskatoon and didn't even participate in the 1983 Entry Draft.

Federko took the Blues to the conference championship in 1986, and despite not making it to the Final, he and teammate Doug Gilmour led the playoffs in scoring with 21 points each, a feat duplicated only once before or since (by Peter Forsberg in 2002). Federko was named team captain in 1988. He was traded to Detroit the very next year, though, and after one season he retired at age 33.

For all the years he waited to get into the Hockey Hall of Fame, Federko was the only player with 1,000 career points not inducted, but the Blues knew his value to the team much sooner and retired his number a year after his final season with Detroit.

CEREMONY

St. Louis Blues forward Brendan Shanahan was the emcee for the 10-minute ceremony prior to a bitter clash against rivals Chicago Blackhawks. He sported a bright green jacket for the occasion and teammate Rick Meagher gave Federko a framed number 24 sweater. Federko was joined by plenty of family members, notably parents Nick and Natalie; wife Bernadette; sons Jordy, Dustin, and Drew; and older twin brothers Don and Ron.

Federko then addressed the crowd: "In 1976, a boyhood dream of mine came true. I was drafted by a National Hockey League team, the St. Louis Blues. To be honest, I didn't know where St. Louis was, or what it was all about. Now, 15 years later, I realize how lucky I was to become a part of this great city that will always be a big part of both my family and me. I thank all the hockey fans for all the wonderful support they have given me, both on and off the ice. It was a lot of fun.

"The Blues have given me the greatest compliment an athlete can have by retiring my number, an honour I will cherish forever. I will always be grateful to them. The Bluenote will always be tattooed to my heart. The great friends I have made through the years—and there have been many—I will never forget. Hopefully, someday, I will be able to repay all of you wonderful people who have brought smiles to my wife, Bernadette, our sons Jordy, Dustin, and Drew, and me. St. Louis will always be home in our hearts."

THE GAME: Chicago Blackhawks 3–St. Louis Blues 2

The game started well for the home Blues when Brett Hull nailed his 79th goal of the season on an early power play. The Hawks tied it up, but Bob Bassen put St. Louis ahead, 2–1, on a short-handed goal in the second period, but that lead, too, went by the wayside.

Jeremy Roenick made it 2–2 just three and a half minutes later, and Steve Larmer scored what proved to be the game winner at 9:24 of the middle period when his bad-angle shot hit goalie Pat Jablonski's stick and caromed in.

Try as they might, though, the Blues couldn't tie the score over the last half of the game. Ed Belfour was excellent in the Chicago net, improving his season record to 40–18–5.

Said coach Brian Sutter of the Blues: "We wanted to win the game. We played hard. The other team played hard. They got the break and won the game."

12

STAN
SMYL

VANCOUVER CANUCKS
NOVEMBER 3, 1991

Born: Glendon, Alberta, January 28, 1958
Position: Right wing
Shoots: Right
Height: 5'8"
Weight: 185 lbs.

HONOURS
- Drafted 40th overall by Vancouver 1978
- Played his entire career with Vancouver Canucks
- Won Memorial Cup with New Westminster Bruins 1977, 1978

NHL CAREER STATS

	Regular Season					Playoffs				
Years	GP	G	A	P	Pim	GP	G	A	P	Pim
1978–91	896	262	411	673	1,556	41	16	17	33	64

CAREER

The first player from Vancouver to have his number retired, Stan Smyl gave his entire career to the Canucks, one that spanned 13 years and included every major offensive record in team history. He was a first-rate prospect with the New Westminster Bruins, winning consecutive Memorial Cup titles in 1977 and 1978, after which the Canucks selected him 40th overall in the Amateur Draft.

Stocky and tough as nails, he was a power forward who had no problem fighting as well as scoring, both of which he did very well. After a rookie season of 14 goals, he rattled off eight straight seasons of 20 goals or more, but the highlight of his career came at the end of the 1981–82 season when the team advanced to the Cup Final. There they faced the New York Islanders, and although the Islanders won, the Canucks believed they had the foundation to win.

Such was not the case, though. Smyl was named captain at training camp in 1982, and remained so until his final year, 1990–91, when the duties were split among three other players. The Canucks were quickly eliminated in the playoffs his first two years wearing the "C" and the team missed the post-season altogether for four straight seasons after that. At this point, Smyl's production began to dip.

He retired in 1991 as the team's career leader in games played (896), goals (262), assists (411), and points (673), but stayed with the organization as an assistant coach, watching from behind the bench as the Canucks went to the Final in 1994 before losing game seven to the Rangers. He has been with the team ever since in a variety of administrative positions.

CEREMONY

They called him the "Steamer," and for his 13 years of faithful play the Canucks retired his number 12 after his last season. Smyl was an assistant coach with the team at the time, but he couldn't have imagined how special the night would be. Gifts included a truck and a motorcycle, a portrait by sports artist Glen Green, and a $12,000 donation to the Canuck Foundation, his charity of choice.

With his wife, Jennifer, and their three children by his side, Smyl gave a heartfelt thanks to the fans. "You made me a better player and a better person," he said from centre ice. "The faith that you had in the Steamer made the game worthwhile to me."

THE GAME: Vancouver Canucks 7–Edmonton Oilers 2
Before the players took to the ice, captain Trevor Linden stood up in the dressing room and made the night's priority clear. "Let's make this a complete day for Stan," he said, imploring the team to win for their old number 12. And they did. The Canucks came out on all cylinders in the first period, scoring three times to the Oilers' one.

The pattern repeated itself in the second, and after 40 minutes the home side held a comfortable 6–2 lead. Igor Larionov had a hat trick for the Canucks, and coach Pat Quinn couldn't have been happier with the effort. "I think our performance had to do with that ceremony," he said, stating the obvious. "You think about the reasons that sweater is up there, and it has nothing to do with physical skill. Character, heart, courage. Those are the things that are important. Hopefully our team will learn some of these things."

"This tops them all," assistant coach Smyl beamed after the lopsided win. "This is the best gift I've received."

7

TED LINDSAY

DETROIT RED WINGS
NOVEMBER 10, 1991

Born: Renfrew, Ontario, July 29, 1925
Position: Left wing
Shoots: Left
Height: 5'8"
Weight: 163 lbs.

HONOURS
- **Stanley Cup** 1950, 1952, 1954, 1955
- **Art Ross Trophy** 1950
- **NHL All-Star Game** 1947, 1948, 1949, 1950, 1951, 1952, 1953, 1954, 1955, 1956, 1957
- **NHL First All-Star Team** 1948, 1950, 1951, 1952, 1953, 1954, 1956, 1957
- **Hockey Hall of Fame** 1966

NHL CAREER STATS

	Regular Season					Playoffs				
Years	GP	G	A	P	Pim	GP	G	A	P	Pim
1944–65	1,068	379	472	851	1,808	133	47	49	96	194

CAREER

Ted Lindsay may have been only about 5'8" and 160 pounds in his birthday suit, but make no mistake—he was as feared as he was talented, and he could use his stick to score and spear with equal effect. By the time he retired in 1965, at age 39, he was the highest scoring left winger in NHL history.

"Terrible Ted" entered the NHL in 1944 before he earned that moniker, and by his third year he developed into a superstar thanks to the presence of rookie Gordie Howe and the leadership of Sid Abel. Abel, the grizzled veteran, played on the Production Line with these two kids, and they immediately became the top-scoring threesome in the game. In 1949–50, they finished 1-2-3 in scoring, Lindsay leading the way with 78 points, the only time he led the league.

Along with Red Kelly on defence and Terry Sawchuk in goal, the Red Wings of this era could compete any time, anywhere against Toronto and Montreal, the

other top teams of these years. Indeed, Detroit finished in first place seven straight years and won the Stanley Cup four times—1950, 1952, 1954, and 1955. Lindsay and Howe, best friends on and off the ice, led the charge during this golden era, and Lindsay in particular was as fist happy as he was goal savvy, drawing the ire of opponents for his tough play, and then scoring to rub salt in the wounds.

Lindsay's passion for the game, and his combative and competitive personality, got him into trouble with the team and league in the late 1950s when he tried to form a players' union. He met with top players on the Leafs and Canadiens in secret to try to forge a unified front against the dictatorial owners, but his efforts were eventually quashed and he was traded to lowly Chicago in 1957, then the worst team in the league. His courage did not go forgotten, though, and a few years later a young Toronto lawyer named Alan Eagleson did, in fact, form a union to give the players their first code of rights and bargaining power.

No man who ever played hockey had more commitment to his team and to the game, and no man has had greater influence off ice than Ted Lindsay. The retirement of his number 7 sweater was not just common sense; it was essential to the integrity of the game.

In 2010, Lindsay received a unique honour from the Players' Association. It re-named the Lester B. Pearson Award the Ted Lindsay Award to commemorate forever his contribution to the players.

10 ALEX DELVECCHIO

DETROIT RED WINGS
NOVEMBER 10, 1991

Born: Fort William, Ontario, December 4, 1932
Position: Forward
Shoots: Left
Height: 6'
Weight: 195 lbs.

HONOURS
- **Stanley Cup** 1952, 1954, 1955
- **Lady Byng Trophy** 1959, 1966, 1969
- **Lester Patrick Trophy** 1974
- **Played entire career with Detroit and later coached the team**
- **Hockey Hall of Fame** 1977

NHL CAREER STATS

	Regular Season					Playoffs				
Years	GP	G	A	P	Pim	GP	G	A	P	Pim
1950–74	1,549	456	825	1,281	383	121	35	69	104	29

CAREER

No player in NHL history spent his entire career with only one team longer than Alex Delvecchio. From the time he entered the league on March 25, 1951, to the day he retired to become its coach, November 7, 1973, he played for Detroit and no other. Such was his devotion and longevity that he cut across two eras of Red Wings players. In the early days, he played on the Production Line with Gordie Howe and Ted Lindsay replacing Sid Abel who was traded to Chicago, and a much later incarnation of the line had him and Howe combining with Frank Mahovlich.

Although he was a consistent scorer, Delvecchio was known more as a playmaker. He wasn't fast on his skates, but he was smooth, gliding seemingly above the ice with grace and strength. The opposite to Howe and Lindsay, he was a pacifist and a gentlemanly player, winning the Lady Byng Trophy three times during his career.

He was also resilient. Although he missed 22 games in 1956–57 because of an ankle injury, he missed only 21 other games in those 24 years, finishing with 1,549 regular-season games to his credit, among the leaders in this category when he retired. He joined the Red Wings when it was in its greatest days, winning the Stanley Cup in his first full season, 1951–52, and twice more in 1953–54 and 1954–55.

The team remained competitive throughout the 1960s until expansion, after which it went through very difficult times and missed the playoffs five out of his last six years. Delvecchio retired early in the 1973–74 season to become the team's coach, a position he held with only moderate success for the next three and a half years.

Delvecchio took over as captain from Gordie Howe in 1962 and retained the "C" for the next 11 years. He was nicknamed "Fats" because of his round face, although in his later days, his hair now silver-white, he was also corpulent of body. Good natured and affable, he was beloved by fans and respected by opponents. Three years after retiring he was inducted into the Hockey Hall of Fame, although he had to wait another 14 years to have his number 10 raised to the rafters of the Joe Louis Arena.

CEREMONY

The 20-minute, pre-game honour was highlighted by a dual ceremony at centre ice for Ted Lindsay and Alex Delvecchio. These were the second and third numbers retired by the team after Gordie Howe's number 9. Deadpanned Lindsay: "When they raise the sweater, well, what more can they do for you? That means you've been hung. What really counts," he continued, "is who we're hung with—the greatest athlete in any sport that I've ever seen."

Delvecchio was given a number 10 sweater by current Red Wings forward Jimmy Carson. Carson had been sporting the number himself, so on this night he removed the number 10 for the last time and switched to number 12, this despite leading the team in scoring. "I hope this doesn't jinx him," Delvecchio joked. When asked what Carson should do if it did jinx him, Fats replied, "then he'd better put the [number 10] sweater on again."

Current captain Steve Yzerman presented Lindsay with a number 7 sweater and then both banners with name and number were raised to the rafters of the Joe Louis Arena.

THE GAME: Detroit Red Wings 6–St. Louis Blues 4

The star of the night was Bob Probert, whose old style of play was reminiscent of Lindsay's era. He scored the first and last goals of the game, was by turns physical and skilful all night, and was a key factor in the win.

He opened the scoring at 8:06, and by the end of the period the Red Wings had built a 3–1 lead. The Blues evened the count midway through the game after goals by Nelson Emerson and Ron Sutter, but Steve Yzerman and Shawn Burr restored the two-goal lead after 40 minutes.

Brett Hull brought the Blues to within one goal early in the third, but a late power-play marker from Probert proved to be the final goal of the game.

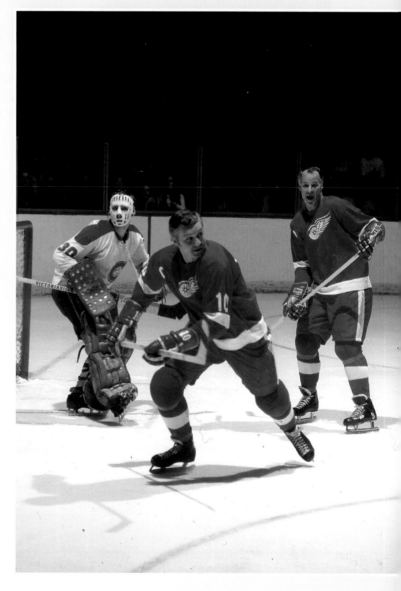

5

DENIS
POTVIN

NEW YORK ISLANDERS
FEBRUARY 1, 1992

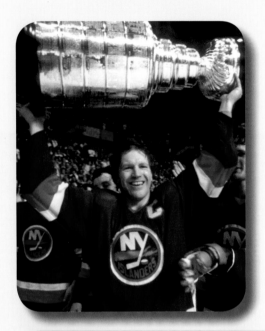

Born: Ottawa, Ontario, October 29, 1953
Position: Defence
Shoots: Left
Height: 6'
Weight: 205 lbs.

HONOURS
- **Stanley Cup** 1980, 1981, 1982, 1983
- **Calder Trophy** 1974
- **Norris Trophy** 1976, 1978, 1979
- **NHL All-Star Game** 1974, 1975, 1976, 1977, 1978, 1981, 1983, 1984, 1988
- **Played for Canada in Canada Cup** 1976, 1981
- **Hockey Hall of Fame** 1991

NHL CAREER STATS

	Regular Season					Playoffs				
Years	GP	G	A	P	Pim	GP	G	A	P	Pim
1973–88	1,060	310	742	1,052	1,356	185	56	108	164	253

CAREER

Although Denis Potvin rushed the puck, he wasn't a daredevil like his influence, the great Bobby Orr. This meant he wasn't as exciting to watch, but it also meant his career endured well beyond Orr's. Potvin retired in 1988 after playing 1,060 regular-season games and scoring 1,052 points, the first defenceman to reach the thousand mark and the all-time leader in goals (310) and assists (742) as well.

Drafted first overall by the New York Islanders in 1973, the 19-year-old Potvin stepped into the lineup that fall and started moving the puck up ice with confidence. He had had a stellar junior career with the Ottawa 67's, partnering with Ian Turnbull on the blue line and setting a record with 123 points in his final year.

At the end of his rookie season with the Islanders, in which he had 54 points and a career-high 175 penalty minutes, he was awarded the Calder Trophy. He

earned plenty of ice time, led the power play, and brought another dimension to a team in need of anything conducive to winning.

Starting the next year, Potvin began a stretch of nine out of 12 seasons with at least 20 goals, culminating in 1978–79 when he scored 31 goals and earned a total of 101 points, a personal best. That summer he was named team captain after winning his third Norris Trophy in four years. Indeed, when he won for the first time, in 1976, he was the first player not named Orr to win it since Harry Howell in 1966.

Ironically, as Potvin's offensive totals declined, the team started to win the Stanley Cup, testament both to his abilities inside his own blue line as well as confirming the old axiom that defence wins championships. Four times in a row he hoisted the Cup, from 1980 to 1983, leading the Islanders to a dynasty that still remains the last of its kind.

Potvin also played in the two Canada Cup tournaments, winning with Canada in 1976, and losing in 1981. He played in nine All-Star Games, and by the time he retired it was clear his number would one day hang in the rafters.

CEREMONY

The Islanders' glory days had passed, and on this night only 11,715 fans made it through the turnstiles to honour one of their greats. Nonetheless, the evening was special for Denis Potvin; his wife, Valerie; daughter, Madeleine; and son, Christian.

Potvin waved to the crowd and blew kisses to the seats before speaking of his many years with the team when it was winning the Stanley Cup. "These were the very best years of my life," he said. "I grew up here. I came here as a teenager and went as a man. This is where my playground was. I now feel like I really, really belong, and I'm never going away."

The Islanders gave him gold cufflinks with his number 5 engraved on them as a token of their thanks.

THE GAME: New York Islanders 5–Philadelphia Flyers 5 (OT)

Times had changed, and now the once-dominant Islanders were like many other teams, fighting for a playoff spot. They blew a two-goal lead after two periods and had to rally to force overtime and get a single point in the standings, the result of which only kept them out of last place in the Patrick Division, ahead of the Flyers by a single point.

The Islanders trailed 2–1 after the first period but took control of the game in the second when they scored three times to take a 4–2 lead. But they in turn were pushed around by the Flyers in the third as Philadelphia scored three times in the first half of the period to take a 5–4 lead.

New York tied the game with only 1:06 left in regulation. Derek King, with his team-best 31st goal of the season, converted a shot by Tom Kurvers on the power play, beating Ron Hextall and sending the game to overtime. In the New York net, goalie Mark Fitzpatrick was by turns brilliant and weak. "I wasn't happy with my game," he said. "On a couple of goals, I was a little too deep and it cost us. You've got to be consistent. Five goals should be enough to win."

"We kind of blew a great opportunity," said coach Al Arbour, behind the bench during Potvin's heyday and still the bench boss of the Isles. "I'm not very pleased."

8
BILL
GOLDSWORTHY

MINNESOTA NORTH STARS
FEBRUARY 15, 1992

Born: Waterloo, Ontario, August 24, 1944
Died: Minneapolis, Minnesota, March 29, 1996
Position: Right wing
Shoots: Right
Height: 6'
Weight: 190 lbs.

HONOURS
- **NHL All-Star Game** 1970, 1972, 1974, 1976
- **Played for Canada in 1972 Summit Series**

NHL CAREER STATS

	Regular Season					Playoffs				
Years	GP	G	A	P	Pim	GP	G	A	P	Pim
1964–78	771	283	258	541	793	40	18	19	37	30

CAREER

Perhaps the first superstar in the history of the Minnesota North Stars, Bill Goldsworthy was certainly its finest scorer in the 1970s, at a time when the team had limited success. And, like dozens of players of his era, he was given new life in 1967 when the NHL expanded from six to 12 teams.

As a teen, Goldsworthy had been discovered by the Boston Bruins, and as a result he played junior hockey for the Niagara Falls Flyers. Between 1964 and 1967, however, he played only 33 games with the Bruins while spending most of his time in the minors. The 1967 Expansion Draft changed everything for him. The Minnesota North Stars claimed the right winger, and he immediately became a top forward for the fledgling team.

In his third season with the North Stars, Goldsworthy scored 36 goals, his first of seven straight seasons of at least 24 goals. In the 1968 playoffs he led all scorers

with eight goals and 15 points, but the team lost to the St. Louis Blues in the division final. In 1973–74, he was one of the top goal scorers in the league with 48, but the team enjoyed only moderate playoff success during the decade.

Few players are famous for their goal celebrations, but Goldsworthy's "Goldy Shuffle" was one such example. In all, he scored 267 goals with the North Stars over nine and a half seasons before being traded to the Rangers and later moving to the WHA at the end of his career. Yet Goldsworthy was always associated with Minnesota first and foremost, and his number 8 was only the second to be retired by the team (after Bill Masterton's 19).

MINNESOTA NORTH STARS ™

CEREMONY

The celebration began when current player Jim Johnson first agreed happily to give up the number 8 he had been wearing. He moved down to number 6, and Goldsworthy's 8 went up to the rafters of the Met Center.

The brief ceremony included speeches from Goldsworthy himself, former teammate Tom Reid, and the Minnesota North Stars first coach, Wren Blair.

"When they called me to tell me they were going to retire my jersey," Goldsworthy said the previous day, "I was shocked. I almost fell out of my chair."

THE GAME: Minnesota North Stars 5–Pittsburgh Penguins 2

This was a key game in the playoff race, particularly for the North Stars, which solidified their hold on a post-season date. And they beat the team that hammered them 8–0 to win the Stanley Cup the previous year. "This was a really big win," said Ulf Dahlen. "Now we've got to keep putting them together."

Mario Lemieux made a great pass to Larry Murphy for the opening goal by the visitors, but Dave Gagner answered on the power play at 12:24 to make it a 1–1 game after 20 minutes. The North Stars scored the only two goals of the middle period, thanks to Gaetan Duchesne and Dahlen, but the Penguins tried to mount a rally early in the third when Murphy scored again.

The North Stars continued to press and refused to be intimidated, scoring two late goals and muscling out an impressive win. "I thought our defence as a group was really good and the goaltending was outstanding," Stars coach Bob Gainey said, specifically in reference to netminder Darcy Wakaluk. "He made two or three terrific saves in the second period that kept us in the game. And he gave us confidence in the third when the game closed up."

22

MIKE
BOSSY

Born: Montreal, Quebec, January 22, 1957
Position: Right wing
Shoots: Right
Height: 6'
Weight: 186 lbs.

HONOURS
- **Stanley Cup** 1980, 1981, 1982, 1983
- **Lady Byng Trophy** 1983, 1984, 1986
- **Calder Trophy** 1978
- **Conn Smythe Trophy** 1982
- **Played for Canada in Canada Cup** 1981, 1984
- **Hockey Hall of Fame** 1991

NHL CAREER STATS

	Regular Season					Playoffs				
Years	GP	G	A	P	Pim	GP	G	A	P	Pim
1977–87	752	573	553	1,126	210	129	85	75	160	38

CAREER

One of the purest, greatest, and most consistent scorers in NHL history, Mike Bossy was prevented from possibly becoming the highest scorer due to a deteriorating back injury that forced him to retire at age 30 after only 10 years in the league.

Surprisingly, given that in junior he averaged 77 goals a season, he was drafted only 15th overall by the Islanders in 1977. But scouts believed poor skating and a lack of attention to defence would do him in. They were wrong. Bossy had the best snap shot in the game and a release as fast as a gun. He played on the Trio Grande Line with centre Bryan Trottier and left winger Clark Gillies, the former being the set-up man the latter the mucker and chaser down of loose pucks and corner-board battles.

Bossy shattered the rookie scoring record by recording 53 goals in his first year and winning the Calder Trophy. It was the first of nine consecutive 50-goal seasons,

a record not even Wayne Gretzky or Mario Lemieux matched. Five times he eclipsed the 60-goal mark, and in 1980–81 he tied Maurice Richard's 35-year-old record by scoring 50 goals in the first 50 games of the season. Bossy had 48 going into his 50th game, against Quebec, but he scored midway through the game and then again with less than two minutes to go to tie an incredible record.

Such was the on- and off-ice relationship Trottier and Bossy had that they earned the nickname "Bread and Butter." Trottier was the set-up man who worked perfectly with Bossy, the finisher. Together they led the Islanders to the Stanley Cup in 1980 and each of three seasons after that. Bossy led the playoffs in goals for those second, third, and fourth victories, each time netting 17. In the 1982 playoffs he was awarded the Conn Smythe Trophy.

During his career Bossy played the game with gentlemanly sportsmanship, earning him three Lady Byng Trophies, but more than that he was a vocal advocate for fair play at all levels of the game. He had just 210 penalty minutes in his decade in the league, and it was more than a little ironic that his back injury was the result of constant crosschecks. He was the poster boy for clean play, both in words and in deed.

In all, Bossy retired in 1987 with 573 goals to his credit in only 752 games played, a remarkable ratio for any era.

CEREMONY

A 30-minute ceremony prior to the Montreal-Islanders game honoured the team's greatest scorer, a Hall of Famer, and one of the main reasons the Isles won the Stanley Cup four years in a row. Bossy was introduced on the video scoreboard by longtime line mate Bryan Trottier, who was playing for Pittsburgh at the time and unable to attend the event in person.

Bossy was given several gifts, spoke in English and French, and finished by turning the tables on the 14,085 fans who were in attendance. "I would like to give you a hand. Thank you," he said, raising his arms and clapping as he turned to acknowledge the people who cheered him on for his entire playing career.

THE GAME: Montreal Canadiens 4–New York Islanders 3

The game was one of the most exciting of the season, but in the end the Canadiens prevailed with a late goal to win, 4–3. Brent Gilchrist provided the killer, scoring his second of the game with just 2:21 left in regulation to give the visitors the win.

"We didn't play that bad," said Pierre Turgeon of the Islanders, "but they scored one more than us."

Indeed, the New Yorkers jumped into an early 2–0 lead thanks to goals from Uwe Krupp and Turgeon, but Kirk Muller scored twice late in the period to erase that deficit before the first intermission. There was no scoring in the second period, and Gilchrist got his first midway through the third, but Turgeon equalized at 14:42. The game looked to be headed to overtime until Gilchrist took a pass from Sylvain Lefebvre and beat goalie Mark Fitzpatrick for the game winner at 17:39.

This was the NHL debut for two Islanders players who had just played for the United States at the 1992 Olympics in Albertville—Scott Lachance and Marty McInnis.

8 FRANK
FINNIGAN

OTTAWA SENATORS
OCTOBER 8, 1992

Born: Shawville, Quebec, July 9, 1900
Died: Shawville, Quebec, December 25, 1991
Position: Right wing
Shoots: Right
Height: 5'9"
Weight: 165 lbs.

HONOURS
- **Stanley Cup** 1927, 1932
- **Played in Ace Bailey Benefit Game** 1934

NHL CAREER STATS

	Regular Season					Playoffs				
Years	GP	G	A	P	Pim	GP	G	A	P	Pim
1923–37	553	115	88	203	407	38	6	9	15	22

CAREER

It's not often that there's a good explanation for keeping a player waiting more than 55 years to have his sweater number retired, but in the case of Frank Finnigan, there *is* a worthy story. Finnigan was a great star with the Ottawa Senators, to be sure, but the original Senators of the 1920s. The team folded soon after he left and it didn't return to the NHL until 1992, by which time Finnigan had passed away at age 91.

Finnigan got his start with the Senators in 1923 when he was just 20 years old. It took him a couple of years to get used to the faster, more experienced players of the NHL after having played at a much lower level the previous two seasons, but by 1926 he was starting to gain a little confidence. He scored 15 goals in 36 games in 1926–27, and the Senators won the Stanley Cup. This was the first of four straight seasons of at least 15 goals for the right winger, but it was to be his only Cup with the team.

In all, Finnigan played eight seasons with Ottawa, but the team suffered financially and had to trade away or sell many of its stars, Finnigan among them. He ended up with the Maple Leafs in 1931 and was part of that team's Cup win the following spring in its first season at Maple Leaf Gardens. After one season he was able to return to the Senators.

When the Senators moved to St. Louis in 1934, Finnigan went back to Toronto, returning to Ottawa to work in the business world after his playing days were done. In the early 1990s, the city was intent on bringing NHL hockey back, and Finnigan was recruited to promote the new owners and a new era of hockey in the nation's capital. After the NHL awarded Ottawa an expansion franchise, the team announced that Finnigan's number 8 would be retired at the opening ceremonies of the first home game. Although he was aware of this honour, he passed away before the actual occasion.

CEREMONY

It was an historic night for hockey in Ottawa as the NHL returned to the city for the first time in 65 years. Bruce Firestone, the man behind the successful return, was given a thunderous ovation in the tiny downtown Civic Centre where 10,449 fans squeezed in to welcome back the Senators. Ground had been broken for the new arena in the suburb of Kanata, but was still years away from completion.

Indeed, the retiring of Frank Finnigan's number 8 was one of only several momentous occasions on this night, and that was just fine for all involved, including his son, Frank Jr., who was part of the ceremonies on behalf of his late father.

The team raised banners for the original team's Stanley Cup victories as well, so Finnigan had immediate company in the rafters. The ceremonial faceoff and player introductions lengthened the drama leading to the opening faceoff.

THE GAME: Ottawa Senators 5–Montreal Canadiens 3

The Ottawa Senators, a rag-tag group of draft choices, free agent signings, and castoffs, gave the fans what they wanted: a win on opening night. No one could have known this night, but the Montreal Canadiens went on to win the Cup and the Sens finished dead last in the overall standings. No matter.

The first period was scoreless thanks only to Sens goalie Peter Sidorkiewicz and Habs netminder Patrick Roy. Neil Brady scored the first Ottawa goal just 26 seconds into the second period to give the home side a 1–0 lead, and halfway through the period Doug Smail made it 2–0. Goals from each side made it a 3–1 Ottawa lead after 40 minutes, but Vincent Damphousse cut the lead with a goal early in the third.

Ottawa opened another two-goal lead after Sylvain Turgeon ripped a low shot past Roy from the slot, and two goals in the final minute closed out the scoring. If the Sens were to win only once all year, this was the game they knew they had to win.

And they did.

5 BILL
BARILKO

TORONTO MAPLE LEAFS
OCTOBER 17, 1992

Born: Timmins, Ontario, March 25, 1927
Died: Cochrane, Ontario, August 26, 1951
Position: Defence
Shoots: Right
Height: 5'11"
Weight: 180 lbs.

HONOURS
- **Stanley Cup** 1947, 1948, 1949, 1951
- **NHL All-Star Game** 1947, 1948, 1949

NHL CAREER STATS

	Regular Season					Playoffs				
Years	GP	G	A	P	Pim	GP	G	A	P	Pim
1946–51	252	26	36	62	456	47	5	7	12	104

CAREER

Bill Barilko packed as much into such a short life as any player to pass through the NHL, and by the time he perished in a plane crash at the tender age of 24, he was already a legend at Maple Leaf Gardens.

He got his start by playing for the Hollywood Wolves in California, a most unlikely place to get a hockey education, as it were. But his blue line partner was Tommy Anderson, a much-respected, well-travelled pro who told Conn Smythe of Barilko's attributes. The youngster was called up to Toronto late in the 1946–47 season, and just a few weeks later he was celebrating his first Stanley Cup.

Far from the strongest or biggest defenceman, Barilko nonetheless hit opponents with vim and energy such that his teammates nicknamed him "Bashin' Bill." The next season, 1947–48, he also led the league in penalty minutes, but the Leafs won the Cup again. Ditto for his third season.

It was the 1950–51 season when the Barilko legend took hold. Montreal and Toronto played in the Cup Final that year, and all five games of the series went into overtime, the first and only time this has happened. In the last of these games, Barilko swooped in from the point and swatted at a loose puck as he dove head first toward the net. He beat Habs goalie Gerry McNeil, and the Leafs won the big prize for the fourth time in five years.

That summer he went on a camping trip to the remote Ontario North, accessible only by small plane. It was there he met his fate. The plane crashed, but its remains weren't discovered until June 7, 1962. The Leafs, who had been without a Stanley Cup win since Barilko's disappearance, had won the Cup again that April, thus giving rise to the story that the team was cursed until Barilko's body was given a proper burial.

His life has been celebrated in many ways, most famously by a Tragically Hip song called "Fifty Mission Cap" that includes the lyrics "the last goal he ever scored/won the Leafs the Cup." In loving memory of the man and player, no one wore number 5 for the Leafs after that goal in 1951.

CEREMONY

Although no player ever wore the number 5 for the Maple Leafs after Barilko, it was not hoisted to the rafters until October 17, 1992, along with Ace Bailey's number 6. Captain Wendel Clark helped with the ceremony prior to the game, as did Joyce Bailey, representing her father, Ace, and Ron Ellis, who was the only other player to wear number 6 after Bailey. Barilko was represented by his younger sister, Ann Barilko-Klisanich and former captain and teammate Ted Kennedy. This marked the first—and still only—time numbers have been retired by the Leafs.

THE GAME: Toronto Maple Leafs 4–Chicago Blackhawks 3

The Leafs got the better of the Hawks on this night thanks to a pair of goals in each of the first two periods and some solid goaltending from Grant Fuhr along the way.

Glenn Anderson got the first goal for Toronto at 5:06 of the opening period, and Doug Gilmour made it 2–0 on a power play. Chicago wiped that lead away before the end of the period, though.

Toronto got the only two goals of the second, the first thanks to Nikolai Borshevsky and the second, on the power play again, at 19:34 from Anderson. In the third, Chicago tried to mount a comeback, but only a goal from Igor Kravchuk in the final minute made the score a little closer.

Ed Belfour, who much later also played for the Leafs, was the goalie of record for the Blackhawks.

31

BILLY SMITH

NEW YORK ISLANDERS
FEBRUARY 20, 1993

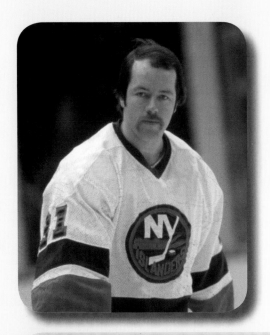

Born: Perth, Ontario, December 12, 1950
Position: Goalie
Catches: Left
Height: 5'10"
Weight: 185 lbs.

HONOURS
- **Stanley Cup** 1980, 1981, 1982, 1983
- **Vezina Trophy** 1982
- **Conn Smythe Trophy** 1983
- **Jennings Trophy** 1983 (with Roland Melanson)
- **First NHL goalie to be credited with a goal** (November 28, 1979, vs. Colorado Rockies)
- **Hockey Hall of Fame** 1993

NHL CAREER STATS

Regular Season

Years	GP	W-L-T	Mins	GA	SO	GAA
1971–89	680	305-233-105	38,431	2,031	22	3.17

Playoffs

Years	GP	W-L-T	Mins	GA	SO	GAA
1971–89	132	88-36-0	7,645	348	5	2.73

CAREER

They called him "Battlin' Billy" because he was not averse to chopping the ankle or back of the leg of an opponent encroaching on his goal crease, but that quality carried him to four Stanley Cup wins in a row, a trip to the Hockey Hall of Fame, and a ceremony to honour his number 31.

Billy Smith is so associated with the New York Islanders' success that few fans remember he started his career with the Los Angeles Kings. He was claimed by the Islanders at the 1972 Expansion Draft when he was just 22 years old, and it was with that team that he spent the next 17 years.

Smith came to a team that would soon have several great young players, notably Bryan Trottier, Mike Bossy, Bob Nystrom, and Clark Gillies. Together they

grew up on and off the ice, and although the team lost to and learned from the Montreal Canadiens in the late 1970s, the Isles won their fair share and developed a dynasty.

Smith wasn't one of those goalies who had a sparkling goals-against average or who stopped everything thrown at him. More, he was cut from the same cloth as Gerry Cheevers and Grant Fuhr: a goalie who gave up his share of goals over a playoff series or season, but who was called a "playoff goalie" because when the chips were down he was virtually unbeatable. Coach Al Arbour happily gave his second goalie, "Chico" Resch, plenty of playing time, but in the playoffs, Resch was on the bench and Smith secured one win after another for the team.

Indeed, between 1980 and 1985, Smith won 69 playoff games, a remarkable rate of success. He won the Conn Smythe Trophy for the team's final Cup win, in 1983, and then it was New York who taught Edmonton about losing. In 1984, the Islanders' dynasty gave way to Wayne Gretzky's Oilers.

Only one of Smith's 305 career wins came with Los Angeles, and when he retired in 1989 it was clear his legacy was ensured for eternity. His playoff record of 88 wins and only 36 losses is one of the best ratios of all time.

CEREMONY

Smith appeared on ice at the Islanders goal with many who were near and dear to him, starting with his wife, Debbie, and several teammates, namely Denis Potvin, Bryan Trottier, Butch Goring, and Clark Gillies. Also in the group was Bill Torrey, the longtime general manager who helped build the dynastic Islanders of the early 1980s.

The Smiths were given trips to Europe and Jamaica, an exercise machine, and 31 cases of beer. Then the lights went down and a spotlight opened on the large banner with the number 31 on it. "You don't know how much this means to me," an emotional Smith told the crowd as he became only the third player so honoured (after Mike Bossy and Denis Potvin).

THE GAME: New York Islanders 4–Pittsburgh Penguins 2

This turned out to be a vital and prescient win for the Islanders. For starters, it moved the team into fourth spot in the Patrick Division, one point ahead of the Rangers, for the final playoff spot in the division. More important, it presaged the second-round, game-seven playoff battle, which pitted the two-time defending Cup champion Penguins against the underdog Islanders, in which the Islanders won 4–3 in overtime.

On this night the hero was Pierre Turgeon, the 23-year-old star forward who was already in his sixth NHL season. He had three goals for the victors, but had to share the spotlight with goalie Glenn Healy who'd made some big saves at the right time.

The Isles scored the only goal of the first thanks to Turgeon, and the Pens got the only one of the middle period from Jaromir Jagr, but the 1–1 deadlock opened early in the third. The Penguins had a flurry of great chances but couldn't beat Healy, and on the ensuing rush up ice Turgeon scored to give the Isles a lead. He scored again just 77 seconds later to make it 3–1.

Larry Murphy pulled the Pens to within a goal, and the rest of the game was tight and exciting until Uwe Krupp scored the final goal into the empty Pittsburgh net with goalie Tom Barrasso on the bench for a sixth attacker.

TERRY
SAWCHUK

DETROIT RED WINGS
MARCH 6, 1994

Born: Winnipeg, Manitoba, December 28, 1929
Died: Long Beach, New York, May 31, 1970
Position: Goalie
Catches: Left
Height: 5'11"
Weight: 195 lbs.

HONOURS
- **Stanley Cup** 1952, 1954, 1955, 1967
- **USHL Rookie of the Year** 1948
- **AHL Rookie of the Year** 1949
- **Calder Trophy** 1951
- **Vezina Trophy** 1952, 1953, 1955, 1965 (with Johnny Bower)
- **Lester Patrick Trophy** 1971
- **NHL All-Star Game** 1950–56, 1959, 1963–64, 1968
- **Hockey Hall of Fame** 1971

NHL CAREER STATS

Regular Season

Years	GP	W-L-T	Mins	GA	SO	GAA
1949–70	971	447-338-172	57,194	2,389	103	2.51

Playoffs

Years	GP	W-L-T	Mins	GA	SO	GAA
1949–70	106	54-48-0	6,290	266	12	2.54

CAREER

Of all Original Six goalies, Terry Sawchuk reigns supreme. He was rookie of the year in the United States Hockey League (USHL) in 1947–48, rookie of the year the next year in the AHL, and got into his first NHL games the year after. In his first full season with the Detroit Red Wings, he won the Calder Trophy. In fact, he was so good that GM Jack Adams traded his starting goalie, Harry Lumley, because he knew Sawchuk would be around for many years to come.

He backstopped the Red Wings to the Stanley Cup in 1952, 1954, and 1955, but it was his first win that might have been the greatest playoff year for a goalie in Cup history. Sawchuk allowed just 5 goals, recorded four shutouts, and won in

the minimum number of games required—at the time it was eight—to win the NHL's greatest prize.

In the regular season he was a warrior, playing every minute of the 1950–51 and 1951–52 seasons. He led the league in wins five straight years (1950–55), and, of course, he piled up the shutouts. By the time he passed away in 1970, he had 103 regular season shutouts and 12 more in the playoffs, all but eight coming with the Red Wings.

When he was 12, Sawchuk broke his arm and didn't tell anybody. The break healed badly and caused him serious pain for many years before he underwent corrective surgery. He suffered an eye injury and punctured lung, was hit in the face by a Bobby Hull slapshot, and had his hand skated over by Bob Pulford, resulting in torn tendons. His hunched-over style of play was not because of some brilliant tactic or forward-thinking coach; it was the result of ruptured vertebrae.

Yet, by 1970, there was little question he was the greatest of them all. His bravery and style, his ability and willingness to do anything and everything to stop the puck, made him the best of the best. Ironically, as he got older and his career was in its twilight, he found it impossible to retire. He and Johnny Bower combined to win one final Stanley Cup with Toronto, in 1967, and then Sawchuk went on to play a season with Los Angeles, Detroit again, and the Rangers.

By the end of his career, he led the league in every major statistical category. He played an incredible 971 games, recorded 447 wins, played in 57,194 NHL minutes, and had a sparkling GAA of 2.51. But those 103 shutouts stood out, testament to Sawchuk's genius in the crease—usually the Detroit crease.

CEREMONY

The fourth number to be retired by Detroit—after Howe, Lindsay, and Delvecchio—Sawchuk's number 1 was honoured prior to an afternoon game at Joe Louis Arena. All three great men were at centre ice for the much-deserved celebration, as were owners Mike and Marian Ilitch. Joining them were NHL commissioner Gary Bettman and six of Sawchuk's seven children. "I want to thank Mr. and Mrs. Ilitch [Mike and Marian]," Jerry Sawchuk, a son, said. "I just can't put it into words . . . Thank you very much."

The players donated $2,500 to Ronald McDonald House, the charity of choice for Sawchuk's family.

THE GAME: Buffalo Sabres 3–Detroit Red Wings 2

Although the home side didn't win, Terry Sawchuk's spirit couldn't have been too unhappy because Sabres goalie Dominik "Dominator" Hasek—as unorthodox to his generation as Sawchuk was to his—turned in a magnificent crease performance. "Dominik was awesome," Buffalo coach John Muckler effused after. "He's the hottest goalie in the NHL."

Incredibly, Detroit outshot Buffalo 17–5 in the first period and sat in the dressing room after 20 minutes trailing 1–0. That's how good Hasek was, and how fortuitous the visitors were when Doug Bodger scored in the dying seconds while short-handed.

Teams exchanged goals in the second, and Buffalo took control with a goal from Yuri Khmylev midway through the third. A goal by Steve Yzerman at 19:54 made the score closer. Overall, Detroit held a 45–22 advantage in shots on goal.

16

MICHEL GOULET

QUEBEC NORDIQUES
MARCH 16, 1995

Born: Peribonka, Quebec, April 21, 1960
Position: Left wing
Shoots: Left
Height: 6'1"
Weight: 195 lbs.

HONOURS
- **NHL All-Star Game** 1983, 1984, 1985, 1986, 1988
- **NHL First All-Star Team** 1984, 1986, 1987
- **Played for Canada in Canada Cup** 1984, 1987
- **Hockey Hall of Fame** 1998

NHL CAREER STATS

Years	Regular Season					Playoffs				
	GP	G	A	P	Pim	GP	G	A	P	Pim
1979–94	1,089	548	604	1,152	825	92	39	39	78	110

CAREER

March 16 is a date Michel Goulet will always remember, which is a good thing because it means the head injury that ended his career caused no permanent damage. On March 16, 1994, 33-year-old Goulet crashed head-first into the boards, suffering a bad concussion and ending his career on the spot. He had been wearing a helmet, but one which wouldn't pass any reputable safety test today. On that date a year later, his number 16 was retired by the Quebec Nordiques in honour of his exceptional career.

Like many of the best players in the 1970s, Goulet benefited from the existence of the WHA. He played only a year and a half in junior and then signed with the Birmingham Bulls as an 18-year-old in 1978. That buffer year prepared him for the NHL for the following season when the Nordiques joined the league, which ended the WHA's existence.

Goulet was a pure scorer with lightning speed and a great shot. He improved his goal totals in each of the first four seasons, from 22 to 32 to 42 to 57. The 57 season started a string of four straight 50-goal years, after which he had 49 and 48. All this time the team had violent and emotional playoff battles with provincial rivals, the Montreal Canadiens. They won some, they lost some, but every game was a war for both sides. Such was his ability, Goulet also played for Canada at the 1984 and 1987 Canada Cup tournaments, victories both for the home side in the pre-eminent best-on-best event. The left winger was traded to Chicago late in the 1989–90 season after a contract dispute disrupted the start of his season. However, he was never the same player away from his spiritual home in Quebec.

Four and a half years later he suffered his career-ending head injury, but his legacy in his home province was long established. Four years later, he was inducted into the Hockey Hall of Fame, his 1,152 career points in 1,089 regular-season games proof of his dynamic contributions to the league and game.

CEREMONY

Goulet came out onto the ice in full equipment for the 20-minute ceremony, where he was joined by his mother, Alphonsine; father, Jean-Noel; his wife, Andree; and their three children, Dominique, Nicholas, and Sylvain.

He was given a two-minute standing ovation, and he also received two important telegrams. One, from teammate Peter Stastny, read in part: "You must be proud of what you have accomplished. All the best in your second career."

The other, from Dale Hunter, began with: "Dear Michel, I had the opportunity to develop alongside the best left winger in the NHL . . . Congratulations."

The visiting Penguins presented Goulet with a set of golf clubs. His own team gave him two around-the-world plane tickets as well as a Charlevoix painting.

"When they say hockey is in the roots of Quebeckers, I'm the proof," he said. He then recounted his childhood, skating on the frozen ponds near his home in Peribonka, Quebec.

THE GAME: Quebec Nordiques 3–Pittsburgh Penguins 2
The game started a bit slowly for the home side but ended as any home fan would have liked, in victory. Jaromir Jagr scored early for the Penguins to rattle the Nordiques, and it wasn't until 20 minutes later, early in the second period, that Peter Forsberg tied the game, 1–1.

Luc Robitaille, who had known Goulet growing up in Quebec, made it 2–1 Pittsburgh just two minutes later, but Owen Nolan again equalled for the Nordiques before the end of the period. Nolan got the only goal of the final period on an early power play, and at the final horn Mike Ricci scooped up the puck and gave it to Goulet.

Forsberg and Nolan played on a line with Bob Bassen, and this three-some was matched all night against Jagr, Robitaille, and Ron Francis, adding to the evening's drama for the 15,399 fans stuffed into Le Colisée on this night.

23

BOB
NYSTROM

NEW YORK ISLANDERS
APRIL 1, 1995

Born: Stockholm, Sweden, October 10, 1952
Position: Right wing
Shoots: Right
Height: 6'1"
Weight: 200 lbs.

HONOURS
- **Stanley Cup** 1980, 1981, 1982, 1983
- **NHL All-Star Game** 1977

NHL CAREER STATS

	Regular Season					Playoffs				
Years	GP	G	A	P	Pim	GP	G	A	P	Pim
1972–86	900	235	278	513	1,248	157	39	44	83	236

CAREER

A Swede by birth, Bob Nystrom moved to Canada with his family when he was four years old and grew up out west. He was drafted in 1972 by the expansion New York Islanders and made the team his first year, as a 20-year-old.

Nystrom was solid yet unspectacular in all aspects of the game. He could score and make plays, but he could also check tenaciously, work hard along the boards, and fight if need be. In short, he was the quintessential two-way player. He skated on a line with Bob Bourne and Wayne Merrick, and the three constituted the most effective third line in the league. Nystrom had seven seasons of 20 goals or more, but he was one of those rare players who excelled in the playoffs.

His most memorable moment came the night of May 24, 1980. The Stanley Cup Final featured the New York Islanders and Philadelphia Flyers, and with the Isles leading the series three games to two, game six went to overtime. Nystrom's

goal at 7:11 in OT gave the team its first Stanley Cup, the first of four in a row as history showed. In all, he scored four overtime goals in the playoffs during his career.

Nystrom played 14 seasons and 900 games with the team, never playing with anyone but the Islanders. His career came to a sudden end early in the 1985–86 season when he was struck in the eye by teammate Gerald Diduck's stick in practice, and he moved behind the bench as an assistant coach for the rest of the year. On the last day of the season, though, Nystrom had 899 games to his credit. Coach Al Arbour asked if he'd like to play in one more game to round his total off to an even 900, and Nystrom obliged. He took the opening faceoff, stayed out for about five seconds, and then headed to the bench, his career over and done.

Never the most talented player, he exuded that confidence and tenacity that marked the Islanders' dynasty. Nystrom was also among the more popular players with the fans both for his play and personality on ice and his tireless charity work in the community. Although his number was retired in 1995, three other Islanders wore it after he stopped playing.

CEREMONY

The fourth Islanders number to be retired from their 1980s dynasty, Bob Nystrom's number 23 joined Denis Potvin's 5, Mike Bossy's 22, and Billy Smith's 31 in the rafters of Nassau Coliseum.

"These guys are Hall of Fame guys," Nystrom said of the other retired numbers honourees. "I'm just a journeyman." Perhaps that's true, but he did score the biggest goal in team history, that one at 7:11 of overtime in 1980 against Philadelphia to give the team its first Stanley Cup.

Teammates Lorne Henning, John Tonelli, Gerry Hart, Richie Hansen, Gord Lane, Jean Potvin, Garry Howatt, Ken Morrow, as well as former coach Al Arbour, were part of the festivities, presenting Nystrom with a framed number 23 sweater before helping raise a banner in the player's honour. Nystrom was joined by his wife, Michelle, daughter Marissa, and son, Eric, a future NHLer himself. Parents Thor and Gunnel were also there as well as sister Annika.

Clark Gillies gave Nystrom a set of golf clubs on behalf of the alumni, which Nystrom ran, and several players and sponsors donated a total of $13,500 to charities in Nystrom's name.

THE GAME: Buffalo Sabres 5–New York Islanders 1

It didn't take long for the cheers for Nystrom to turn to boos for the current team as the Islanders limped to their 11th loss in 14 games. Bob Sweeney scored two short-handed goals, including the only goal of the first period of this afternoon game, to lead the offense.

"We were trying to key off Bobby, obviously," Islanders coach Lorne Henning said angrily after. "A little hard work, teamwork, inspiration, from Bobby—and we certainly didn't."

Vladimir Malakhov tied the game for the Islanders early in the second, but the rest of the game belonged to the visitors. The Sabres rattled off three unanswered goals to conclude the middle period, and Donald Audette finished the scoring midway through the third with his 18th of the season. Dominik Hasek stopped all but one of the 25 shots he faced while Jamie McLennan faced 31 shots in the New York end.

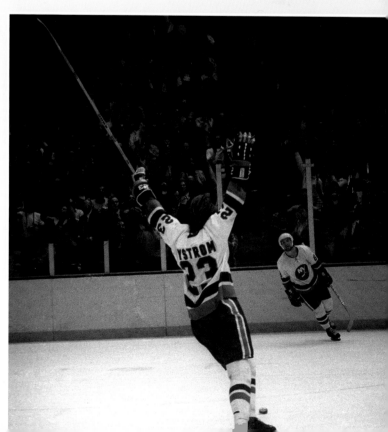

18

DAVE TAYLOR

LOS ANGELES KINGS
APRIL 3, 1995

Born: Levack, Ontario, December 4, 1955
Position: Right wing
Shoots: Right
Height: 6'
Weight: 190 lbs.

HONOURS
• **Played entire career with Los Angeles Kings; captain** 1985–89
• **Bill Masterton Trophy** 1991
• **King Clancy Memorial Trophy** 1991
• **NHL All-Star Game** 1981, 1982, 1986, 1994
• **Played for Canada at World Championship** 1983, 1985, 1986

NHL CAREER STATS

	Regular Season					Playoffs				
Years	GP	G	A	P	Pim	GP	G	A	P	Pim
1977–94	1,111	431	638	1,069	1,589	92	26	33	59	145

CAREER

The only member of the famed Triple Crown line to play his entire career in Los Angeles, Dave Taylor averaged nearly a point a game for more than 1,100 games over his 17-year career. In addition, he was a solid two-way player, a scorer in the offensive end and a capable defender inside his own blue line.

Taylor was a success story right from the start. Drafted a lowly 210th overall in 1975, he was passed over so many times by so many teams it was clear no one expected him to survive, let alone thrive, in the NHL. Yet he scored 22 goals as a rookie, and the next year, when he was added to the line with Marcel Dionne and Charlie Simmer to create the Triple Crown, Taylor nearly doubled his output to 43.

Despite the line's tremendous success as one of the top scoring threesomes in the league, their goals didn't equate to playoff success. The Kings were eliminated

in the first round in each of Taylor's first four seasons (1977–81), making it to the second round the year after before failing to qualify altogether in four of the next five years. Yet Taylor kept doing his part, reaching new personal bests in 1980–81 and 1981–82 with 112 and 106 points, respectively.

He was named Kings captain in the summer of 1985, but happily turned the "C" over to Wayne Gretzky when the "Great One" arrived in 1988. With Gretzky on board, the Kings had many of their best years in franchise history. The climax to this success came in 1993 when the team advanced to the Stanley Cup Final for the first time ever, only to lose to Montreal in five games.

Taylor won his only two individual trophies in 1991: the Masterton and King Clancy trophies. He also represented Canada three times at the World Championship, and by the time he retired in 1994, he had recorded 1,069 points in 1,111 games.

CEREMONY

The 30-minute pre-game ceremony to honour the team's current assistant to the general manager was only the third for a Kings player, following goalie Rogie Vachon and Hall of Famer Marcel Dionne.

Taylor took in the on-ice festivities with his wife, Beth; daughters, Jamie and Katie; and parents, Andy and Margaret. Charlie Simmer was there, as was commissioner Gary Bettman. There was a video tribute to Taylor, and Vachon spoke warmly to the cheering crowd in praise of his former teammate. "During this franchise, there have been a lot of ups and downs, but we could always count on number 18 to play every night."

The visiting Edmonton Oilers presented Taylor with a plaque, and the league made a donation to the Cystic Fibrosis Foundation, a charity close to Taylor's heart. The players gave him a Rolex watch while the front office gave him an SUV and a cruise to Alaska.

THE GAME: Los Angeles Kings 7–Edmonton Oilers 2

The Kings couldn't have made this a better night for Taylor than they did, scoring early and often and not surrendering a goal until the third period, by which time they were dominating to the tune of 7–0. Two early goals in the first were added to by a hat trick in the middle period from Tony Granato and a second goal from John Druce. Randy Burridge made it 7–0 early in the third before Todd Marchant and Igor Kravchuk added some small level of respect to the final score line.

Los Angeles held a 46–31 margin in shots and Kings goalie Kelly Hrudey was not nearly as busy as Bill Ranford at the other end. The only slight disappointment was that UCLA was playing in the NCAA championship game that night, so although the announced crowd was a 16,005 sellout, there were empty seats, as Taylor himself noted in his speech, thanking those who came to the game for their loyalty.

Once the game was out of reach (i.e., early in the second), play got more than a little chippy. The Kings had three of their goals scored over eight power-play chances and both Oilers' goals came with the extra man midway through the third.

12 SID
ABEL

DETROIT RED WINGS
APRIL 29, 1995

Born: Melville, Saskatchewan, February 22, 1918
Died: Detroit, Michigan, February 7, 2000
Position: Forward
Shoots: Left
Height: 5'11"
Weight: 170 lbs.

HONOURS
- **Stanley Cup** 1943, 1950, 1952
- **Hart Trophy** 1949
- **NHL All-Star Game** 1949, 1950, 1951
- **NHL First All-Star Team** 1949, 1950
- **Hockey Hall of Fame** 1969

NHL CAREER STATS

	Regular Season					Playoffs				
Years	GP	G	A	P	Pim	GP	G	A	P	Pim
1938–54	612	189	283	472	376	97	28	30	58	79

CAREER

In the old days, when players stayed on one team for many years, continuity produced lines that could develop together, and this in turn produced great names for the lines. Abel was on two threesomes of note, one before the Second World War, the other after.

Abel joined Detroit midway through the 1938–39 season and played an ever more important role with the team over the next few seasons. By his second full season he was playing on the Liniment Line with Don Grosso and Eddie Wares, and in 1942–43 this threesome led the Red Wings to the Stanley Cup. The team finished first overall in the regular-season standings and then swept the Boston Bruins aside in four games of the final, Abel finishing second on the team with 13 points in the 10 playoff games.

This was to be Abel's last hockey for nearly three years as he returned to Canada

and joined the RCAF. He returned to civilian life and the Red Wings late in the 1945–46 season, and at the start of the next year the centre formed a line with two youngsters named Gordie Howe (right wing) and Ted Lindsay (left wing). The resultant line, dubbed the Production Line, played havoc with every goalie in the league.

They created an innovative set play that is often used today. Abel, now team captain, would shoot the puck into the opposition corner—left or right side—and the puck would bank into the area near the crease where a blazing winger, Lindsay or Howe, would swoop in for an uncontested shot on goal. The defending team had little way to prevent the play, and it often resulted in a goal.

In 1948–49, the three men finished 1-2-3 in league scoring, and Abel was named winner of the Hart Trophy. A year later, the team won another Stanley Cup. This marked the start of the Red Wings' greatest glory as they finished first overall in the regular season for seven straight years. The team won the Cup again in 1952 after which Abel was sold to the Chicago Black Hawks. A year and a half later, he retired.

Abel later coached Detroit for a decade in the late 1950s and through the '60s, but although he took the team to the Cup Final four times, he never won again. Late in life, when owner Mike Ilitch had the team well in hand and wanted to pay homage to the great early years, the team retired Abel's number 12, in 1995.

CEREMONY

An enormous pleasure associated with retiring numbers is reuniting old teammates and friends, and no finer example of this can be found than in the case of Sid Abel at age 77, whose number 12 was raised to the rafters fully 41 years after he played his final game with the Red Wings.

In his case, that reunion took place at centre ice with his famous—and younger—line mates, Gordie Howe (age 67) and Ted Lindsay (age 69). "Sid taught us so much," Howe recalled the night of the ceremony. "We used to sit up in the trains for hours after the game, and he'd go over everything. He'd take us through the whole game, pointing out what we did right and what we did wrong. I think I learned more on the trains than I did on the ice."

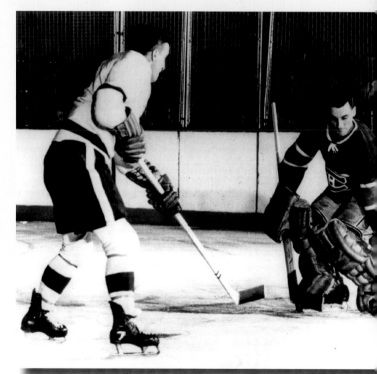

Lindsay picked up the story: "He'd take us into what they called the 'smoker' at one end of the car. I guess you'd call it a bathroom these days, but they had only one john and about six sinks. They had benches against three of the walls, and we'd just sit in there and listen to him."

THE GAME: Detroit Red Wings 4–Dallas Stars 2

Abel's night went off perfectly once the game began as the Red Wings, in first place overall, skated to an impressive win. The only thing they didn't do was get the first goal. That honour went to the Stars' Derian Hatcher at 7:35 of the first period, but defenceman Nicklas Lidstrom got that back less than five minutes later, and the team never looked back.

Detroit got the only two goals of the middle period to build a 3–1 lead, Shawn Burr and Ray Sheppard, with his 30th of the year, leading the attack. Dallas made it close early in the third when Hatcher connected again, this time on a power play, but Dino Ciccarelli iced the game with an empty netter in the final minute.

"It's a good feeling to be the best team in the league," goalie Chris Osgood said, "but we still have other goals."

25

THOMAS
STEEN

WINNIPEG JETS
MAY 6, 1995

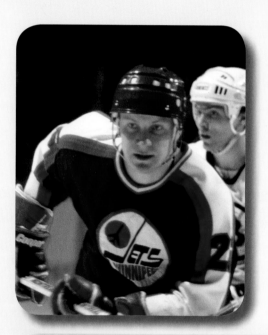

Born: Grums, Sweden, June 8, 1960
Position: Centre
Shoots: Left
Height: 5'11"
Weight: 190 lbs.

HONOURS
- Played entire NHL career with Winnipeg Jets
- Played for Sweden at Canada Cup 1981, 1984, 1991

NHL CAREER STATS

	Regular Season					Playoffs				
Years	GP	G	A	P	Pim	GP	G	A	P	Pim
1981–95	950	264	553	817	753	56	12	32	44	62

CAREER

Only three European players have had their numbers retired by NHL teams, and Thomas Steen was the first (the others are Peter Stastny and Jari Kurri). He had an outstanding career with Leksand in Sweden before signing with the Winnipeg Jets in 1981, two years after the team joined the NHL from the WHA.

Steen was offensively gifted, a great skater who could both shoot and pass. He was joining a team steeped in Swedish and European tradition, for it was the WHA Jets that had created the first truly international line featuring Canadian Bobby Hull and Swedes Ulf Nilsson and Anders Hedberg.

In his 14 years with the Jets, Steen averaged nearly a point a game and was an important part of the team's offense, along with Dale Hawerchuk. The team made the playoffs 10 times during his career, but it never went far because the Jets almost always had to face the Oilers in the early rounds and could never beat Wayne

Gretzky, Mark Messier, and the rest of the incredible Edmonton teams.

In addition to his NHL career, Steen represented Tre Kronor, Sweden's national team, internationally many times, most notably during the 1984 Canada Cup. Playing on a line with Kent Nilsson and Hakan Loob, the team advanced to the final before losing to Canada. Steen also played at the 1981 and 1991 Canada Cup events as well as three World Championships.

Steen's career ran out of steam after the lockout-shortened season of 1994–95. The Jets missed the playoffs, and he moved back to Europe to close out his playing days in Germany. Almost immediately after his final game with the Jets, the team retired his number, only the second player after Bobby Hull to be so honoured. When the team moved to Phoenix, the Coyotes kept Steen's number 25 out of circulation.

CEREMONY

There was sadness as well as joy on the night Thomas Steen's number 25 was raised to the rafters. And there was no game. The 100-minute ceremony came after the Jets had played their last game in Winnipeg before moving to Phoenix, Arizona, to continue as the Coyotes. To make matters worse, Steen had been released from hospital only the Friday before, suffering from stress and a bad back, and here he was 24 hours later attending an honour dedicated to him.

Steen was surrounded by his two families, the one on the ice and the one off. His wife, Mona, was accompanied by their three children—Alexander, Cassandra, and Hamilton—as well as "little Amadeus, who's up there somewhere," Steen said, remembering their infant son who'd died five years previous.

His on-ice family included the 17 members of the Jets who were still in the city. They all came out in uniform, and some 15,000 fans packed the Arena to say thanks and good-bye to a team that had had such success since joining the WHA in 1972. Steen was as shaken and upset as any native Winnipegger by the loss of 23 years' of history.

The retiring of Steen's number was the culmination of a stirring evening that started with many of the players addressing the crowd, notably Randy Gilhen, Kris King, Russ Romaniuk, Darrin Shannon, Keith Tkachuk, Teemu Selanne, and Ed Olczyk, who promised to return to the 'Peg with the Stanley Cup if the team ever won it.

Shannon waxed eloquent on Steen's importance off ice. "Everybody knows what he can do on the ice. He's a great player. What a lot of people don't know is the fact he's a sensitive guy who cares a lot. He's probably gone through more hell in the last two months [because of his back] than every one of us combined. Just look at Thomas's golf tournament. Everybody's got a charity tournament, which is great, but nobody else includes kids in his tournament. He's thinking of opening a hockey clinic and camp. His whole summer is doing hockey schools for kids."

After all was said and done, the entire building sang "Auld Lang Syne," and the players retired to their dressing rooms for one final visit. Said longtime Jets defenceman Teppo Numminen: "It's a sad, sad day for Winnipeg. We had this chance to retire Thomas's sweater, and it was just a pleasure to be here and be involved. But this is so tough."

THE GAME

No game, only celebrations and tears for a team lost.

JACQUES
PLANTE

MONTREAL CANADIENS
OCTOBER 7, 1995

Born: Shawinigan Falls, Quebec, January 17, 1929
Died: Geneva, Switzerland, February 26, 1986
Position: Goalie
Catches: Left
Height: 6'
Weight: 175 lbs.

HONOURS
- **Stanley Cup** 1953, 1956, 1957, 1958, 1959, 1960
- **Hart Trophy** 1962
- **Vezina Trophy** 1956, 1957, 1958, 1959, 1960, 1962, 1969 (with Glenn Hall)
- **NHL All-Star Game** 1956, 1957, 1958, 1959, 1960, 1962, 1969, 1970
- **Hockey Hall of Fame** 1978

NHL CAREER STATS

Regular Season

Years	GP	W-L-T	Mins	GA	SO	GAA
1952–73	837	435-247-145	49,493	1,964	82	2.38

Playoffs

Years	GP	W-L-T	Mins	GA	SO	GAA
1952–73	112	71-36-0	6,651	237	14	2.14

CAREER

If Glenn Hall was the greatest goalie of the Original Six then surely Jacques Plante was the most influential. Not only were his career accomplishments remarkable, but he actually changed the way his position was played.

Plante made his debut with the Montreal Canadiens at the start of the 1952–53 season, helping the team to a Stanley Cup as a rookie. The next year he and Gerry McNeil were the two goalies, but by season's end it was clear Plante was superior, a player who could be a star for years to come. He led the Canadiens to the Cup Final in each of the next six years, losing to Detroit in 1955 and then winning five in a row to close out the decade. He also won the Vezina Trophy each of these Cup-winning seasons, and in 1961–62 he won both the Vezina and Hart trophies, the last goalie to be named league MVP until Dominik Hasek in 1997.

Hockey history was made the night of November 1, 1959. In a Rangers–Canadiens game, Andy Bathgate's shot hit Plante square in the face, and the goalie had to leave the ice for stitches. Plante returned to the game a few minutes later, however, but he was sporting a face mask. With one exception, he never played bare-faced again. His coach, Toe Blake, disapproved of the so-called cowardly protection, but Plante was adamant. Over the course of the next decade and more, one goalie after another donned a mask until finally there were no netminders crazy enough to play without one. The game had become too fast, slapshots too dangerous.

Plante was traded to the Rangers in 1963 and later played with St. Louis, Toronto, and Boston. In addition to being a great puckstopper, he was an innovator. He was the first goalie to raise his hand on an iced puck, to alert teammates that a whistle was forthcoming. He communicated with his defenceman and wandered from his crease to play the puck. He even wrote a book about his position, making a clinical study of a position once considered merely the place for the guy who couldn't skate or for the teammate most overweight.

CEREMONY

Although Plante had passed away nearly a decade earlier, he was represented on this night by family and colleagues: his son, Michel, and daughter, Audrey; and notable Montreal goalies Gerry McNeil and Gump Worsley. Interestingly, the first Canadiens player to wear number 1 was Georges Vezina, but the digit was not retired in his honour.

Michel and Audrey were given a painting depicting their father by renowned Quebecois artist, Michel Lapensée.

THE GAME:

Philadelphia Flyers 7–Montreal Canadiens 1
The table was set for a great night, but Patrick Roy, of all people, wasn't ready once the game started. The heroic Habs goalie lasted only 22:12 of this game, surrendering five goals on 15 shots en route to a lopsided loss. "I thought I was ready for the game," he said later. "I felt ready, but..."

Patrik Juhlin scored just 3:02 into the game for the Flyers, and this score was followed by goals from Eric Lindros, John LeClair, and Rob DiMaio before the first period had ended. When backup goalie Patrick Labrecque allowed a sixth goal just a few minutes after taking over for Roy early in the second period, the game was pretty much over. Only a Mark Recchi shorthanded goal midway through the second prevented visiting goalie Ron Hextall from recording a shutout.

The 17,646 fans at the Forum had little else to cheer about once the Plante festivities were over. Rod Brind'Amour had a goal and two assists for the Flyers, as did Juhlin.

7

RICK
MARTIN

BUFFALO SABRES
NOVEMBER 15, 1995

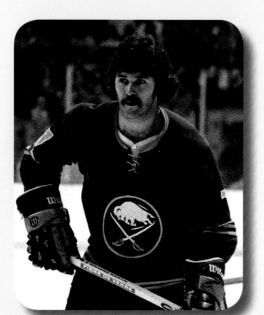

Born: Verdun, Quebec, July 26, 1951
Position: Left wing
Shoots: Left
Height: 5'11"
Weight: 180 lbs.

HONOURS
- **NHL All-Star Game** 1972, 1973, 1974, 1975, 1976, 1977, 1978
- **NHL First All-Star Team** 1974, 1975
- **NHL Second All-Star Team** 1976, 1977

NHL CAREER STATS

| Years | Regular Season | | | | | Playoffs | | | | |
	GP	G	A	P	Pim	GP	G	A	P	Pim
1971–82	685	384	317	701	477	63	24	29	53	74

CAREER

The defining threesome of the 1970s was the Buffalo Sabres French Connection Line of Gilbert Perreault, René Robert, and Rick Martin (whose Anglo name betrayed his Quebecois heritage). Together these three had speed, skill, and chemistry, and for several years scored more goals than any other line. In Martin's case, he averaged more than 40 goals in his nine full seasons with the team, peaking in 1973–74 and 1974–75 when he had back-to-back seasons of 52 goals. Perreault might have had the slick moves, but Martin had the deadliest slapshot in the game.

Drafted fifth overall by Buffalo in 1971, Martin fit in perfectly with the expansion Sabres, a team in its second season. It had drafted Perreault first overall in its inaugural season and added Robert midway through Martin's rookie season, and coach Punch Imlach quickly put the three speedsters together to great effect.

Buffalo made it to the Cup Final in 1975 against Philadelphia, but the Flyers prevailed and the Sabres didn't make it as far again until 1999.

As a rookie, Martin scored 44 goals and despite being just 21 years old he was invited to Team Canada's training camp for the 1972 Summit Series. He never played, but just being around the best players in the world gave Martin both education and inspiration. He became a key player for his country four years later at the first Canada Cup.

Martin never scored fewer than 28 goals in a season, but his career came crashing back to earth the night of November 9, 1980, in a game against the Washington Capitals. Flying down his left wing, he crashed into goalie Mike Palmateer who had come out to challenge him. The collision damaged Martin's knee. He played just four games in two years before heeding doctors' advice that any more contact could cause permanent injury.

Martin retired at age 30, many years of hockey still left in all parts of his body except the one knee. Nonetheless, he scored 382 of his 384 goals with Buffalo, and all members of the French Connection Line have since had their numbers hoisted to the rafters in perpetuity.

14

RENÉ ROBERT

BUFFALO SABRES
NOVEMBER 15, 1995

Born: Trois-Rivières, Quebec, December 31, 1948
Position: Right wing
Shoots: Right
Height: 5'10"
Weight: 184 lbs.

HONOURS
- **NHL All-Star Game** 1973, 1975
- **NHL Second All-Star Team** 1975

NHL CAREER STATS

	Regular Season					Playoffs				
Years	GP	G	A	P	Pim	GP	G	A	P	Pim
1970–82	744	284	418	702	597	50	22	19	41	73

CAREER

The meteoric rise of René Robert could not have been predicted. After all, the 1967 expansion was supposed to give any top player who had been previously shut out of the NHL the chance to play, perhaps with a poor team. Yet after his junior career in Quebec, Robert was signed by the Leafs late in the 1967–68 season and immediately assigned to the minors. In two more years with the team, he played just five games in the NHL. The following year he finally made a name for himself with Pittsburgh, but even the Penguins traded him to Buffalo, in 1971.

And then Robert's career shot into the sky. Coach Punch Imlach put him on a line with Gilbert Perreault and Rick Martin, and Robert scored 40 goals. The French Connection Line was born. Robert had an off year in 1973–74, however, the next season he not only hit the 40 mark again but finished with 100 points—an incredible total. Perreault had 96 that year and Martin 95, making them one of the

highest-scoring lines in the league. More important, the team went to the Stanley Cup Final before losing to Philadelphia.

Robert had eight straight years scoring at least 20 goals, but he was an equally adept passer, especially when he had line mates who could also put the puck in the net. But when Imlach was replaced by Scotty Bowman as coach, Robert's career fell off the rails. He was traded to the Colorado Rockies and later back to the Toronto Maple Leafs, but his days of glory were done.

Nonetheless, he and his line mates all had their numbers retired by the Sabres for several years of thrilling play. The team's success hinged almost entirely on their effectiveness. Despite being an expansion team, they made it to the Cup Final in only their fifth season, and they missed the playoffs only twice while Robert was there.

CEREMONY

The evening was incredibly special not only for Rick Martin and René Robert, who were being honoured together, but also for their line mate, Gilbert Perreault. This evening marked the first time the three had appeared on Auditorium ice since that fateful day in 1980 when the French Connection Line was split by Robert's trade.

Indeed, it was such an anticipated event that it turned into a week-long festival, highlighted by a private reception on Tuesday, the actual sweater retirement on Wednesday, and then a Legends of Hockey charity game on Friday, in which all three skated.

All three players appeared on ice in their full equipment for the raising of Martin's number 7 and Robert's 14, and once the banners were raised to join Perreault's number 11, fans saw another banner, a broad strip emblazoned with the words "The French Connection," ensuring that the honours were equally distributed by the longtime line mates.

The highlight of the ceremony arrived when it was time for team CEO Seymour Knox to present the traditional silver sabre to the players. Both Martin and Robert knelt before Knox, and the CEO didn't miss a beat, touching the shoulders of both men with the blade to complete the honours. All three players skated several laps around the ice for the adoring fans, and after the banners were in position it was time to play hockey.

THE GAME: Buffalo Sabres 2–Dallas Stars 1

Although Todd Harvey opened the scoring for Dallas off a scrambly play at 2:20 of the first period, Buffalo settled down and produced an impressive, if workmanlike, win for the French Connection trio. Randy Burridge tied the game midway through the opening period and then Pat LaFontaine got the winner midway through the second period.

Goaltending was the difference as Dominik Hasek was excellent for the Sabres, turning aside all but one of 30 shots he faced as his team nursed a one-goal lead for the better part of 28 minutes.

"It was great to see those guys on the ice, and it took us a little while to get over that," coach Ted Nolan said of Buffalo's slow start. "Once we did, I thought we played a really sound hockey game. We're slowly starting to get things going here."

2

MILES "TIM"
HORTON

Born: Cochrane, Ontario, January 12, 1930
Died: St. Catharines, Ontario, February 21, 1974
Position: Defence
Shoots: Right
Height: 5'10"
Weight: 180 lbs.

HONOURS
- **Stanley Cup** 1962, 1963, 1964, 1967
- **NHL All-Star Game** 1954, 1961, 1962, 1963, 1964, 1968, 1969
- **NHL First All-Star Team** 1964, 1968, 1969
- **Hockey Hall of Fame** 1977
- **Number 7 also an Honoured Number with Toronto Maple Leafs**

NHL CAREER STATS

	Regular Season					Playoffs				
Years	GP	G	A	P	Pim	GP	G	A	P	Pim
1949–74	1,446	115	403	518	1,611	126	11	39	50	183

CAREER

Tim Horton's number 2 was retired by the Buffalo Sabres in tribute to his NHL career almost as much as what he contributed to the team itself. After all, he played in the NHL for some 24 years and a then-record 1,446 games, but only his final two seasons, the second cut short by his sudden death, came with Buffalo.

One of the strongest players in the game, he was pacifist more than antagonist, famous for his bear hug to quell a disturbance and prevent a player from becoming involved in a fight. He made his debut with Toronto late in the 1949–50 season and for most of the next 20 seasons was a force on the team's blue line.

Horton had poor eyesight and was the first NHLer to wear contact lenses during games, and, with one notable exception, he was a durable player, appearing in every game of 12 seasons. That exception came during the latter stages of the 1954–55 season and forced him to miss nearly a year with a broken leg after a dev-

astating collision with the Rangers' Bill Gadsby.

He returned as good as ever, though, and continued to be a skater with a powerful stride and offensive ability. Horton was with the Leafs during their greatest years of the 1960s, when the team won three Stanley Cups in a row (1962–64) and a fourth in 1967. But later in the 1969–70 season he was traded to the Rangers for nothing more than future considerations.

Still, Horton continued to play and was reunited in Buffalo with Punch Imlach, his longtime coach with the Leafs. His career and life came to a tragic end on a highway while driving back to Buffalo after a game at Maple Leaf Gardens. He crashed his car and died as a result of his injuries.

CEREMONY

It was a dignified and formal occasion, one that would have been different had Horton been alive or had he been honoured by the Leafs, for whom he played most of his career. But his wife, Lori, and her grandson, came out to centre ice to participate in the ceremony that saw Horton's number 2, which he wore for only 124 games over a year and a half, lifted to the rafters.

Before and after the game, Sabres old and young talked about Horton's influence on their lives and careers. Said assistant general manager Larry Carriere, a 22-year-old defenceman when Horton signed with the Sabres: "I think I speak for everyone who ever played with him if I say I felt fortunate just to have known him. He helped all of us out, not just on the ice but off it, too. I never met anyone who didn't admire and respect Tim Horton. He was that kind of man."

THE GAME:

Buffalo Sabres 3–Toronto Maple Leafs 1
Toronto coach Pat Burns admitted he wrote two words on the chalkboard before the game—"respect Buffalo." He was referring to the Sabres' sense of desperation this night with the playoff race tightening, and he was right.

The Sabres raced out to a 2–0 first-period lead and never looked back, playing one of their best games of the season. Dave Hannan and Brad May scored the early goals, and Pat LaFontaine added a third late in the second. Dave Andreychuk replied just 20 seconds later to make it a 3–1 game after two periods, but the Sabres battened the proverbial hatches in the third and protected goalie John Blue to preserve the victory.

"We executed well all night long," said Hannan. "Our concentration was a key. We made the big plays defensively."

"I was really happy with our quick start," said Buffalo coach Ted Nolan. "We had made some adjustments in our defensive zone coverage this week, and we held them to five shots in the first period."

26

PETER STASTNY

QUEBEC NORDIQUES
FEBRUARY 4, 1996

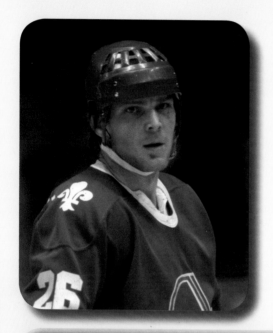

Born: Bratislava, Czechoslovakia (Slovakia), September 18, 1956
Position: Centre
Shoots: Left
Height: 6'1"
Weight: 200 lbs.

HONOURS
- **Calder Trophy** 1981
- **NHL All-Star Game** 1981, 1982, 1983, 1984, 1986, 1988
- **Played for Czechoslovakia at Olympics** 1980
- **Played for Canada at Canada Cup** 1984
- **Played for Slovakia at Olympics** 1994
- **Hockey Hall of Fame** 1998

NHL CAREER STATS

	Regular Season					Playoffs				
Years	GP	G	A	P	Pim	GP	G	A	P	Pim
1980–95	977	450	789	1,239	824	93	33	72	105	123

CAREER

Anyone who would care to argue that Peter Stastny was not the best European player in NHL history would have to put up quite an argument. In the 1980s, he was, after all, the player who scored more points than every other NHLer, with one exception—Wayne Gretzky.

Stastny and his brothers, Anton and Marian, played in Czechoslovakia in the 1970s, a time and place that was unrelated to the West and the NHL. Peter and Anton were the first to defect, in 1980, an act so daring, brave, and dangerous that it couldn't possibly have been for hockey that they risked their own lives and the lives of their families.

Making their way to Quebec, the brothers took the NHL by storm with their tic-tac-toe passing and shooting at top speed. Peter had 39 goals and 109 points and caused controversy when he won the Calder Trophy. Critics pointed out that

this "rookie" was 24 years old and a veteran of many pro seasons in the Czech league and had won two gold and two silver medals at the World Championships, but since this was his first year in the NHL, the trophy was his.

Stastny hit the 100-point mark in each of his first six seasons, the second being more gratifying than the first because Marian had managed to defect, too, ensuring the entire family was safe in Quebec City doing what they did best—playing hockey.

Peter played almost 10 years with the Nordiques and later moved on to the New Jersey Devils and the St. Louis Blues. By the time he left the NHL in 1995, he had played 977 games and recorded an astounding 1,239 points. He had played in the All-Star Game six times and proved beyond a shadow of a doubt that he was one of the most exciting and skilled players in the game. His vision and imagination with the puck, his patience and calm under pressure, were his trademarks and what made him so effective.

The Nordiques retired his number 26, but when the team moved to Colorado it put the number back into circulation. Peter didn't object—it gave his son, Paul Stastny, the opportunity to wear Dad's digits.

CEREMONY

By the time the Nordiques celebrated Stastny's career, the team had moved to Denver as the Colorado Avalanche. As a result, his number 26 retirement took place prior to an alumni game between Nordiques oldtimers and NHL oldtimers, a game scheduled expressly for the occasion and one in which he and his brothers participated.

"This is such a great honour from the people of Quebec," Peter said, "and is a further sign of my love for this city. My family and I have been honoured to be accepted by the people of Quebec."

Stastny was accompanied by his two Quebec City-born sons, Yan and Paul, who both later played in the NHL, as well as two other children and his wife, Darina.

"Every day I played was a happy one for me," Stastny told the crowd. "I loved the competition, and I always played with one goal in mind—to win. The money and fame, and everything else were a bonus. The banner you raise for me today represents all that I tried to do with the Nordiques in these regards."

Of course, the humble Stastny distributed the credit. "My teammates are the ones who helped me become the player I was," he continued. "And the people of Quebec, as I tell everyone, are the greatest hockey fans in the world."

THE GAME: NHL Oldtimers 6–Quebec Nordiques Oldtimers 5

Quebec's legends included goalie Richard Brodeur as well as Marc Tardif, Réal Cloutier, Michel Goulet, Mario Marois, Jacques Richard, Pierre Lacroix, and Wilf Paiement. The team was coached by Michel Bergeron.

The NHL's lineup featured many former Canadiens, including goalie Steve Penny as well as Gille Lupien and Yvon Lambert. Other Quebeckers who didn't necessarily play for the Habs included the French Connection Line of Gilbert Perreault, René Robert, and Rick Martin.

The 14,127 fans who crammed into Le Colisée for the game were treated to a light-hearted game of gentlemanly play. Jean-Francois Sauve was named player of the game after his hat-trick performance. The game-winning goal was scored by Gaston Therrien with just 22 seconds left in the third period. Other NHL goals were scored by André Dupont and Pierre Plante.

Quebec got goals from Christian Bordeleau, Alain Cote, Goulet, Cloutier, and Paiement.

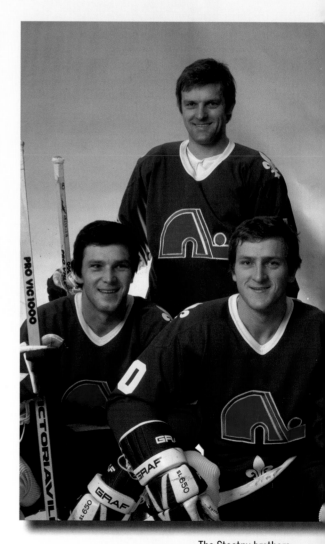

The Stastny brothers.

9

CLARK GILLIES

NEW YORK ISLANDERS
DECEMBER 7, 1996

Born: Moose Jaw, Saskatchewan, April 7, 1954
Position: Left wing
Shoots: Left
Height: 6'3"
Weight: 215 lbs.

HONOURS
- **Stanley Cup** 1980, 1981, 1982, 1983
- **NHL All-Star Game** 1978
- **NHL First All-Star Team** 1978, 1979
- **Played for Canada in Canada Cup** 1981
- **Hockey Hall of Fame** 2002

NHL CAREER STATS

	Regular Season					Playoffs				
Years	GP	G	A	P	Pim	GP	G	A	P	Pim
1974–88	958	319	378	697	1,023	164	47	47	94	287

CAREER

One of the first power forwards to make an impact in the game, Clark Gillies was an integral part of the New York Islanders' teams that won the Stanley Cup in four straight seasons (1980–83). His reputation was unique, though, because opponents reminded themselves not to "wake him up." That is, Gillies had the habit of playing lazy hockey sometimes, but then he'd take a big hit, get mad, and become a force in the game. Teams that left him to his own devices, with nothing to motivate him, were often more successful, except that few were able to follow through on the plan to leave him alone.

Selected by the Islanders fourth overall in 1974, Gillies came out of the Regina Pats of the WHL after winning the Memorial Cup and made the NHL team at his rookie camp at age 20. He had an immediate impact, scoring 25 goals, after which he rattled off four seasons of at least 33 goals. He was named captain for nearly

two years, but he felt uncomfortable shouldering the extra responsibility and begged off "C" duties starting in 1979. He played on the Trio Grande Line with Bryan Trottier and Mike Bossy, two other young and developing players who were key ingredients to playoff success.

The New York Islanders made their breakthrough in 1980 when they defeated the Philadelphia Flyers in overtime of game six of the Stanley Cup Final, starting a stretch of four years when they were unbeatable in the playoffs. One of the keys to this first win was Gillies' willingness to fight the Boston Bruins in the quarter-finals, a series won by the New Yorkers in five games, each one an exhausting battle.

After that, winning became easier once it was in their minds, and Gillies sailed along scoring and fighting as needed. In 1977, he set a record by scoring the game-winning goal in four straight playoff games, and in 1979 he was named Team NHL MVP of the Challenge Cup, the best-of-three showdown against the Soviets in a short series that replaced the All-Star Game that year.

Not surprisingly, Gillies' style meant he had a shorter shelf life than most top players, and as the dynasty had run its course, so, too, had his body. Banged up and battered, he kept going a while longer, but was left exposed by the Islanders in the Waiver Draft. He played 86 games with Buffalo over a year and a half until finally a knee injury ended his playing days once and for all.

CEREMONY

Clark Gillies made a name for himself not only by smooth skating, pinpoint passing, and great shooting around the goal; he led by example, by determination, by brute force. In his honour, the team showed video clips not of his pure skill but of his tough play, the Gillies highlight reel a cornucopia of fistic success during his career with the Isles.

He was given gifts and feted by family and friends at centre ice, among whom was John Hunter, one of his coaches from childhood.

THE GAME:

New York Islanders 2–Washington Capitals 0

Players came out for the warm-up all wearing number 9 sweaters with the Gillies nameplate, and once the game started the current Islanders were all business. The first two periods featured hard hitting, several fights, and end-to-end action, but the game's first goal had to wait until the third period.

Bryan Smolinski scored at 4:22 on a smart play. Zigmund Palffy skated in over the blue line and fired a sizzling shot that goalie Jim Carey saved, but the puck squirted off to the side. Smolinski raced in and fired right away from a terrible angle, the puck banking off the goalie's skate and into the net as Carey tried to re-establish position.

Niklas Andersson scored into an empty net to seal the win, and Tommy Salo recorded his second shutout of the season, both coming at the expense of the Capitals. "I just wanted them to play hard tonight, and they did," coach Mike Milbury said later of his team's win.

66
MARIO
LEMIEUX

PITTSBURGH PENGUINS
NOVEMBER 19, 1997

Born: Montreal, Quebec, October 5, 1965
Position: Centre
Shoots: Right
Height: 6'4"
Weight: 230 lbs.

HONOURS
- **Stanley Cup** 1991, 1992
- **Hart Trophy** 1988, 1993, 1996
- **Art Ross Trophy** 1988, 1989, 1992, 1993, 1996, 1997
- **Lester B. Pearson Award** 1986, 1988, 1993, 1996
- **Conn Smythe Trophy** 1991, 1992
- **Bill Masterton Trophy** 1993
- **Played for Canada at Canada Cup** 1987
- **Won gold medal with Canada at Olympics** 2002
- **Hockey Hall of Fame** 1997

NHL CAREER STATS

	Regular Season					Playoffs				
Years	GP	G	A	P	Pim	GP	G	A	P	Pim
1984–2006	915	690	1,033	1,723	834	107	76	96	172	87

CAREER

In a 17-year NHL career beset by injuries and retirement, Lemieux averaged nearly two points a game, a pace comparable to Wayne Gretzky's. Had he had a full and healthy career, he might even have equalled number 99's career totals of 2,857 points (in 1,487 games), such was the extraordinary skill of number 66.

Lemieux scored on his first NHL shift and became only the third rookie to record 100 points in a season. He won the Calder Trophy, and the next year went from 100 points to 141, finishing second in scoring to Gretzky. He continued to produce at a tremendous pace, but not one that yet showed his full potential.

During practice at the Canada Cup in 1987, Gretzky tore a strip off the talented star, telling him to strive for more, to reach higher. Lemieux went out and scored the winning goal in the best-of-three final for Canada against the Soviets, led the tournament with 11 goals (nine assisted by Gretzky), and then won the Art

Ross and Hart trophies after scoring 168 points in the 1987–88 NHL season.

In 1988–89, Lemieux had 199 points, one shy of joining Gretzky as the only player ever to have 200 in a single season (Gretzky did it four times).

Soon after, the injuries started to exact a toll. Lemieux missed most of 1990–91 due to an off-season back surgery, yet rallied down the stretch to lead the Penguins to their first ever Stanley Cup. The next season he missed 18 games, yet still won the Art Ross Trophy and led the team to a second straight Cup, winning the Conn Smythe Trophy both years.

In 1992–93, Lemieux again missed many games, this time with Hodgkin's lymphoma. Yet again, he returned to score at an incredible pace, winning another scoring title despite playing only 60 games.

Lemieux retired in 1997 and had his number 66 retired by the team soon after, but he came back three and a half years later—again as though no time had passed. He had a goal and three assists in his first game, and finished with 76 points in just 43 games. His back caused him to miss most of the 2003–04 season, but he returned after the 2004–05 lockout to play with his number-one draft choice, Sidney Crosby. A heart condition forced him to retire early in the season, and he settled into his full-time job as the team's owner, his place in hockey long established among the greatest of the greats.

CEREMONY

The 30-minute ceremony for Mario Lemieux honoured one of the greatest players ever to skate on a sheet of ice. The fans knew it, and gave him several lengthy ovations worthy of his incredible play. "One thing I want to say," he told the crowd. "Thank you for making the last 13 years of my life the best years of my life."

The presents were endless. His former teammates, knowing his oenological ambitions, gave him a five-magnum bottle of cabernet sauvignon in a customized box. The two owners of the team, Howard Baldwin and Roger Marino, gave him a gold medallion and a cheque for $250,000 for the Mario Lemieux Foundation. They also gave Lemieux's parents a cruise and his wife, Nathalie, a charm bracelet. His three daughters were given gold necklaces and his only son, Austin, got a plaque.

Although the NHL didn't accord him the same honour as Wayne Gretzky by retiring his number league-wide, such was his respect that no other NHLer has worn number 66 since Mario hung up the blades.

THE GAME: Pittsburgh Penguins 3–Boston Bruins 3 (OT)

Without Lemieux, the Penguins were not the same team, and on this night, with Jaromir Jagr in the press box nursing a sore hip, they were even less impressive, having to settle for a 3–3 tie with the visiting Bruins. The tie gave the Pens a mediocre 9–9–3 record so far in the young season, disappointing this night because they had a lead going into the final period.

Jason Allison got an early goal for Boston at 2:21, but just 86 seconds later Alexei Morozov tied it for Pittsburgh. Ed Olczyk had the only goal of the second for the home side, but Don Sweeney caught a break early in the third period when his shot banked off a skate and past a helpless Tom Barrasso in the Penguins net.

Neil Wilkinson got a lucky one on a shot from nearly centre ice that Jon Casey missed, but again the Bruins fought back, this time on a Ray Bourque point shot, to make it 3–3 and giving each team a point.

5

ROD
LANGWAY

WASHINGTON CAPITALS
NOVEMBER 26, 1997

Born: Maag, Formosa (Taiwan), May 3, 1957
Position: Defence
Shoots: Left
Height: 6'3"
Weight: 218 lbs.

HONOURS
- **Stanley Cup** 1979
- **Norris Trophy** 1983, 1984
- **NHL All-Star Game** 1981, 1982, 1983, 1984, 1985, 1986
- **Played for United States in Canada Cup** 1981, 1984, 1987
- **Hockey Hall of Fame** 2002

NHL CAREER STATS

	Regular Season					Playoffs				
Years	GP	G	A	P	Pim	GP	G	A	P	Pim
1978–93	994	51	278	329	849	104	5	22	27	97

CAREER

To say that Rod Langway played old-school defence is an understatement. He could have fit right into an Original Six lineup and enjoyed an outstanding career in the 1950s, but instead he was born a couple of generations later and played from 1978 to 1993.

Amazingly, Langway attended the University of New Hampshire on a football scholarship, but he also played hockey. The Montreal Canadiens were impressed enough to draft him in 1977, but the two parties couldn't agree on a contract so the defenceman signed with the Birmingham Bulls of the WHA. A year later he was playing for the Habs.

Langway's rookie season ended in Stanley Cup triumph, but the next three years were difficult for him. He was playing on a great team steeped in tradition and success, but that also meant being one of many important parts and not

always playing every night or playing very often over the course of a game. He was more than happy to be traded to the lowly Washington Capitals in 1982 where he could be counted on as a leader.

Langway played a very simple game. He had no offensive ambitions and desired only to take his man, prevent scoring chances, and get the puck out of his own end. Not only was he very good at this, he made history by winning the Norris Trophy in consecutive years: 1982–83 and 1983–84. These were historic in the sense that since Bobby Orr's arrival in 1966, the best defenceman always meant the most offensively talented. Winners between 1966 and 1982 included Orr, Larry Robinson, and Dennis Potvin. In his two winning seasons, Langway had a grand total of three and nine goals, respectively.

Upon arriving in Washington, D.C., Langway was named captain and remained so until he retired. He was everything he was billed to be, and his play internationally only bolstered his reputation. Langway played at the three Canada Cup tournaments in the 1980s ('81, '84, and '87) for the United States at a time when the team didn't have the skills it developed throughout the 1990s and beyond.

One of his greatest skills was blocking shots, and after he retired the Hockey Hall of Fame sought him out to ask for his now famous shin pads. He declined, suggesting they were too meaningful for him to part with just yet.

CEREMONY

The retirement of Rod Langway's number 5 took place the night of the Capitals' final game at their old arena, US Airways Arena. Nine days later they played for the first time in the swishy new MCI Center, where his banner went also. "I know now that I will always be remembered," Langway said. "As long as they have hockey in D.C. and [owner] Abe Pollin is associated with it, I will be remembered."

The sellout crowd applauded him for his 11 years of service, during which time the team went from worst in the league to a consistent and respectable playoff team. Langway received golf clubs and a golf cart, a portrait, and a silver hockey stick in appreciation of his years of service.

THE GAME: Montreal Canadiens 6–Washington Capitals 5

The Montreal Canadiens were the opposition, appropriately given that Langway was traded to Washington from Montreal on September 10, 1982. Although it was a high-scoring game, the visitors got the best of the Capitals, jumping into a 2–0 lead on a pair of goals from Shayne Corson. Richard Zednik scored two of his own, one late in the first and another early in the second to tie the game 2–2, but the Canadiens scored three of the next four goals in the period to head to the dressing room with a 5–3 lead after 40 minutes.

The teams exchanged goals early in the third and then Mark Tinordi drew the Caps to within a goal at 8:30, but the home side couldn't get the tying marker in the last half of the period. At the game's end, balloons were released and players skated around the ice as "Auld Lang Syne" played for one last time at the old arena.

7

NEAL BROTEN

MINNESOTA NORTH STARS/ DALLAS STARS
FEBRUARY 7, 1998

Born: Roseau, Minnesota, November 29, 1959
Position: Centre
Shoots: Left
Height: 5'9"
Weight: 175 lbs.

HONOURS
- **Stanley Cup** 1995
- **Lester Patrick Trophy** 1998
- **Hobey Baker Award** (NCAA—University of Minnesota) 1981
- **Played for United States in Canada Cup** 1981, 1984
- **NHL All-Star Game** 1983, 1986

NHL CAREER STATS

	Regular Season					Playoffs				
Years	GP	G	A	P	Pim	GP	G	A	P	Pim
1980–97	1,099	289	634	923	569	135	35	63	98	77

CAREER

Although Neal Broten played most of his nearly 1,100 regular-season games in the NHL with the Minnesota/Dallas franchise, he is perhaps better known for his pre-NHL career as a member of the United States "Miracle on Ice" team of 1980.

Broten scored two goals during the 1980 Olympics, an historic victory in Lake Placid by a group of university students who shocked the Soviets, 4–3, in the penultimate game of that event and went on to win Olympic gold. Virtually every player from that team went on to play in the NHL, some for just a few games, others for much longer. Broten fell into the latter category. After playing one more year at the University of Minnesota, one in which he was honoured with the Hobey Baker Award, he joined the North Stars and continued along on a 17-year career.

A centreman and gifted scorer, he helped the North Stars go to the Cup Final

twice, the first time in 1981 when the team lost to the Islanders, and a decade later when they lost to Mario Lemieux and the Pittsburgh Penguins.

Given his success in 1980, it isn't surprising that he was also asked to play for his country at the 1981 and 1984 Canada Cup tournaments. What is surprising is that after he retired from the NHL in 1997, he had yet to play his final hockey game. A year later, the United States finished 12th at the World Championship and needed to win a qualifying tournament to compete in the top pool the next year.

Not to win would have been a colossal embarrassment for the Americans, but this qualifying event took place during the NHL season, so no pros could play. The three Broten brothers—Neal, Aaron, and Paul—led the charge and dressed for three more games, giving the Americans the needed victory.

CEREMONY

Broten made this event an important moment in his life. He invited some 50 family and friends down to Dallas for the week leading up to the on-ice ceremony, and they all enjoyed a reunion and played a little golf at the same time. Among this number were former teammates Stu Gavin and Craig Hartsburg; wife, Sally; and daughters, Brooke and Larissa.

It was also a bit of a strange celebration. Although he played some 13 years for the Minnesota North Stars, his Dallas Stars career, after the team moved south, was limited to just 116 games. So, he was, in effect, being honoured by one city for his career in another.

But coach Ken Hitchcock explained the situation perfectly before the game. "I think this is more of an honour for our organization than for Neal Broten," he began. "When you have the opportunity to retire a sweater, it means that that player has done a tremendous amount of good. He's the most identified, U.S.-born player in the history of the game. He's played in this league since 1980. Neal Broten has meant everything to USA Hockey, from his college days to the Olympic team to the North Stars. He was hockey in Minnesota at the pro level; he came down here and was the most identifiable player we had. We should be honoured to have his number up there."

The brisk, 10-minute ceremony was hosted by Ralph Strangis, radio announcer for the team who had moved with the Stars to Texas. He introduced a video tribute by saying that Broten, "came from a town you never heard of, where he would walk two miles in bitter cold to play with the bigger kids. And folks—Neal always beat the bigger kids."

Broten received several gifts, including the last sweater he ever played in (presented by team president, James Lites), a painting, a watch, and a crystal objet d'art.

THE GAME: Dallas Stars 3–Chicago Blackhawks 1
The Stars continued their hot play of late, winning for the eighth time in their last 10 games. Defenceman Sergei Zubov got the only goal of the first for the home side, and then a late flurry in the second period rounded out the scoring.

First, Michal Sykora tied the game at 16:26. Just 51 seconds later, Pat Verbeek restored the Dallas lead, and at 18:40 he scored again to make it 3–1 after 40 minutes. Goalie Roman Turek was excellent in goal for the Stars, who were now six points ahead of Detroit and Colorado in top spot in the Western Conference.

18

DENIS SAVARD

CHICAGO BLACKHAWKS
MARCH 19, 1998

Born: Pointe Gatineau, Quebec, February 4, 1961
Position: Centre
Shoots: Right
Height: 5'10"
Weight: 175 lbs.

HONOURS
- **Stanley Cup** 1993
- **Drafted third overall by Chicago** 1980
- **NHL All-Star Game** 1982, 1983, 1984, 1986, 1988, 1991, 1996
- **Hockey Hall of Fame** 2000

NHL CAREER STATS

	Regular Season					Playoffs				
Years	GP	G	A	P	Pim	GP	G	A	P	Pim
1980–97	1,196	473	865	1,338	1,336	169	66	109	175	256

CAREER

Although he never scored 50 goals in a season, Denis Savard did break the 100-point mark on five occasions during a career that took him to the Hockey Hall of Fame three years after he retired in 1997. The cornerstone of the Chicago Blackhawks for most of his 17 NHL seasons, he won his only Stanley Cup not as a leader, as he was with the Hawks, but as more a role player in the twilight of his career, in Montreal, in 1993.

Savard was a centreman in the 1980s, during a time of many great centremen. Consequently, he never won any individual honours or led the league in any one offensive category, but he was nonetheless one of the most electrifying and exciting players ever to don the Chicago sweater.

As a rookie in 1980–81 he scored 28 goals and displayed his trademark razzle-dazzle with the puck. Specifically, Savard was the master of the spin-o-rama in the

offensive end. He'd skate full throttle at a defender and seem to run out of room, only to do a full turn and whiz by the opponent who anticipated a move in the other direction.

Savard reached 119 points in his second season, and despite being only 21 years old he was already in the prime of his career. He increased his goal production in each of his first six seasons, to a career high of 47 in 1985–86, but the one thing the team lacked was playoff success. The team's best two runs came in 1984–85 and 1989–90, when it lost in the conference championship, and in the former Savard was dynamite, scoring 29 points in just 15 games. But it wasn't enough.

The Hawks traded him for local boy Chris Chelios in the summer of 1990, a wildly unpopular deal with fans because Savard was so well liked. He stayed three seasons with the Canadiens, but fan expectations for the Quebecois star exceeded his abilities now that he was 30 years old and a step slower. Still, he played a solid if unspectacular role with the team and won the Cup in 1993, although he played only 14 games in the playoffs when he was often a healthy scratch.

After a brief stint with Tampa Bay, Savard returned to the Windy City late in the 1994–95 season and spent the final two and a half years of his career in his adopted city. He retired with 1,338 points in 1,196 regular-season games, and he kept this point-a-game pace up during 169 playoff games as well. Savard played in an era dominated by Wayne Gretzky, Mario Lemieux, Steve Yzerman, and Peter Stastny, but he was, by any measure, a superstar centre all the same.

CEREMONY

The 40-minute ceremony to honour Denis Savard was an emotional one for both player and 22,242 fans stuffed in the United Center, the NHL's largest arena. It began with a video tribute, highlighted by the classic spin-o-rama he made famous.

Savard was with his wife, Mona, and daughter, Tanya, as they welcomed a parade of players from Savard's time and earlier. Al Secord and Steve Larmer were the first introduced; the trio were one of the highest-scoring lines in the 1980s. Tony Esposito and Stan Mikita, whose numbers already adorned the rafters, came out, as did owner Bill Wirtz, who presented Savard with framed sweaters of the last three variations of the Hawks' logo.

Savard finished his 10-minute speech with a heartfelt tribute: "To my wife and daughter. After a tough loss, you always found a way to get my spirits up. Thank you for being the most unselfish people in the world. I will remember this night forever and ever."

THE GAME: Chicago Blackhawks 1–Montreal Canadiens 0
Goalie Jeff Hackett made sure this night remained special in Savard's memory thanks to his shutout performance against the Canadiens. Chad Kilger got the only goal of the game, at 19:03 of the middle period, off a great pass from Greg Johnson. Hackett did the rest, stopping all 24 Montreal shots.

"It was such an honour to be on the ice with a classy guy like Denis," the goalie said after. "[The ceremony] could have gone on for two hours because he deserved it so much. It was his time, his day. We wanted to make sure we had a good effort."

Hackett preserved his seventh shutout of the year by making several big saves in the second period when the game was still scoreless.

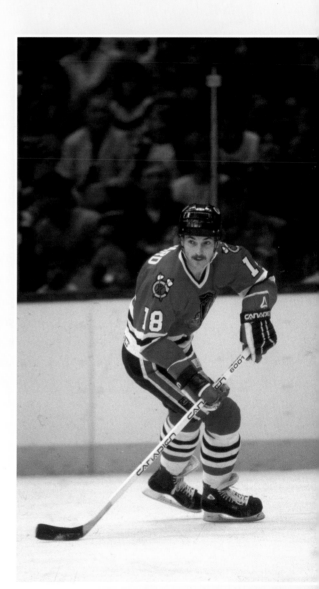

GLENN
HALL

CHICAGO BLACKHAWKS
NOVEMBER 20, 1988

Born: Humboldt, Saskatchewan, October 3, 1931
Position: Goalie
Catches: Left
Height: 5'11"
Weight: 180 lbs.

HONOURS

- **Stanley Cup** 1961
- **Calder Trophy** 1956
- **Vezina Trophy** 1963, 1967 (with Dennis DeJordy), 1969 (with Jacques Plante)
- **Conn Smythe Trophy** 1968
- **NHL All-Star Game** 1955, 1956, 1957, 1958, 1960, 1961, 1962, 1963, 1964, 1965, 1967, 1968, 1969
- **NHL First All-Star Team** 1957, 1958, 1960, 1963, 1964, 1966, 1969
- **Hockey Hall of Fame** 1975

NHL CAREER STATS

Regular Season

Years	GP	W-L-T	Mins	GA	SO	GAA
1952–71	906	407-326-163	53,484	2,222	84	2.49

Playoffs

Years	GP	W-L-T	Mins	GA	SO	GAA
1952–71	115	49-65-0	6,899	320	6	2.78

CAREER

Terry Sawchuk was the king of the shutout, and Jacques Plante was the man who brought the mask to the goalie. But Glenn Hall set a record that will never be broken. Not ever. From the start of the 1955–56 season until November 8, 1963, Hall played every minute of every game for Chicago, regular season and playoffs. That constituted a streak of 502 straight games in the regular season and 50 more in the playoffs.

Of course, such a streak is only attainable if the player is skilled, and Hall was that and then some. He played briefly in 1952–53 and 1954–55 with Detroit, but because he was in favour of the players organizing a union he and teammate (and

union organizer) Ted Lindsay were traded to Chicago—the worst team in the league—prior to the start of the 1957–58 season. The trade worked wonders on a team that already had a young Bobby Hull and a host of other talents, and in 1961 the Black Hawks won the Stanley Cup.

Hall was known for one other characteristic few want to emulate. Prior to every game he played, he threw up. This sounds almost like a parody of Greek mythology, but the truth is that he got that nervous before every game and hated the position more than he could describe. It just so happened he was particularly good at his job as well.

In all, Hall played an even 10 years with the Hawks, years that accounted for most of his 407 career wins. His style was unique, and he might well be considered the first goalie to use the butterfly. He kept his knees together but skates apart in an effort to protect as much of the net as possible.

Although Hall never won another Cup after 1961, he was claimed by the expansion St. Louis Blues in 1967 and took the team to the Final in 1968. Hall was so remarkable in the post season that despite the Blues being swept by Montreal in four games, he was named winner of the Conn Smythe Trophy.

35

TONY ESPOSITO

CHICAGO BLACKHAWKS
NOVEMBER 20, 1988

Born: Sault Ste. Marie, Ontario, April 23, 1943
Position: Goalie
Catches: Right
Height: 5'11"
Weight: 185 lbs.

Honours
• **Stanley Cup** 1969
• **Calder Trophy** 1970
• **Vezina Trophy** 1970, 1972 (with Gary Smith), 1974 (with Bernie Parent)
• **NHL All-Star Game** 1970-74, 1980
• **Hockey Hall of Fame** 1988

NHL CAREER STATS

Regular Season

Years	GP	W-L-T	Mins	GA	SO	GAA
1968–84	886	423-306-151	52,585	2,563	76	2.92

Playoffs

Years	GP	W-L-T	Mins	GA	SO	GAA
1968–84	99	45-53-0	6,017	308	6	3.07

CAREER

It is the oddities of circumstance that make the career of Tony Esposito so intriguing. After all, he won his only Stanley Cup during a rookie season (1968–69) in which he played a mere 13 games as a part-time backup for the Montreal Canadiens. After that, he played another 873 NHL games in the regular season, set records and was a dominant goalie, but never got his name on the Cup a second time.

Like Ken Dryden, "Tony O" was a rare example in the 1960s of a player getting to the NHL via an American college. In his case, it was Michigan Tech, and once he graduated in 1967, only the Canadiens were interested in signing him. Yet after just one season the Habs left his name available in the Intra-League Draft, and Chicago snapped up his rights. It was there Esposito remained for the next 15 years and 418 wins.

To this day he remains, with Grant Fuhr, one of the greatest left-handed goalies in the game's history. But more than merely wearing the catching glove on his right hand, he established a goaltending style that continues to this day. Rather than play standing up, pads together, Esposito liked to keep his knees together and his feet apart, to cover more of the lower part of the net. Of course, this left a gap between his pads (now called the "five-hole") but tell a player to shoot in the middle of a goalie's pads in the 1970s and he would have thought you were crazy.

Esposito won a league-best 38 games as a rookie in 1969–70, but more amazingly recorded a modern-era best of 15 shutouts, a record that still stands today. He won the Calder Trophy and Vezina Trophy as well that season and was on his way to a Hall of Fame career.

Esposito and the Black Hawks came closest to a Stanley Cup the next year, 1970–71. He again led the league in wins (with 35) and the team advanced to the Final, only to be bested by Montreal and another rookie goalie, Dryden. In all, Esposito won at least 30 games in each of his first seven seasons, another record that remains unchallenged. He is a member of the elite 400-win club for goalies, and he has the distinction of having played for two countries during his international career.

He and Dryden split the goaltending duties during the historic Summit Series, but later Esposito became an American citizen and played for the United States at the 1981 Canada Cup.

CEREMONY

Glenn Hall and Tony Esposito were co-honoured by the Blackhawks as the two greatest goalies in the team's long and illustrious history. Esposito appeared with his wife, Marilyn, while Hall and his wife, Paula, came out to centre ice along with owner Bill Wirtz. Both goalies received lengthy ovations for their contributions to the team, and then their respective numbers were raised to the rafters.

THE GAME: Vancouver Canucks 7–Chicago Blackhawks 4
These were not the glorious Blackhawks of days gone by, and on this night it was especially disappointing for coach Mike Keenan to see his goalie, Darren Pang, turn in a bad effort. Pang, though, was by no means alone, as the team's defensive play left plenty to be desired.

"It was difficult to determine how I played," Pang said. "They only had 23 shots, but they had three power-play goals and those shots from in front of the net."

Much of the game was determined by special teams. Vancouver had three goals on seven power plays while Chicago had but one goal on 10 chances with the extra man. The Canucks led 3–1 after the first and 6–2 after 40 minutes and coasted to victory in the third.

"Except for tonight, we played well for the month of November," Keenan noted encouragingly. "This is a terrible loss, but I don't think the club is down or at the same [low] level of play it was in October."

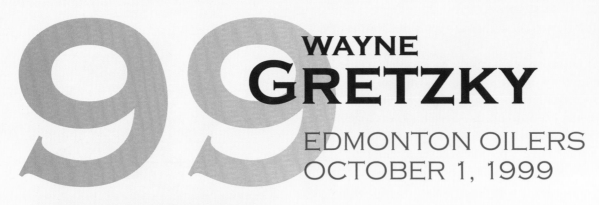

99
WAYNE GRETZKY

EDMONTON OILERS
OCTOBER 1, 1999

Born: Brantford, Ontario, January 26, 1961
Position: Centre
Shoots: Left
Height: 6'
Weight: 185 lbs.

HONOURS

- **Stanley Cup** 1984, 1985, 1987, 1988
- **Hart Trophy** 1980, 1981, 1982, 1983, 1984, 1985, 1986, 1987, 1989
- **Lady Byng Trophy** 1980, 1991, 1992, 1994, 1999
- **Art Ross Trophy** 1981, 1982, 1983, 1984, 1985, 1986, 1987, 1990, 1991, 1994
- **Lester B. Pearson Award** 1982, 1983, 1984, 1985, 1987
- **Conn Smythe Trophy** 1985, 1988
- **NHL All-Star Game** 1980, 1981, 1982, 1983, 1984, 1985, 1986, 1988, 1989, 1990, 1991, 1992, 1993, 1994, 1996, 1997, 1998, 1999
- **Played for Canada at Canada Cup** 1981, 1984, 1987, 1991
- **Played for Canada at World Cup** 1996
- **Played for Canada at Olympics** 1998
- **Hockey Hall of Fame** 1999

NHL CAREER STATS

Years	Regular Season					Playoffs				
	GP	G	A	P	Pim	GP	G	A	P	Pim
1979–99	1,487	894	1,963	2,857	577	208	122	260	382	66

EDMONTON CAREER

The nine years that Wayne Gretzky played in the NHL with Edmonton were nine years that may never be replicated in the annals of the game. The 18-year-old kid who played his first NHL game in October 1979 gave way to the weeping captain, Stanley Cup winner, and record setter who was traded in the summer of 1988. But in between those markers history was forged, records obliterated, memories of greatness set forever in the city that embraced his every move.

Gretzky was blessed by having the WHA as an intermediary league between junior and the NHL. He left the Ontario Hockey League (OHL) in 1978 to play a

year in the WHA, first with the Indianapolis Racers then soon after with the Edmonton Oilers. By the time the team joined the NHL a year later, he was already in his prime and ready for greatness. The "kid" scored 51 goals and led the league with 86 assists, but although his 137 points tied with Marcel Dionne for top spot, Dionne got the Art Ross Trophy because he had more goals (53). No matter, Gretzky led the league in scoring every other year he was in Edmonton except the last, in which he missed 18 games because of injury.

In his second season he took care of two records, his 109 assists leaving Bobby Orr's 102 in second place and his 164 points bettering by a dozen Phil Esposito's previous mark. This was just the beginning. In 1981–82, he started by setting perhaps his most untouchable record, scoring 50 goals in the first 39 games of the season. He ended the year with another untouchable one, 92 goals in a season. And he became the first player to reach 200 points in a year, finishing with 212.

Over the course of his Edmonton years Gretzky improved his records to include 163 assists in a season and 215 points in a year. Indeed, there were three years when he had more assists than any other player in the league had total points. But with all these incredible records, it was the Stanley Cup that was the ultimate chase. The Oilers, like any other great team, had to lose before they could win, and after a particularly bitter loss to the Islanders in the 1983 Final, they vowed never to lose again.

The team won its first Cup the next year, and won four of the next five, losing only in 1986 on a fluky own goal against Calgary that might have cost them a place in history alongside Montreal as the only teams to win five in a row. In addition, Gretzky suited up for Team Canada whenever he could, and this meant playing in the Canada Cup in 1981, 1984, 1987, and 1991.

The first was a disastrous loss to the Soviets; the second a victory against surprise finalists, Sweden; the third, an historic showdown against the Soviets, the best-of-three called by many the finest hockey games ever played. Gretzky's set-up of Mario Lemieux's series winner with less than two minutes to go is one of the greatest goals in Canadian history along with Paul Henderson's heroics in 1972 and Sidney Crosby's Olympic gold winner in overtime on February 28, 2010.

Of course, all good things must come to an end, and Gretzky's trade to Los Angeles shocked the entire country. He left Edmonton having scored more than 1,600 points by age 27 and given the city four Stanley Cup parades. The "Great One" would go on to play another 11 years in the NHL, but he never won another Cup. His Edmonton legacy was beyond dispute.

CEREMONY

The Edmonton Oilers vowed not to retire another number until Gretzky's 99 went up, and on October 1, 1999, they proved true to their word. Gretzky was at centre ice with wife, Janet, and their children, Paulina, Ty, and Trevor, as well as his parents, Walter and Phyllis. The 55-minute tribute began with bagpipes and continued with a video tribute highlighting the dozens of great moments he brought to Edmonton.

There were presents, too, of course. Teammates Mark Messier, Jari Kurri, and Dave Semenko gave him an oil painting by local artist Wei Lunan. Former head coach and general manager Glen Sather spoke eloquently about Gretzky's first

days with the team when the teenager lived with him and his wife, Ann, for several weeks as he adjusted to life in Edmonton.

"He came to us a boy, became a man and then a legend," he said. "We'll always think of Wayne as ours. Playing for the Oilers was a perfect fit."

Joey Moss, the team's equipment manager, was there for hugs and tears, and the house dissolved when broadcaster and emcee Rod Phillips said, "These words will never be heard in the building again . . . Hockey fans, tonight's first star—Wayne Gretzky."

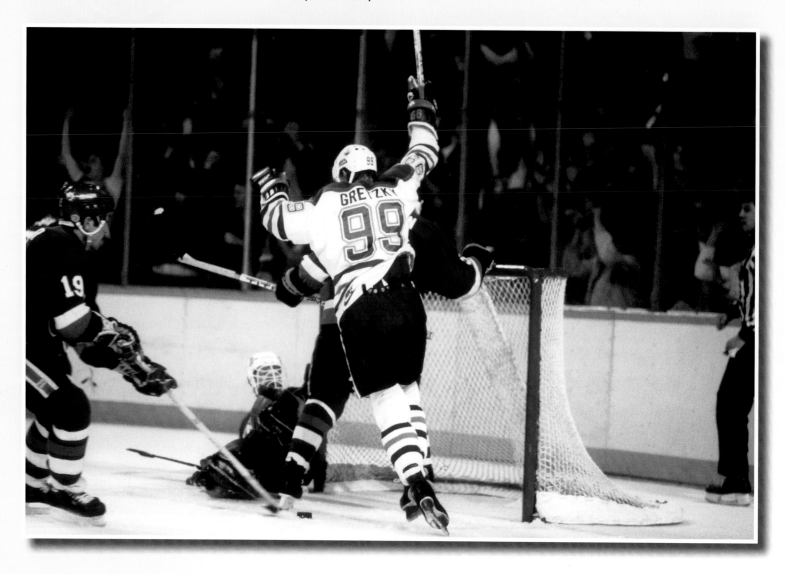

The celebrations and honours began earlier in the day when thousands of fans gathered at City Hall for a public tribute to Gretzky. Mayor Bill Smith, along with Sather and Phillips, took part in the tribute that included renaming a freeway Wayne Gretzky Drive. The highlight of the afternoon came when nine lucky children got to ask Gretzky one question each. Andrew Kuxy asked him what was his greatest memory with Edmonton, to which number 99 replied, "Most memorable experience was, by far, the very first Stanley Cup we won."

The ceremony ended with snowfall, and then everyone took a break before heading over to Skyreach Centre for the sweater retirement.

THE GAME: Edmonton Oilers 1–New York Rangers 1

Kevin Lowe, a longtime friend and teammate of Gretzky, had made his head-coaching debut with the Edmonton Oilers the previous night, and his promise of returning to high-flying hockey looked good this night during an entertaining 1–1 tie with Gretzky's last team, the New York Rangers.

Both goals came in the second period, the first from Ryan Smyth, who had just signed a new contract with the team, and then Tim Taylor a few minutes later for the Blueshirts. Rangers' goalie Mike Richter was the star of the game as the Oilers held a decided edge in play.

"The guys played a pretty good game," Lowe said after. "It was one of those games where we had our chances . . . I thought we had enough to deserve a win."

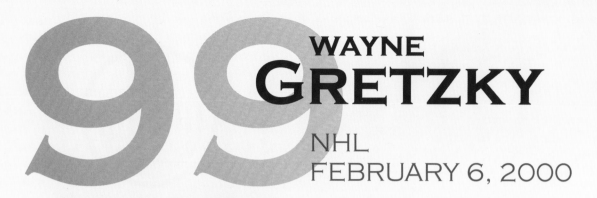

99
WAYNE
GRETZKY

NHL
FEBRUARY 6, 2000

Born: Brantford, Ontario, January 26, 1961
Position: Centre
Shoots: Left
Height: 6'
Weight: 185 lbs.

HONOURS
- **Stanley Cup** 1984, 1985, 1987, 1988
- **Hart Trophy** 1980, 1981, 1982, 1983, 1984, 1985, 1986, 1987, 1989
- **Lady Byng Trophy** 1980, 1991, 1992, 1994, 1999
- **Art Ross Trophy** 1981, 1982, 1983, 1984, 1985, 1986, 1987, 1990, 1991, 1994
- **Lester B. Pearson Award** 1982, 1983, 1984, 1985, 1987
- **Conn Smythe Trophy** 1985, 1988
- **NHL All-Star Game** 1980, 1981, 1982, 1983, 1984, 1985, 1986, 1988, 1989, 1990, 1991, 1992, 1993, 1994, 1996, 1997, 1998, 1999
- **Played for Canada at Canada Cup** 1981, 1984, 1987, 1991
- **Played for Canada at World Cup** 1996
- **Played for Canada at Olympics** 1998
- **Hockey Hall of Fame** 1999

NHL CAREER STATS

	Regular Season					Playoffs				
Years	GP	G	A	P	Pim	GP	G	A	P	Pim
1979–99	1,487	894	1,963	2,857	577	208	122	260	382	66

CEREMONY

Although the league had already made clear—and every player, coach, and general manager in his right mind knew as much—it was at the 2000 All-Star Game in Toronto that number 99 was officially retired league-wide. A special banner was raised to the rafters of the Air Canada Centre in Gretzky's honour before a stage that was all too familiar with his greatness. Gretzky held many All-Star Game records, so it was only fitting he be honoured at the annual showcase of talent.

Commissioner Gary Bettman had first announced the league-wide retiring of the number before Gretzky's final game, but it wasn't until this day that it was

made official. "When I started wearing this number in junior hockey in 1977," he said, "I didn't expect that one day they wouldn't let anybody else wear it. It's a great honour."

In commemoration of the event, 28 children came out onto the ice, each wearing a sweater of one of the NHL teams. Gretzky's son, Ty, was among them. "He was very excited about being out there," the proud father said later. "It was very cute."

THE GAME: World 9–North America 4

Gretzky dropped the puck during pre-game ceremonies at centre ice. He was accompanied by Bettman; and Jaromir Jagr and Paul Kariya happily watched as their old opponent dropped the puck to the ice.

It was the Russians who shone brightest this afternoon. Pavel Bure, the game's MVP, had a hat trick and three assists while his brother, Valeri, had two assists. Slava Kozlov added three assists, and Dmitri Yushkevich had a goal and an assist. Eleven points in all for the Russians in a game that was close only in the first half.

North America scored two goals late in the second, after which Team World scored the only four goals of the final period to make it 5–4, thanks to Tony Amonte and Ray Whitney.

Earlier, the skills competition thrilled the fans. Al MacInnis won the hardest shot challenge for the fourth time in six years, registering a blast of 160.2 kilometres per hour. Sami Kapanen won the league's fastest skater contest and Slava Kozlov and Ray Bourque had the most accurate shots.

32

DALE
HUNTER

WASHINGTON CAPITALS
MARCH 11, 2000

Born: Petrolia, Ontario, July 31, 1960
Position: Centre
Shoots: Left
Height: 5'10"
Weight: 198 lbs.

HONOURS
• **NHL All-Star Game** 1997

NHL CAREER STATS

	Regular Season					Playoffs				
Years	GP	G	A	P	Pim	GP	G	A	P	Pim
1980–99	1,407	323	697	1,020	3,565	186	42	76	118	729

CAREER

Few players have had as controversial a career as Dale Hunter, a player who did nothing to make himself popular but who played with heart and gusto for 19 NHL seasons. He holds several unique records, starting with the fact that he is the only career 300-goal scorer (323 in total) never to have recorded one 30-goal season. Also, he took the longest time to reach 1,000 career points (1,308 games). His 3,565 career penalty minutes is far and away the most for any 1,000-point player, and his 186 playoff games is the most of anyone who has not won the Stanley Cup. He is also the only player in NHL history to have scored two series-clinching goals in overtime. What to make of all this?

Hunter was drafted in 1979 by the Quebec Nordiques and played for seven years at Le Colisée. He was traded to Washington and later served as team captain, but he was reviled everywhere he went for unduly physical, if not downright dirty

play. Yet Hunter had skills, of course. Although he never had a 30-goal season, he had nine seasons of at least 20 goals and 11 seasons of more than 200 penalty minutes. Only Tiger Williams served more time in the penalty box than Hunter.

The closest he came to winning the Cup was in 1997–98 with the Capitals. That season, they advanced to the Final, but were swept by Detroit in four straight games (although the first three were all decided by a single goal). He was traded to Colorado late in the 1998–99 season and played 12 games at the end of the regular season and then 19 more in the playoffs as the team advanced to the conference final before losing in seven games to Dallas.

In 1982, Hunter scored one of the biggest goals of his career in the best-of-five opening-round playoff series for Quebec against Montreal. The deciding game went into overtime, and his goal eliminated the dreaded Habs. Six years later, he helped orchestrate another upset, this time while playing for Washington. In game seven of the first round series against Philadelphia, Hunter scored on a breakaway in overtime to eliminate the Flyers.

CEREMONY

The only number 32 retired by an NHL team, Dale Hunter was greeted by a packed chorus of cheers from the 18,672 fans at the MCI Center on hand for his sweater retirement.

Perhaps he could have expected that, but he could not have anticipated what his former teammates gave him as going away presents: an all-terrain vehicle, a horse trailer, and . . . the old penalty box from the Capital Center!

After his number 32 was hoisted to the rafters, Hunter walked by the team's players' bench and shook hands with the Caps, and then headed off ice for the final time.

THE GAME: Washington Capitals 4–New Jersey Devils 2

The Washington Capitals started off like gangbusters, but were soon corralled by the visiting New Jersey Devils before pulling away in the third period thanks to Chris Simon. Simon and Joe Murphy got goals in the first 4:31 of the first period after the inspiring ceremony, but the Devils fought back less than four minutes later to tie the game. The rest of that period and all of the second were goalless, and during the second intermission Simon reminded his teammates that it was a special night.

"He mentioned that you can't have a night like this, honouring one of the organization's greats, and come out flat and lose the game," goalie Olaf Kolzig said after. "It was really important to win it for Dale . . . It was a great tribute to Dale."

With these words in mind, Ulf Dahlen scored the go-ahead goal—and eventual game winner—in the second minute, and Steve Konowalchuk added an empty netter to make it a 4–2 game. The first star of the night was announced as Hunter himself, and everyone went home happy on the home side this night.

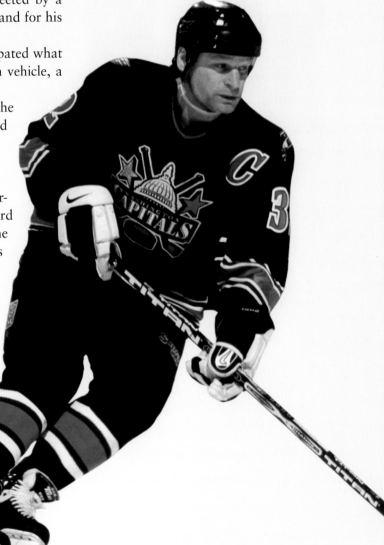

21

MICHEL BRIÈRE

PITTSBURGH PENGUINS
JANUARY 5, 2001

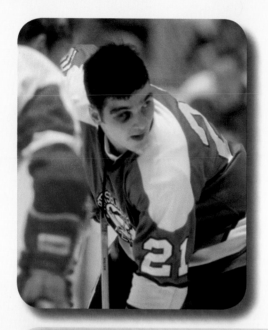

Born: Shawinigan Falls, Quebec, October 21, 1949
Died: Montreal, Quebec, April 13, 1971
Position: Centre
Shoots: Left
Height: 5'10"
Weight: 165 lbs.

HONOURS
• Drafted 26th overall by Pittsburgh 1969

NHL CAREER STATS

	Regular Season					Playoffs				
Years	GP	G	A	P	Pim	GP	G	A	P	Pim
1969–70	76	12	32	44	20	10	5	3	8	17

CAREER

A career that started out with such promise was snuffed out by tragedy after just one season, but the name Michel Brière lives on in the number 21 sweater that will always hang high in the Pittsburgh Penguins' arena.

Brière was a small and swift French-Canadian who had an outstanding junior career in Shawinigan, Quebec. Drafted by Pittsburgh in 1969, he made the team as an 19-year-old, a rare accomplishment in that era. He scored 12 goals during the season, but in the playoffs he became even more effective, scoring the team's first overtime goal in franchise history against Oakland to eliminate the Seals four games to none in the quarter-finals. The Penguins then lost to the Blues in a six-game series, but Brière had five goals in 10 games in the playoffs and three of those were game winners.

Brière returned home for the summer to prepare for a June wedding with his girlfriend, with whom he had an infant son, but on May 15, 1970, he was involved in a single-car crash that proved fatal. He underwent four brain surgeries, and the Penguins played the entire next season carrying his sweater and equipment around from game to game in his honour, hoping he could recover. Unfortunately, on April 11, 1971, Brière succumbed to his injuries, never having come out of a coma sustained 11 months previous.

Although his number wasn't officially retired until 2001, no Pittsburgh player has worn the 21 since. The Penguins also established the Michel Brière Rookie of the Year Award and the Quebec Major Junior Hockey League (QMJHL) renamed its MVP award in his honour as well.

CEREMONY

Words cannot describe the sadness surrounding the retirement of Michel Brière's number 21. Although the event took place some 30 years after his demise, it was made poignant by the presence of Brière's son, Martin, who was just an infant when his father passed away. Mario Lemieux's number 66 was the only other number so honoured by the Penguins, but with Lemieux recently out of retirement and back on the ice, number 21 had the rafters all to itself this day in 2001.

THE GAME: Montreal Canadiens 4–Pittsburgh Penguins 3

Now in his fourth game since coming out of retirement on December 27, 2000, Mario Lemieux picked up another goal and two assists to make it 12 points since his return after a three-and-a-half-year absence. But on this night, it wasn't quite enough as the lowly Montreal Canadiens jumped into a 2–0 lead, which they never relinquished.

Brian Savage and Eric Weinrich scored in the first 6:27 to stake the Canadiens to that lead, and although Alexei Kovalev got one back for the home side soon after, the period ended 2–1 for the visitors. In the second, Montreal opened a two-goal lead and a second from Weinrich in the first minute of the final period put the game out of reach.

The Penguins rallied with goals from Lemieux and Martin Straka, but they could get no closer than the final 4–3 score despite outshooting the Habs, 32–21. "Their goalie was hot," Lemieux said of Jose Theodore. "We had plenty of chances, especially in the third period. He made some key saves."

"We got too many goals behind," line mate Jaromir Jagr added. "It was 4–1 and then we started to play. But then, it was too late. Maybe with five more minutes it would have been a different story."

3 AL HAMILTON

EDMONTON OILERS
APRIL 4, 2001

Born: Flin Flon, Manitoba, August 20, 1946
Position: Defence
Shoots: Right
Height: 6'1"
Weight: 195 lbs.

HONOURS
• **Won Memorial Cup with Edmonton Oil Kings** 1966
• **Played for WHA Team Canada at 1974 Summit**
• **Captain of Alberta/Edmonton Oilers in WHA** 1972–76

NHL CAREER STATS

	Regular Season					Playoffs				
Years	GP	G	A	P	Pim	GP	G	A	P	Pim
1965–80	257	10	78	88	258	7	0	0	0	2

CAREER

The Rexall Place rafters have seven banners honouring players from the Oilers' history, from Wayne Gretzky and Mark Messier, to Jari Kurri, Paul Coffey, Glenn Anderson, Grant Fuhr—and Al Hamilton.

Al who? In fact, Hamilton was the first Oilers player to have his number retired, an honour bestowed upon him for his contributions to the team during its years in the World Hockey Association (WHA). He had been to the Memorial Cup three years in a row, winning with the Edmonton Oil Kings in 1966, and then turning pro, playing first with the New York Rangers and later with the Buffalo Sabres.

When he had the chance, though, he decided to return to Edmonton via the WHA, in 1972. He was named the team's captain, a position he held for four years. Despite being a first-rate defenceman he was beset by long-term injuries

during his career, breaking his knee twice within a few months, suffering a serious eye injury that nearly blinded him, and separating his shoulder.

Hamilton hung in there long enough to play half a season when the team joined the NHL in 1979, after which he retired. For his extraordinary service, fortitude, and dedication to the team, the Oilers took his number 3 out of circulation, and it has been in the rafters ever since.

CEREMONY

Al Hamilton is one of a rare group to have his number retired twice by the same team, in two separate ceremonies more than 20 years apart. The first honour came on October 10, 1980, prior to the Oilers' home opener against Quebec. Hamilton, his first wife, Barb, and their three small children, Stephen, Allison, and Erin, were feted at centre ice, much to the delight of the sold-out crowd of 17,334, at the time the largest crowd to watch a game in Canadian history. "It was a beautiful thing for Al," said Robbie Ftorek, of the Nordiques. "It was first class, for a deserving gentleman . . . it was truly fantastic."

Unfortunately for Hamilton, the man who lured him to Edmonton, Bill Hunter, was unable to attend because he was fundraising for Notre Dame College, made famous by Monsignor Athol "Pere" Murray. "Bill Hunter is the man who talked me into coming here," Hamilton told the crowd. "He said this would become the greatest major league hockey town in Canada. I'm not sure I believed him, but wherever you are tonight, Bill, thank you."

Hamilton received gifts including a microwave, television, stereo, bicycle for two, freezer, trip for two anywhere in the world courtesy of Air Canada, and a pendant with the Oilers' logo and the number 3 engraved.

Fast forward to April 4, 2001. In another ceremony, Hamilton's number 3 was raised again (sometime in between it had been taken down). This time, a much older Hunter was in attendance, and Wayne Gretzky, who'd fed Hamilton a perfect pass for a tap-in goal—the last of his NHL career—delivered a video dedication: "Thanks for the company in the rafters."

Also part of the ceremony was Hamilton's second wife, Jan, and their twin sons, Brett and Andrew, and his three now-grown children from his previous marriage.

THE GAME: Quebec Nordiques 7–Edmonton Oilers 4/Edmonton Oilers 2–Minnesota Wild 2

"We're just not that good in games with pre-game ceremonies," Wayne Gretzky said after the Nordiques downed Oilers 7–4 in 1980. He should know. The last time the Oilers held a ceremony was a year and a half before when number 99 signed a 21-year contract at centre ice. On this night, the Oilers jumped into a 2–0 lead, and the back-and-forth game went one way in the third period when the visitors scored the only four goals to pull away for the victory.

Edmonton fared only a little better 20 years later in Hamilton's second retirement game, tying Minnesota 2–2, after scoring late in the third period to earn a point in the standings. The team was in a fight for the playoffs, and the loss of one point came at a bad time. Stacey Roest scored early for the Wild, but Janne Niinimaa tied the game for the Oilers late in the first. Pavel Patera got the only goal of the second for the visitors, and Doug Weight tied the game at 19:12 on a power play to send the game to a scoreless overtime.

77

RAY BOURQUE

BOSTON BRUINS
OCTOBER 4, 2001

Born: Montreal, Quebec, December 28, 1960
Position: Defence
Shoots: Left
Height: 5'11"
Weight: 220 lbs.

HONOURS
- **Stanley Cup** 2001
- **Calder Trophy** 1980
- **Norris Trophy** 1987, 1988, 1990, 1991, 1994
- **King Clancy Trophy** 1992
- **Lester Patrick Award** 2003
- **Played for Canada at Canada Cup** 1981, 1984, 1987
- **Played for Canada at Olympics** 1998
- **NHL All-Star Game** 1981, 1982, 1983, 1984, 1985, 1986, 1988, 1989, 1990, 1991, 1992, 1993, 1994, 1996, 1997, 1998, 1999, 2000, 2001
- **Hockey Hall of Fame** 2004

NHL CAREER STATS

Years	Regular Season					Playoffs				
	GP	G	A	P	Pim	GP	G	A	P	Pim
1979–2001	1,612	410	1,169	1,579	1,141	214	41	139	180	171

BOSTON CAREER

One could compare Ray Bourque to Ron Francis or Adam Oates rather than to Bobby Orr or Paul Coffey, because Bourque had more consistently high seasons than any truly sensational ones. During his 22 years in the NHL, Bourque played more than 20 seasons with the Bruins, making the playoffs almost every year, setting career scoring records, but never having a 100-point season (as did Orr and Coffey, several times), and never winning the Stanley Cup (until he was traded to the Colorado Avalanche).

Drafted by Boston in 1979, Bourque joined the Boston Bruins that fall and had an immediate impact, setting a record with 65 points for a defenceman in his rookie season and winning the Calder Trophy. He had his best statistical year in 1983–84, scoring 31 goals and 96 points, but the Bruins lost in the first round of the

playoffs as they would the next three years.

In fact, Boston made the playoffs 29 consecutive times, setting a record for a North American sports team. The closest the team came to winning the Stanley Cup was in 1988 and 1990, when they went to the Final, only to lose both years to Edmonton.

Bourque regularly logged 25 minutes of ice time a game and was the anchor of a team that was consistently good for a very long time. He was named co-captain of the Bruins in 1985 and made full-time captain three years later, serving in this capacity until his trade to Colorado in March 2000. In fact, he was the longest-serving captain in league history until Steve Yzerman later surpassed him.

The Bruins missed the playoffs in 1997 and as his career was winding down he asked to be traded to a contender in the hopes of winning the Stanley Cup just once during his career. He got his wish a year and a half later, with the Avalanche.

CEREMONY

Although he spent nearly 21 seasons trying unsuccessfully to bring the Stanley Cup to Boston, Bourque's place in the team and city's spirit was entrenched long ago. The emotional ceremony to retire his number 77 hit several crescendos, the first lasting 3:14 when he was first introduced. None, however, was more poignant than when Phil Esposito walked onto the ice carrying a white 77 sweater and handed it to Bourque. Two decades earlier, when the Bruins retired Espo's number 7, Bourque took that number off his back and switched to 77 in the great forward's honour. Now, Espo could give a little back.

Joining Bourque and Esposito were Bobby Orr, Johnny Bucyk, and Milt Schmidt.

The 31-minute ceremony culminated when Bourque and his family—his wife, Christiane, and their children Melissa, Chris, and Ryan—raised the 77 banner to the rafters as the crowd cheered wildly.

Gifts were plentiful. Commissioner Gary Bettman presented Bourque with a silver stick; the Fleet Center and Bruins employees gave him a black-and-gold snowmobile; and on behalf of the players, Don Sweeney gave him a marble bench with all Bruins names with whom he played engraved on it.

"It is so good to be home," Bourque began, as he addressed the crowd. "I thought I was nervous coming out here tonight, but there's one thing I realized: I'm among friends." He ended in similar fashion. "This is my home. This is where I really grew up. This is where my children were born. And this is where we will stay because we are among friends. I'd like to thank everyone. I love you, Boston!"

THE GAME: Boston Bruins 4–Anaheim Mighty Ducks 2

The opening game of the season couldn't have gone better for the Bruins, who followed the ceremony with a solid win over the Mighty Ducks. The Bruins got the first goal at 5:37 thanks to Nick Boynton, and the lead held up until early in the second when Jeff Friesen tied the game, 1–1.

The Bruins struck for the next two goals thanks to Joe Thornton on the power play and Brian Rolston, and after the Ducks made it 3–2 Sergei Samsonov finished the scoring in the period and game with the Bruins' fourth at 16:26. A goalless third gave the Bruins a win to start the season, but as Rolston acknowledged, Bourque deserved an assist.

"It was incredible to see the support the fans gave," he said. "It gets you fired up. It's something special."

17

JARI KURRI

EDMONTON OILERS
OCTOBER 6, 2001

Born: Helsinki, Finland, May 18, 1960
Position: Right wing
Shoots: Right
Height: 6'
Weight: 194 lbs.

HONOURS

- **Stanley Cup** 1984, 1985, 1987, 1988, 1990
- **Lady Byng Trophy** 1985
- **NHL All-Star game** 1983, 1985, 1986, 1988, 1989, 1990, 1993, 1998
- **Played for Finland at Canada Cup** 1981, 1987, 1991
- **Played for Finland at Olympics** 1980, 1998
- **Played for Finland at World Cup** 1996

NHL CAREER STATS

	Regular Season					Playoffs				
Years	GP	G	A	P	Pim	GP	G	A	P	Pim
1980–98	1,251	601	797	1,398	545	200	106	127	233	123

CAREER

Jari Kurri's famous number 17 is retired in three places, clear indication of the Finn's great career. It hangs in the Edmonton Oilers' Rexall Centre; the Finnish national team took it out of circulation to honour his international career; and his Finnish club team Jokerit raised it to the rafters of Hartwall Arena in Helsinki.

The greatest scorer and offensive player in Finnish history, Kurri joined the Edmonton Oilers in 1980 as a 20-year-old rookie. Coach Glen Sather put him on a line with Wayne Gretzky in Kurri's 19th game of the season, and Kurri had a hat trick—all goals assisted by number 99.

Kurri improved his scoring from 32 goals as a rookie and sophomore to 45, 52, and then 71, the last a record for right wingers. He and Gretzky were magical together, knowing instinctively where the other was, making highlight-reel-worthy, tic-tac-toe passes resulting in tap-in goals and empty-net shots.

Kurri played 10 years with the Oilers, winning all five Stanley Cup titles and leading the playoffs in goals on three occasions. By 1990, however, he was missing his friend and set-up man, Gretzky, who had been traded to Los Angeles. Sather refused to trade Kurri to the Kings, so Kurri packed up and moved back to Finland for a year until Sather relented. Reunited, he wasn't quite the speedy player with the soft hands, but in five years he still managed to score more than 100 goals with Gretzky and the Kings.

By the time he retired in 1998, every notable record by Finns in the NHL belonged to Kurri: most games (1,251), most goals (601), most assists (797), and most points (1,398). More impressive, he played in 200 playoff games, among the all-time leaders in that important measure of success. Incredibly, despite his sensational career, the only individual trophy he won was the Lady Byng Trophy in 1984–85.

In addition to Kurri's great NHL career, he played for his country every chance he got, notably at the 1980 and 1998 Olympics, the 1981, 1987, and 1991 Canada Cup, 1996 World Cup, and four World Championships.

CEREMONY

Kurri began receiving honours even before the official retirement when Edmonton mayor Bill Smith declared the Friday "Jari Kurri Day" during a special reception at City Hall. The best, however, took place the next night at a packed Skyreach Centre.

As was often the case during these special events, the visitors were the Phoenix Coyotes coached by Wayne Gretzky, which made the evening that much more memorable. General manager Kevin Lowe asked Kurri to come out to centre ice in full equipment, and he happily obliged, standing with his twin sons, Ville and Joonas.

Current Oilers forward Rem Murray, who wore number 17 for five years, happily returned the number to Kurri and replaced it with 16. Kurri skated around the ice waving to fans, then Gretzky grabbed a stick and fired a pass to him. He went in on the empty goal and buried a shot, but not without some ribbing from number 99. "From where I was standing, I was worried Jari was going to miss the net."

"Let's have a replay," Kurri rejoined. "It went right into the middle."

Gretzky, godfather to Kurri's sons, laughed. Then, it was time to play hockey.

THE GAME: Edmonton Oilers 6–Phoenix Coyotes 2

The game wasn't as lopsided as the score might indicate, but it was good for the Oilers to get their first win of the season in their home opener after losing their first game on the road days earlier. More important, the team scored two goals in the second period with the extra man after starting the year 0-for-22 in their first four periods of hockey.

As it turned out, the scoreless first period on this night gave way to wide-open play in the middle 20 minutes, Dan Cleary scoring with the extra man just 22 seconds into the period to give the Oilers a 1–0 lead. Ryan Smyth had two more in the period and Claude Lemieux the only Coyotes goal. Captain Jason Smith made it a 4–1 game early in the final period.

Krys Kolanos got Phoenix a little closer, but two goals in the final minute sealed the victory and gave Kurri a final remembrance of his special night. Shots on goal heavily favoured Edmonton, 41–16.

19 BRYAN TROTTIER

NEW YORK ISLANDERS
OCTOBER 20, 2001

Born: Val Marie, Saskatchewan, July 17, 1956
Position: Centre
Shoots: Left
Height: 5'11"
Weight: 195 lbs.

HONOURS
- **Stanley Cup** 1980, 1981, 1982, 1983, 1991, 1992
- **Hart Trophy** 1979
- **Art Ross Trophy** 1979
- **Calder Trophy** 1976
- **Conn Smythe Trophy** 1980
- **King Clancy Memorial Trophy** 1989
- **NHL All-Star Game** 1976, 1978, 1980, 1982, 1983, 1985, 1986, 1992
- **Played for Canada in Canada Cup** 1981
- **Played for United States in Canada Cup** 1984

NHL CAREER STATS

	Regular Season					Playoffs				
Years	GP	G	A	P	Pim	GP	G	A	P	Pim
1975–94	1,279	524	901	1,425	912	221	71	113	184	277

CAREER

As a rookie in 1975–76, Bryan Trottier set a record with 63 assists and 95 points playing on a line with Clark Gillies and Billy Harris. He won the Calder Trophy and became respected around the league for his leadership and dual ability of passing and scoring.

Although his next year saw a decline, his third proved to be the start of five straight seasons of at least 100 points. He was now centreman on the Trio Grande Line with Gillies on left wing and scoring sensation Mike Bossy on the right side.

This threesome was the key to the Islanders' offense, both in five-on-five situations as well as anchoring the power play. In 1979, Trottier became the first player from an expansion team to win both the Art Ross and Hart trophies, and a year later he led the team to its first of four straight Stanley Cup victories. He was named winner of the Conn Smythe Trophy. He had his only 50-goal season in

1981–82, but with Bossy, one of the all-time scoring leaders playing on the wing, Trottier became more concerned with passing the puck than firing it on goal himself.

The Islanders failed to make the playoffs in 1989 after qualifying for the first 13 years of Trottier's career. Not surprisingly, Trottier had a poor year and showed signs of ageing. His point production was halved; Bossy had retired early because of a chronic back condition, and Trottier was less effective with other wingmen.

Trottier signed with the Pittsburgh Penguins in 1990, now more as a defensive player, letting Mario Lemieux and Jaromir Jagr do the scoring. The Pens won consecutive Cups in 1991 and 1992, after which Trottier retired a six-time champion. After a year away from the game, he decided to return to the ice; however, neither his head nor hands were up to the task and he retired for good after 41 games and only four goals.

CEREMONY

By 2001, the key players from the dynasty of the 1980s Islanders all had had their numbers retired—Bossy, Gillies, Bob Nystrom, goalie Billy Smith—but not Trottier. Finally, though, in 2001, player and team came together and agreed that the time was right to honour possibly the most important player on the team, the centreman who set up Bossy for so many goals, the leader who inspired by example, the man who had earned the Conn Smythe Trophy en route to the team's first Cup win in 1980.

The night his number was raised was a special one, indeed. Owner Charles Wang had a good club on his hands, and was happy to share his enthusiasm with the sold-out crowd. "I am proud to welcome on the ice your first-place New York Islanders," he enthused. Indeed, only eight games into the season, the Isles were first in the Atlantic Division with six wins, a tie, and an overtime loss.

As Trottier's banner was raised, the loudspeaker played Mussorgsky's "Pictures at an Exhibition," a poignant offering for the celebration. Trottier was, at this time, an assistant coach with the Colorado Avalanche.

THE GAME: New York Islanders 2–San Jose Sharks 2

The thrilling game was back and forth most of the night, the Sharks taking the early lead and then needing to rally to earn a point on the road. Vincent Damphousse scored late in the first period, and a scoreless second took the game to its final session to decide the outcome.

Kenny Jonsson scored midway through the final period, and then Alexei Yashin seemingly scored the winning goal with exactly one minute left in regulation. But with goalie Miikka Kiprusoff on the bench, the Sharks tied the game with only 5.1 seconds left on the clock, Damphousse doing the damage again. Jonsson hit the post in overtime, but the game ended in a 2–2 tie.

77

RAY BOURQUE

COLORADO AVALANCHE
NOVEMBER 24, 2001

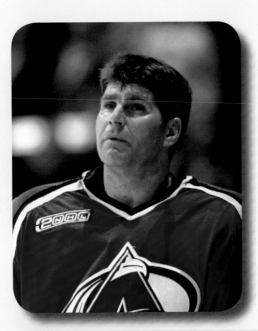

Born: Montreal, Quebec, December 28, 1960
Position: Defence
Shoots: Left
Height: 5'11"
Weight: 220 lbs.

Honours
- **Stanley Cup** 2001
- **Norris Trophy** 1987, 1988, 1990, 1991, 1994
- **King Clancy Trophy** 1992
- **Lester Patrick Award** 2003
- **Played for Canada at Canada Cup** 1981, 1984, 1987
- **Played for Canada at Olympics** 1998
- **NHL All-Star Game** 1981, 1982, 1983, 1984, 1985, 1986, 1988, 1989, 1990, 1991, 1992, 1993, 1994, 1996, 1997, 1998, 1999, 2000, 2001
- **Hockey Hall of Fame** 2004

NHL CAREER STATS

	Regular Season					Playoffs				
Years	GP	G	A	P	Pim	GP	G	A	P	Pim
1979–2001	1,612	410	1,169	1,579	1,141	214	41	139	180	171

COLORADO CAREER

On March 6, 2000, after nearly 21 seasons with the Boston Bruins, Ray Bourque was traded to the Colorado Avalanche along with Dave Andreychuk for Brian Rolston, Samuel Pahlsson, Martin Grenier, and a first-round draft choice. Like any player, Bourque had long dreamed of winning the Stanley Cup, and believing it wasn't going to happen with the Bruins he asked to be traded to a contending team.

His first season with the Avs ended in disappointment again, though, as the team was eliminated by Dallas in the conference final. Bourque returned for a 22nd season, at age 40, still in pursuit of that elusive championship. Early in the 2000–01 season he recorded his 1,528th point to pass Paul Coffey as the all-time scoring leader among defencemen, and two months later he got his 1,137th assist to pass Coffey again for top spot in that department. He led all Colorado

defencemen with 59 points, and in the playoffs his incredible teammates led him to the Cup, just as he'd dreamed.

Patrick Roy was excellent in goal and won the Conn Smythe Trophy for a third time; captain Joe Sakic led all scorers with 13 goals and 26 points; and Rob Blake, a trade deadline acquisition this season, made a significant contribution to the team's defence. At the presentation of the Cup, Sakic, ever the gentleman, swung the Cup over to Bourque so he could be the first to raise the trophy.

The next day, Bourque retired. After 22 seasons, he was the career leader for defencemen in games played (1,612), goals (410), assists (1,169), and points (1,579). And he had his name on the Stanley Cup. He became one of only six players to have their number retired with two teams (Gordie Howe, Wayne Gretzky, Bobby Hull, Mark Messier, and Patrick Roy were the others), and he was inducted into the Hockey Hall of Fame in his first year of eligibility.

CEREMONY

Although Bourque's represented the first number retired by the Avalanche, the earlier incarnation of the team, the Quebec Nordiques, had retired four sweaters—J. C. Tremblay's number 3, Marc Tardif's 8, Michel Goulet's 16, and Peter Stastny's 26.

Colorado general manager Pierre Lacroix gave Bourque a painting of the mountainous countryside and said, "You will always be a part of the Colorado Avalanche family."

Accompanied by his wife and three children, Bourque spoke to the fans for seven minutes, starting with a question: "Have you ever thought about how dreams come true?" He then recounted the events that took him from Boston, where he had played 20 seasons, to Colorado, where he'd played just 94 regular-season games.

"You fans welcomed me with open arms," he continued. "Your energy sparked me every night, and your support kept us going . . . In two short years, Colorado has become a very special place for me and my family, and it always will be."

Bourque and his family then tugged on the ropes to reveal his pennant with name and number, and it began its slow ascent to the rafters.

THE GAME: Colorado Avalanche 2–Edmonton Oilers 0
The players all wore Bourque's 77 sweaters during the warm-up, after which he signed them all for auction, proceeds going to the New York Police and Firemen Widows' and Children's Benefit Fund. By the end of the night, an incredible $190,000 had been raised via the silent auction.

Edmonton had started the season with great success, but on this night the Oilers mustered just 11 shots all game, giving Patrick Roy one of the easiest shutouts of his career. In fact, it was his fourth blank sheet in the last five games, and he extended his shutout streak to 238:47 of play.

Chris Drury scored the first goal of the game at 11:45 of the first, and the defensive play of the Avs made sure that slim lead held up until Shjon Podein potted an empty netter with Tommy Salo on the bench and the visitors looking for the tying goal.

Salo was quite a bit busier, but even the 24 shots he faced hardly goes down as a shotfest in the NHL. Nevertheless, the Avs skated away with a victory in honour of Bourque's special night, and the sellout crowd of 18,007 went home happy.

99
WAYNE
GRETZKY

LOS ANGELES KINGS
OCTOBER 9, 2002

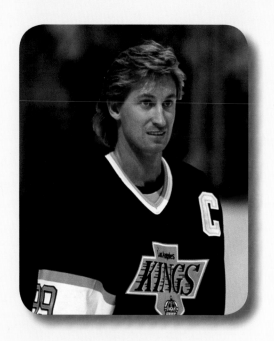

Born: Brantford, Ontario, January 26, 1961
Position: Centre
Shoots: Left
Height: 6'
Weight: 185 lbs.

HONOURS

- **Stanley Cup** 1984, 1985, 1987, 1988
- **Hart Trophy** 1980, 1981, 1982, 1983, 1984, 1985, 1986, 1987, 1989
- **Lady Byng Trophy** 1980, 1991, 1992, 1994, 1999
- **Art Ross Trophy** 1981, 1982, 1983, 1984, 1985, 1986, 1987, 1990, 1991, 1994
- **Lester B. Pearson Award** 1982, 1983, 1984, 1985, 1987
- **Conn Smythe Trophy** 1985, 1988
- **NHL All-Star Game** 1980, 1981, 1982, 1983, 1984, 1985, 1986, 1988, 1989, 1990, 1991, 1992, 1993, 1994, 1996, 1997, 1998, 1999
- **Played for Canada at Canada Cup** 1981, 1984, 1987, 1991,
- **Played for Canada at World Cup** 1996
- **Played for Canada at Olympics** 1998
- **Hockey Hall of Fame** 1999

NHL CAREER STATS

Years	Regular Season					Playoffs				
	GP	G	A	P	Pim	GP	G	A	P	Pim
1979–99	1,487	894	1,963	2,857	577	208	122	260	382	66

LOS ANGELES CAREER

The trade on August 8, 1988, that sent Wayne Gretzky to Los Angeles changed the game forever. First, it was now a given that there was no longer such a thing as an "untouchable" player. Anyone could go anywhere if the price were right.

Second, by getting Gretzky in the prime of his career, the Kings were about to toss off their west coast anonymity and become one of the focal points for the game. Gretzky did his part, on and off the ice. Although the Kings' roster wasn't stocked with players like Mark Messier, Glenn Anderson, Jari Kurri, and Paul Coffey, Gretzky made even the most pedestrian players scorers.

In his first season, he led the league with 114 assists and was second to Mario

Lemieux in scoring with 168 points. He still managed to win the Art Ross Trophy three more times, and the milestones kept piling up. Most notably, he scored his 802nd goal and 1,852nd point to become the all-time leader in those categories, surpassing his childhood hero, Gordie Howe.

Gretzky had his greatest impact in the playoffs in 1993 when he took the Kings to its first—and still only—appearance in the Final. The previous series was a seven-game battle against the Leafs, and in the deciding game he scored a hat trick at Maple Leaf Gardens, a night he later called the greatest NHL playoff game of his career. But in the finals, against Montreal, he and the Kings ran out of gas and lost in five games.

By the 1995–96 season, though, Gretzky's work was done. He was in the last year of his contract, and owner and good friend Bruce McNall faced a jail term for conspiracy and fraud. Gretzky knew his career was in its twilight, and he wanted to settle down for the rest of it. He was traded to St. Louis to be united with friend and scoring star Brett Hull, making his seven and a half years in Los Angeles a thing of the past.

Gretzky's influence on the west coast endured. Kids' leagues, roller hockey, and minor pro leagues all expanded to the west, and a new core of fans embraced the game as never before. Today, in the early 21st century, there are several Californians in the NHL, most of whom have Gretzky to thank for introducing them to the game.

CEREMONY

The last of a seeming parade of sweater retirements for Gretzky, the one in Los Angeles was important because it acknowledged his contributions to a city and a state that had never exactly been a hockey hotbed. Gretzky alone made the sport succeed in southern California, and for that was his number honoured, but he was immortalized in a statue by Eric Blome, which now stands in the plaza outside the new Staples Center.

Gretzky appeared at centre ice with parents Walter and Phyllis, his wife, Janet, and their four children—Paulina, Ty, Trevor, and Tristan. He was also joined by teammates Jari Kurri, Paul Coffey, Kelly Hrudey, Pat Conacher, Dave Taylor, and Luc Robitaille; coach Barry Melrose; general manager Rogie Vachon; commissioner Gary Bettman, and, of course, owner Bruce McNall.

To the fans, Gretzky said: "When I came here in 1988, I never thought we'd have a day like this, believe me. I want to say to all of the fans who treated me and my family so nicely, I want to thank them all."

THE GAME: Los Angeles Kings 4–Phoenix Coyotes 1

The matchup on this night was appropriate, for Gretzky's years with the Kings were spectacular, but he was now 20 per cent owner of the opposition Coyotes. Tonight, player trumped owner as the hometown Kings started slowly and finished strongly in winning their home opener, 4–1.

Although the Kings dominated play in the first 20 minutes, the game's first goal didn't come until 6:32 of the middle period when Eric Belanger staked the Kings to an early lead. Ziggy Palffy made it 2–0 before Daniil Markov got one back for the Coyotes, their only goal of the night as it turned out.

Los Angeles ensured victory midway through the third when they scored twice in a span of 32 seconds, and goalie Felix Potvin held the fort the rest of the way.

24

TERRY
O'REILLY

BOSTON BRUINS
OCTOBER 24, 2002

Born: Niagara Falls, Ontario, June 7, 1951
Position: Right wing
Shoots: Right
Height: 6'1"
Weight: 200 lbs.

HONOURS
• **NHL All-Star Game** 1975, 1978

NHL CAREER STATS

	Regular Season					Playoffs				
Years	GP	G	A	P	Pim	GP	G	A	P	Pim
1971–85	891	204	402	606	2,095	108	25	42	67	335

CAREER

They called him "Taz" because like the cartoon devil he was a maniacal, testoster-one-driven frenzy of excitement every time he stepped on the ice. Terry O'Reilly is a name that does not belong at first blush with the other retired numbers in Bruins history—Bobby Orr, Phil Esposito, Lionel Hitchman, Dit Clapper, Johnny Bucyk, Milt Schmidt, Eddie Shore, and Ray Bourque. Yet a retired number is a team honour, not a Hockey Hall of Fame honour, and O'Reilly was an important member of the Bruins in his own way.

He played all of his 14 seasons and 891 regular-season games with the Bruins, and the team made the playoffs every year from 1972 to 1985. O'Reilly wasn't a scorer so much as a bulldog, the Bobby Clarke of the Bruins, one might say, except tougher and meaner, if that's at all possible. He retired in 1985 at age 33, his body

exhausted from so much fighting and physical play, from dealing with injuries and sitting in the penalty box for more than 2,000 minutes.

He never scored 30 goals in a season, but his ability to fight for the puck created many scoring chances, and he always had his fair share of assists. In 1977–78, he had 90 points, a very respectable scoring stat for a checking right winger. O'Reilly's Bruins made it to the Cup Final three times—in 1974, 1977, and 1978—although they never won, losing first to Bernie Parent's Philadelphia Flyers and then to Ken Dryden's Montreal Canadiens, twice.

O'Reilly symbolized a typical Bruins team. He was the lunch-pail worker coach Don Cherry raved about, a guy who could chase a dump in and turn the lost play into a scoring chance. Beloved by fans for his determined effort despite a lack of skill, he was, to the Bruins, one of the immortals.

CEREMONY

Sons Conor and Evan helped O'Reilly deal with the pressures of having his number retired—some 17 years after his final game—but the evening began in perfect harmony with the way he played the game. O'Reilly was a player who worked hard every day with the limited skills he had, who earned his pay and respect honestly, and who contributed to his team's success in ways other than big goals and end-to-end rushes.

And so to get to the ice for the ceremony, O'Reilly walked down through the stands, among the people with whom he most identified—and who identified with him—and he didn't go to centre ice. He went to the area in front of the penalty box. Given that he'd spent thousands of minutes there during his career, what other part of the ice would most befit number 24?

"I can honestly say that I gave everything I had to the Boston Bruins organization," he told the crowd, "but in my heart and soul I feel that I got more back. You welcomed me with open arms and open hearts. You were patient with me as I stumbled and slipped through my first years—and my last few years."

The video tribute that began the evening exemplified what it means for a team to retire a player's number. O'Reilly was not a Hall of Famer, not a Stanley Cup hero, but he embodied what it meant to be a Bruins player. He was the very symbol of effort, determination, and perseverance, and on those merits the Bruins hierarchy and fans believed he belonged beside Orr and Espo and Schmidt in the rafters.

THE GAME: Boston Bruins 2–Ottawa Senators 2

It wasn't the best or the prettiest game, but the Bruins took a point from their first home game and moved on. All Bruins players came out for the warm-up wearing O'Reilly 24 sweaters, and just 32 seconds later Hal Gill gave the B's an early 1–0 lead after his long shot pinballed off several players in front and past goalie Patrick Lalime. It proved to be the lone score of a feisty period, and in the second it was the visiting Senators who got the only goal, this from captain Daniel Alfredsson.

Both teams scored in the third but neither could net the winner and a 2–2 tie went into the books.

Joe Thornton noted how tough it was playing their home opener under these circumstances, after six games on the road to start the season. "It's not that there's more pressure at home," he explained. "It's just that, obviously, there's a lot of hoopla, especially with Terry's big night. You get cold feet. You get a little bit more nervous in front of the home fans."

31

GRANT
FUHR

EDMONTON OILERS
OCTOBER 9, 2003

Born: Spruce Grove, Alberta, September 28, 1962
Position: Goalie
Catches: Right
Height: 5'10"
Weight: 200 lbs.

HONOURS
- **Stanley Cup** 1984, 1985, 1987, 1988, 1990
- **Vezina Trophy** 1988
- **Jennings Trophy** 1994 (with Dominik Hasek)
- **NHL All-Star Game** 1982, 1984, 1985, 1986, 1988, 1989
- **Hockey Hall of Fame** 2003

NHL CAREER STATS

Regular Season

Years	GP	W-L-T	Mins	GA	SO	GAA
1981–2000	868	403-295-114	48,945	2,756	25	3.38

Playoffs

Years	GP	W-L-T	Mins	GA	SO	GAA
1981–2000	150	92-50-0	8,834	430	6	2.92

CAREER

More than any other goalie, Grant Fuhr was hung out to dry time and again, regular season and playoffs, by the Edmonton Oilers. The Oilers were all about scoring, so if that meant five men around the enemy goal and a possible two-on-the-goalie the other way, so be it. Fuhr was there.

Such was the confidence the team had in their last line of defence that the Oilers became the highest scoring team in NHL history. Why win a game 2–0 when you could win it 7–5? That was their way of doing things. And goalie Fuhr was happy with that philosophy. Winning was what mattered, not goals-against-average (GAA).

In 868 regular season games, he had a mere 25 shutouts. In 150 playoff games, six. His career GAA was 3.38 in the regular schedule and 2.92 in the playoffs—not sparkling numbers. Fuhr's modus operandi wasn't about stopping them all—it was about stopping the last one at the vital time.

In his 10 years with Edmonton, Fuhr was seldom the clear-cut goalie through the 80-game schedule. He often split the duties with Bill Ranford, but in the play-offs coach Glen Sather relied heavily—if not entirely—on Fuhr. A lefty, he had lightning legs, a quick glove, and great stickhandling abilities.

Fuhr was drafted eighth overall by the Oilers in 1981, an uncommonly high selection to use on a goalie in those days. But he made the team at his first camp, played 48 games as a rookie and won 28, and became a key member of a team that strove for offence on every shift.

Fuhr was happy facing one breakaway after another and then firing the puck up ice to create a scoring chance at the other end. And if anyone doubted his true ability to stop the puck, his record internationally was sensational. Fuhr was the only goalie for Canada at the historic Canada Cup in 1987, including the three-game final against the Soviets that all ended 6–5 and which remains arguably the greatest three-game series ever played.

CEREMONY

The fourth Oilers player to have his number retired after Al Hamilton, Wayne Gretzky, and Jari Kurri, Grant Fuhr began the ceremony after the house lights were turned off. A single spotlight on the ice followed him as he skated onto the ice in full equipment and made his way to the Oilers goal, a trip he had made hundreds of times in the past.

On his way he passed four notable teammates, goalies all—Bill Ranford, Ron Low, Eddie Mio, and Eldon "Pokey" Reddick—who served as his backups at various times. He skated a victory lap and settled beside his wife, Candice, and their three daughters—Janine, Rochelle, and Kendyl.

A video tribute moved Fuhr almost to tears, and then he got to say a few words and thank the people most important to the evening—current general manager and former teammate Kevin Lowe; scout Barry Fraser; coach and GM Glen Sather, for drafting him, and giving him the confidence to be number one.

"Watching the video, seeing the goalies, the fans," Fuhr began, "so many great memories. My teammates were my family, one beautiful family. Now that I'm not playing, the thing I miss most is not going down to the rink to see my teammates."

THE GAME: Edmonton Oilers 5–San Jose Sharks 2

The 2003–04 season opener was successful for the Oilers as they pulled away in the third period to win convincingly at the Skyreach Centre. A tentative first period in which they were outplayed by the Sharks gave way to greater confidence in the second.

Shawn Horcoff opened the scoring at 7:25 of that period to give the home side a 1–0 lead after 40 minutes, but Jonathan Cheechoo tied the game early in the third on a San Jose power play.

Soon after, the teams exchanged goals, but the Oilers scored three times in the final five minutes to win handily. Raffi Torres got the eventual game winner at 14:48, but Ryan Smyth's two goals in a span of 72 seconds was really the nail in the coffin.

33

PATRICK
ROY

COLORADO AVALANCHE
OCTOBER 28, 2003

Born: Quebec City, Quebec, October 5, 1965
Position: Goalie
Catches: Left
Height: 6'2"
Weight: 185 lbs.

HONOURS
- **Stanley Cup** 1986, 1993, 1996, 2001
- **Conn Smythe Trophy** 1986, 1993, 2001
- **Jennings Trophy** 1987, 1988, 1989 (with Brian Hayward), 1992, 2002
- **Vezina Trophy** 1989, 1990, 1992
- **NHL All-Star Game** 1988, 1990, 1991, 1992, 1993, 1994, 1997, 1998, 2001, 2002, 2003
- **Hockey Hall of Fame** 2006

NHL CAREER STATS

Regular Season

Years	GP	W-L-T	Mins	GA	SO	GAA
1984–2003	1,029	551-315-131	60,235	2,546	66	2.54

Playoffs

Years	GP	W-L-T	Mins	GA	SO	GAA
1984–2003	247	151-94-0	15,209	584	23	2.30

COLORADO CAREER

Who could know that the destiny of the Colorado Avalanche would be decided on December 2, 1995, in a game between the Montreal Canadiens and the Detroit Red Wings? On that night, Patrick Roy had the worst game of his life. He couldn't stop a beach ball, let alone a puck. The trouble was that coach Mario Tremblay refused to pull Roy even though it was clear that that would have been the smart play.

So, Roy allowed one goal after another, not leaving the game until he had allowed nine in all. He made one simple save and raised his arms in derision as fans cheered equally mockingly. When he skated off the ice, he spoke with team president Ronald Corey, seated behind the players' bench, telling him that he had played

his last game with the team. Taking the vow literally, Corey traded Roy to the Colorado Avalanche, a team that had moved to Denver from Quebec at the start of the season.

In the last half of the season, Roy played 39 games, winning 22, giving the Avs world-class goaltending every night. By the time the playoffs were at hand, he had integrated seamlessly with his teammates and they went on an historic run. Roy played all 22 games, and although captain Joe Sakic won the Conn Smythe Trophy, the goalie's fingerprints were all over this victory.

Roy settled in and played the rest of his career in Colorado, returning to the Cup Final in 2001 and leading the team to victory for the second time in six seasons. He won the Smythe this time for a record third time (1986 and '93 in Montreal). Had Roy not arrived in Colorado, and had the Avs not won two Cups, who knows what fate the team might have enjoyed on its return to Denver?

By the time he retired in 2003, he had set the bar high indeed for other record-chasing goalies. Roy was the first goalie to play 1,000 games (finishing with a total of 1,029), and his 551 wins was also a record (since surpassed by Martin Brodeur) as were his 60,235 minutes played (also bettered by Brodeur, early in the 2009–10 season).

CEREMONY

The brisk 19-minute celebration for Patrick Roy was tasteful and appropriate and covered all the necessary bases, starting with a six-minute video tribute. Roy stepped onto the Pepsi Center ice with his wife, Michele, and their three children, Jonathan, Frederick, and Jana, to a rousing ovation.

Team owner Stan Kronke presented him with a huge oil painting of a mountain scene then Roy delivered a four-minute speech that was honest and from the heart. "It will be more than an honour to see my jersey going beside Ray Bourque's," he said to a loud ovation. "It shows how fast the Avalanche organization has established a winning tradition in such a short time."

On contemplating his arrival in Denver in 1995, he admitted to being, "nervous, facing the unknown, language problems, and especially nervousness about not producing at the level expected of me. But you—the fans and my friends—have made sure that our eight years in Denver will never be forgotten."

"I'm retiring with the feeling I have done everything I could do to be my best. My passion and respect for the game guided me over my career. Once again, thank you all from the bottom of my heart."

THE GAME: Colorado Avalanche 4–Calgary Flames 2

David Aebischer, the heir apparent to Roy in goal, said it best after the victory: "[The win is for] Patrick, and all he did for the organization. I think the whole team worked tonight for him."

A quick start propelled the Avs to victory. They scored the only two goals of the opening period, one from Milan Hejduk, a known scorer, and another from defensive defenceman Adam Foote. Martin Gelinas pulled the Flames to within one goal in the second, but then fourth-liner Jim Cummins scored for the first time in more than two years to give the Avalanche their two-goal lead again.

And again, in the third, Gelinas closed the gap, only to see Rob Blake seal the win with an empty netter with just 30 seconds left on the clock. Aebischer did his part this night, making 26 saves and earning the game's first star for his excellent, Roy-inspired effort.

8

CAM NEELY

BOSTON BRUINS
JANUARY 12, 2004

Born: Comox, British Columbia, June 6, 1965
Position: Right wing
Shoots: Right
Height: 6'1"
Weight: 218 lbs.

HONOURS
• **Bill Masterton Trophy** 1994
• **NHL All-Star Game** 1988, 1989, 1990, 1991, 1996
• **Hockey Hall of Fame** 2005

NHL CAREER STATS

	Regular Season					Playoffs				
Years	GP	G	A	P	Pim	GP	G	A	P	Pim
1983–96	726	395	299	694	1,241	93	57	32	89	168

CAREER

The fact that Cam Neely had to retire at age 30 because injuries had reduced him to being unable to skate properly doesn't diminish the impact he had on the Boston Bruins and NHL during his incredible career. Although he was drafted a lofty ninth overall by Vancouver in 1983, it was his 10 years in Boston that defined his career.

Neely played for the Canucks for three years, and in retrospect these were apprentice years during which he learned the game and grew mentally and physically. By the time he was traded to Boston in 1986 with a first-round draft choice (Glen Wesley) for Barry Pederson, he was ready to become a superstar and render the deal one of the most lopsided in league history.

The term power forward was created with Neely in mind. Big and strong, he used his physical play to create scoring chances. He fought when he had to, which was plenty often, and when he wasn't fighting he was using his hands to let

go bullet shots and score a bucketful of goals. The problem was that the more physically he played, the more often he was hurt. However, his first five seasons with the Bruins were all fairly healthy ones.

The Bruins made it to the Stanley Cup Final twice during these early years, in 1988 and 1990, losing both times to Edmonton. Neely had two seasons of 55 and 51 goals, respectively, in 1989–90 and 1990–91, but then over the next two years he played just 22 games. A knee injury cost him most of one season, and a hip and thigh injury, which proved his final undoing, cost him another.

But just when it seemed he was down and out, he rallied in extraordinary fashion. He started the 1993–94 season as if in perfect health, and scored 50 goals in the first 49 games, one of a small group of players to reach 50 in 50. Ironically, the night he scored his 50th goal, his hip became a problem again and he missed the rest of the season.

His final two years were also failed attempts to regain his health and scoring touch, although he still managed 27 and 26 goals. Despite his woes, he retired in 1996 with 395 career goals and was known as one of the toughest and purest goal scorers of his era. Had he been healthy and played a full career, who knows how many goals he might have scored? Sadly, we'll never find out.

CEREMONY

The retiring of Neely's number 8 was not just for a player but for a style of play. There was no purer scorer in the game, but there was also no one tougher and more combative, either. He was the very embodiment of power forward, and when he stepped on the ice in full equipment one last time the Bruins fans gave him a thunderous ovation as they had for so many of his big hits and big goals.

Neely was joined by his wife, Paulina; son, Jack; and daughter, Ava. They all helped raise the number 8 to the rafters where it settled in between Phil Esposito's 7 and Johnny Bucyk's 9. Also participating were Milt Schmidt, Ray Bourque, Terry O'Reilly, and Bucyk.

THE GAME: Boston Bruins 4–Buffalo Sabres 3

It seemed like the Boston Bruins were playing catch-up all night long, yet in the end they emerged victorious to close out Neely's special night. Buffalo Sabres' Daniel Brière scored a little more than four minutes after the opening faceoff, and Joe Thornton tied the game for the Bruins five minutes later. Before the end of the period, however, Jochen Hecht had put the Sabres ahead again.

Jason Botterill put Buffalo in the driver's seat with an early goal in the second, but just when it seemed the Sabres had the game well under control Patrice Bergeron gave the Bruins life. His late goal made it 3–2, and it was all Boston in the third. The Bruins scored the only two goals, thanks to Bergeron and Sergei Samsonov, and the Sabres had their chances to tie but couldn't convert. In the end, the 17,565 fans left the Fleet Center happy, as did their greatest power forward, Cameron M. Neely.

35

MIKE
RICHTER

NEW YORK RANGERS
FEBRUARY 4, 2004

Born: Abington, Pennsylvania, September 22, 1966
Position: Goalie
Catches: Left
Height: 5'11"
Weight: 185 lbs.

HONOURS
- Stanley Cup 1994
- Lester Patrick Award 2009
- NHL All-Star Game 1992, 1994, 2000
- Led USA to World Cup of Hockey victory 1996 (named tournament MVP)
- Won silver medal with United States at Olympics 2002
- U.S. Hockey Hall of Fame 2008

NHL CAREER STATS

Regular Season

Years	GP	W-L-T	Mins	GA	SO	GAA
1988–2003	666	301-258-73	38,183	1,840	24	2.89

Playoffs

Years	GP	W-L-T	Mins	GA	SO	GAA
1988–2003	76	41-33-0	4,514	202	9	2.68

CAREER

The combination of playing for the Rangers in New York and representing the United States internationally makes Mike Richter the pin-up boy for American hockey. A gentleman and gracious player who was among the world's best goalies of his generation, he accomplished just about everything a kid might dream about.

A 1985 draft choice, Richter didn't make it to the NHL until four years later, but by this time he had already appeared in two World Junior (U20) Championships, two World Championships, and the 1988 Olympics. He joined a team on the upswing and shared the goaltending duties with John Vanbiesbrouck, but eventually it was clear that two number-one goalies was one too many.

Vanbiesbrouck was traded in the summer of 1993, and not coincidentally Richter's increased work schedule coincided with the team's historic run to the Stanley Cup. That 1993–94 season saw him play 68 games and win a league-best 42, and in the playoffs he was nothing short of outstanding. The New York Rangers and the Vancouver Canucks went the full seven games for the Cup, the Blueshirts emerging victorious for the first time since 1940.

Richter had two other moments of particular greatness during the 1990s. He led the United States to victory over Canada in the inaugural World Cup in 1996, almost single-handedly keeping his team in the best-of-three Final and being named tournament MVP. He then played for his country at the first NHL-led Olympics in Nagano in 1998. In 2002, however, he made amends, leading the Americans to the gold-medal game before losing to Canada, 5–2, and settling for a silver medal.

By the time Richter retired prematurely in 2003, the result of a concussion, his place in both Rangers and Team USA history had been well established.

CEREMONY

One of the most beloved Rangers of all time was given one of the greatest send-offs in the game. The 45-minute ceremony, hosted by John Davidson, started with a video of highlights from Richter's career. Then a veritable who's who of teammates and former greats was introduced—Walt Tkaczuk, Steve Vickers, Jan Erixon, Ron Greschner, Glenn Anderson, Nick Kypreos, Stephane Matteau, Adam Graves, Rod Gilbert, and Ed Giacomin.

Captain Mark Messier said a few words, finishing with, "Every time past, present, and future Rangers look up there—" he motioned to the rafters "—they'll know what a champion is supposed to look like."

Richter was presented with some fantastic gifts befitting his 14 years with the team: a photo collage depicting his career, a silver-plated net with the names of all 219 teammates engraved on the posts and crossbar, and a scholarship fund in his name. Then, the Zamboni doors opened to allow a reproduction of a 1940 Cris Craft mahogany boat to slide onto the ice.

Richter was joined by his wife, Veronica, and their two sons, Thomas and James. Appropriately, the banner raising took place right above the home goal, where the number would watch over all future Rangers goalies.

THE GAME: Minnesota Wild 4–New York Rangers 3

The Rangers thought they had overcome a sluggish start, but just when it seemed they were confident of victory, the Wild rallied and claimed the two points.

Minnesota jumped into a 2–0 lead early in the second period thanks to goals from Antti Laaksonen early in the first and Sergei Zholtok early in the second, but then the Rangers newly acquired star Jaromir Jagr took over and almost single-handedly gave the Rangers a 3–2 lead. He set up Petr Nedved's goal less than two minutes after Zholtok had scored, and then Jagr scored twice later in the period to give the home side a 3–2 lead after 40 minutes.

The third was all Minnesota, though, as Zholtok got his second of the game and Marian Gaborik scored the winner at 13:34. Mike Dunham was the New York goalie and didn't have a Richter-like night in net.

"In between the second and third we talked about getting a jump on them," Gaborik said of the comeback.

7

PAUL COFFEY

EDMONTON OILERS
OCTOBER 18, 2005

Born: Weston, Ontario, June 1, 1961
Position: Defence
Shoots: Left
Height: 6'
Weight: 205 lbs.

HONOURS
- **Stanley Cup** 1984, 1985, 1987, 1991
- **Norris Trophy** 1985, 1986, 1995
- **NHL All-Star Game** 1982, 1983, 1984, 1985, 1986, 1988, 1989, 1990, 1991, 1992, 1993, 1994, 1996, 1997
- **NHL First All-Star Team** 1985, 1986, 1989, 1995
- **Played for Canada in Canada Cup** 1984, 1987, 1991
- **Played for Canada in World Cup** 1996
- **Hockey Hall of Fame** 2004

NHL CAREER STATS

	Regular Season					Playoffs				
Years	GP	G	A	P	Pim	GP	G	A	P	Pim
1980–2000	1,409	396	1,135	1,531	1,802	194	59	137	196	264

CAREER

There is surely no disputing that as Bobby Orr was to the 1960s and '70s, Paul Coffey was to the 1980s and '90s. The defenceman with the powerful, brilliant, and free-flowing stride was a genius with the puck, perhaps the purest skater the game has ever known. Drafted sixth overall by Edmonton in 1980, he joined the Oilers that fall as a 19-year-old and embarked on a career with three distinct parts: his glory years in Edmonton, his mature years in Pittsburgh, and his wandering years with a variety of teams.

Coffey joined the Oilers at a time when there were many young players on the cusp of greatness, growing and developing on and off the ice. Of course, these included Wayne Gretzky, Mark Messier, Glenn Anderson, Jari Kurri, and Grant Fuhr.

For Coffey, that meant setting his sights on Orr-like production. In his second season he had 29 goals, 29 again in his third, and then rattled off years of 40, 37,

and 48 goals. This last was a single-season record, eclipsing Orr's 46. He finished that year with 138 points, one shy of tying Orr's points record for a blueliner.

Coffey was cut from the same cloth as Number Four. A pure skater, he liked to rush the puck, join the attack, close in on goal, and be a part of the offense as a fourth forward. In his seven years with the team he produced more than 650 points, but he was the first of the great nucleus to become disenchanted in Edmonton.

The summer of 1987 was a stressful one for him. He played for Canada at the Canada Cup, coached by Sather, but the two men were also involved in acrimonious contract talks. After the great Canadian win, Coffey didn't report to Edmonton's training camp, and several weeks later Sather traded him to Pittsburgh.

He stayed nearly five years with the Penguins, and why not? Mario Lemieux was leading that team to greatness, and Coffey did more than his share to contribute, recording back-to-back seasons of more than 100 points and winning the Cup with the Penguins in 1991. He was traded to Los Angeles midway through the next year, though, and missed out on the second Pittsburgh Cup. That's when Coffey's wandering ways set in. Over the last nine years of his career he played for no fewer than seven teams.

In retrospect, Coffey's years with Edmonton were the highlight of his career. No defenceman except Orr could be said to skate and move the way he did, and his incredible teammates produced more offence as a group than even Orr, Esposito, Hodge, and the Bruins of the early 1970s.

CEREMONY

As was becoming tradition, Coffey came out for the ceremony dressed as if ready to play, full equipment right down to the shoulder pads. He skated a few laps around the ice, picking out familiar faces in the crowd, season's ticket holders, friends, people who continued to sit in the same seats game after game, year after year.

Almost all of the old Oilers were there. Wayne Gretzky was back, coaching the opposition Coyotes on this night, as was general manager and former defenceman Kevin Lowe. Jari Kurri flew in, and Charlie Huddy was also on hand. Coffey's family, of course, was by his side: wife Stephanie, daughter Savannah, sons Blake and Christian.

Former coach Glen Sather, now with the Rangers, taped a message for "Coff," who ended the night by taking a pass from Huddy and skating in alone before firing the puck into the net one last time. Then the number 7 banner was unfurled and raised to the rafters to stand beside Fuhr's.

THE GAME: Phoenix Coyotes 4–Edmonton Oilers 3 (OT)
Gretzky turned out to be a stronger factor than Coffey on this night as the visiting Coyotes skated away with a 4–3 win in overtime. Derek Morris beat Jussi Markkanen with a wrist shot at 1:00 of the extra period on a power play to give Phoenix the victory and spoil a fine comeback by Edmonton.

The Coyotes scored the only two goals of the first period, both by Oleg Saprykin. Igor Ulanov got one back in the second, but Shane Doan, again with the extra man, made it 3–1 early in the third.

That's when Edmonton took over. Michael Peca made it 3–2 at 4:38 and then Marty Reasoner tied the game, 3–3, just over three minutes later, to send the game to overtime.

12 DICKIE MOORE

MONTREAL CANADIENS
NOVEMBER 12, 2005

Born: Montreal, Quebec, January 6, 1931
Position: Left wing
Shoots: Left
Height: 5'10"
Weight: 168 lbs.

HONOURS
- **Stanley Cup** 1953, 1956, 1957, 1958, 1959, 1960
- **Art Ross Trophy** 1958, 1959
- **NHL All-Star Game** 1953, 1956, 1957, 1958, 1959, 1960
- **NHL First All-Star Team** 1958, 1959
- **Hockey Hall of Fame** 1974

NHL CAREER STATS

| Years | Regular Season | | | | | Playoffs | | | | |
	GP	G	A	P	Pim	GP	G	A	P	Pim
1951–68	719	261	347	608	652	135	46	64	110	122

CAREER

Few bodies have been put through the paces the way Dickie Moore's had by the time he retired from hockey in 1963, again in 1965, and finally in 1968. Born with weak knees, he broke his leg twice as a kid, but he kept on pursuing his NHL dream with quiet resolve. He won the Memorial Cup with the Montreal Royals in 1949 and again the next year when the team was known as the Jr. Canadiens.

The Habs eased Moore into the lineup over the course of three seasons (1951–54), the last of these ensuring his full-time status the next year after he led the '54 playoffs in assists and points and helped the team to the Stanley Cup Final. Moore was also part of the Habs teams that won five Cups in a row (1956–60), but his most amazing feat came during the 1957–58 season. He broke his wrist halfway through the schedule, but rather than sit at home and recuperate he asked doctors to fit him with a cast that would allow him to keep playing.

Not only did he play all 70 games of the season, he led the league with 36 goals and won the Art Ross Trophy for his 84 total points. The next year, he led the NHL with 55 assists and established a single-season record of 96 points, besting Gordie Howe's previous mark by one point.

Moore had the pleasure of playing on a line with Maurice Richard and Jean Béliveau, and Béliveau was quick to point out to one and all that while he and the Rocket got most of the credit for the line's success, it was Moore who kept the threesome efficient and focused on each player's duties. Moore was more responsible for going to the corners or retrieving loose pucks, while the others were required to go to the net or the opening ready for a pass.

Moore had at least 20 goals in six of seven seasons during his prime, this despite suffering three shoulder separations among his many injuries. He retired in 1963 because his body could take no more, but after a year and a half of rest he decided that, well, his body could take more after all. He played the 1964–65 season with the Leafs but scored only two goals in 38 games before retiring again.

Still, Moore came back to play one more time, this after a break of two years. St. Louis coach Scotty Bowman convinced the veteran that he could help with the expansion team, and Moore dressed for 27 more games, scoring only five goals. In the 1968 playoffs, though, he rounded into form, helping the Blues to the Cup Final and averaging nearly a point a game, just like the old days. The team lost in four straight games, though, to his former Habs. After that, he retired a third and final time.

12

YVAN COURNOYER

MONTREAL CANADIENS
NOVEMBER 12, 2005

Born: Drummondville, Quebec, November 22, 1943
Position: Right wing
Shoots: Left
Height: 5'7"
Weight: 178 lbs.

HONOURS
- **Stanley Cup** 1965, 1966, 1968, 1969, 1971, 1973, 1976, 1977, 1978, 1979
- **Conn Smythe Trophy** 1973
- **NHL All-Star Game** 1967, 1971, 1972, 1973, 1974, 1978
- **Played for Canada in 1972 Summit Series**
- **Hockey Hall of Fame** 1982

NHL CAREER STATS

Years	Regular Season					Playoffs				
	GP	G	A	P	Pim	GP	G	A	P	Pim
1963–79	968	428	435	863	255	147	64	63	127	47

CAREER

They called him "Roadrunner" because he was small and fast. Very, very fast. He was also a winner, a fully active member of two dynasties with the Canadiens, one in the 1960s and another in the later '70s. In all, Cournoyer won the Stanley Cup 10 times.

He joined the Habs for five games during the 1963–64 season, scoring four times and leaving no doubt as to his capabilities. The next year he scored only seven times in 55 games, but no matter—he had made the team. The trouble was that coach Toe Blake wanted more from Cournoyer than just speed, and the player was reluctant to play in a way that would compromise his offensive talents. So, he played mostly on the power play. Even still, Cournoyer managed 25 and 28 goals in 1966–67 and 1967–68, respectively, but when Blake resigned at the end of the year and Claude Ruel took over, the Roadrunner got more ice time and responded with 43 goals.

The combination of speed and strength made him a force, even if he was only 5'7". More to the point, he was also one of those players whose performance improved the bigger the game. In the 1973 playoffs, he set a league record with 15 goals in just 17 games and led all players with 25 points, as well. That year the Habs won the Cup, his sixth, and he added the Conn Smythe Trophy to his booty.

In 1975, Cournoyer was named captain, a position he held until early in the 1978–79 season when he retired because of a serious and persistent back injury. Although he never won the Lady Byng Trophy, he was among the very cleanest players in the game, accruing a mere 255 penalty minutes over his 16 seasons.

Cournoyer played for Canada at the 1972 Summit Series and was the first person to hug Paul Henderson in the final minute of game eight after Henderson had scored the winning goal. Although he would have to wait until 2005 to see his number 12 in the rafters, no one wore it after him and he was inducted into the Hockey Hall of Fame as soon as he became eligible.

CEREMONY

Dick Irvin and Richard Garneau were joined by Jean Béliveau as hosts of the ceremony, which saw both Dickie Moore and Yvan Cournoyer have their number 12 retired.

Gifts for both men included a painting from artist Michel Lapensée, a commemorative watch from Birks with the number 12 engraved on it, and a donation of $25,000 to their charity of choice courtesy of the Canadiens Children's Foundation.

Montreal assistant captains Richard Zednik and Craig Rivet helped to release the banners to the rafters while captain Saku Koivu joined both honourees at centre ice. Béliveau introduced Moore, an easy assignment given they were highly productive line mates for many years. "When there was a battle for the puck in the corner, guess who came out with the puck?" Béliveau asked, rhetorically. He also provided the easy answer: "Dickie did."

In his speech, Moore thanked his mother for helping him get to the NHL, and finished by thanking his coach, who was so critical to the team's many successes. "Our coach, Toe Blake, who brought us five Stanley Cups—what a gentleman! He helped me through life, and not only hockey."

THE GAME: Toronto Maple Leafs 5–Montreal Canadiens 4 (OT)
Despite losing a back-and-forth game to Toronto, 5–4 in overtime, Montreal still maintained the top spot in the Eastern Conference after picking up one point in the standings. The Habs trailed 2–0 and 3–2, took the lead 4–3, and then watched the win slip away late in the third period and then again in overtime.

The damage was done first by a lucky goal from Jason Allison with less than three minutes to go to tie the game for Toronto. Then, in the final minute of the five-minute overtime, the Leafs, with the league's best power play, were given a man advantage courtesy of a too-many-men penalty to the home side. Jeff O'Neill made no mistake with his shot, giving the Leafs the win.

"It was a miscommunication on our bench, a lack of concentration during a line change," coach Claude Julien admitted after the game. "We were the better team tonight, there's no denying that. We took it to them early and never stopped working. It was a good team effort overall."

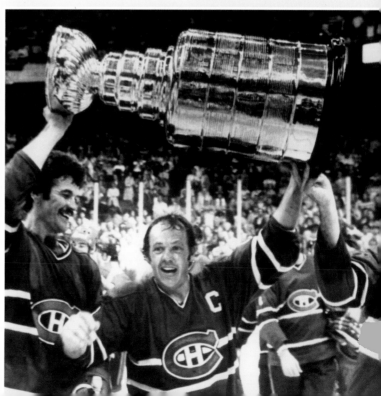

18

DANNY GARE

BUFFALO SABRES
NOVEMBER 22, 2005

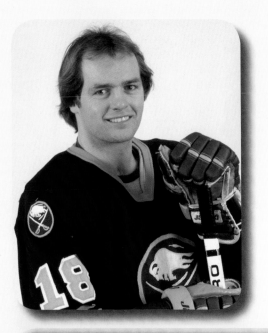

Born: Nelson, British Columbia, May 14, 1954
Position: Right wing
Shoots: Right
Height: 5'9"
Weight: 175 lbs.

HONOURS
- NHL All-Star Game 1980, 1981
- NHL Second All-Star Team 1980
- Reached 50 goals in 1975–76 and 56 goals in 1979–80

NHL CAREER STATS

	Regular Season					Playoffs				
Years	GP	G	A	P	Pim	GP	G	A	P	Pim
1974–87	827	354	331	685	1,285	64	25	21	46	195

CAREER

Players get only one crack at scoring in their first NHL game, and Gare not only managed this feat but came mighty close to one of the oldest and toughest records to break—Gus Bodnar's first goal just 15 seconds into his NHL career, in 1943. Gare scored his first goal just 18 seconds after stepping onto an NHL sheet of ice, but far from this being his only claim to fame, it was a portent of things to come.

Gare was a high-scoring junior who was deemed too small for the bigger, tougher world of the NHL. While Bruce Boudreau, another small, talented player of the 1970s, got precious few chances to prove himself with the Toronto Maple Leafs, though, Gare joined the Buffalo Sabres in the fall of 1974, the same year the team had drafted him 29th overall. He scored 31 goals as a rookie and made it clear size was not an issue for him. The team also went to its first Stanley Cup Final, losing to Philadelphia in six tough games.

The next year, Gare hit the 50 mark for the first time, but injuries limited him to 35 games and 11 goals the next year. He slowly worked his way back, scoring a career-best 56 times in 1979–80, but the team had little success in the playoffs. After one more excellent season (46 goals), Gare stumbled noticeably and his production dropped. He was traded to Detroit, a weak Red Wings team that played only six playoff games in five years, and Gare retired in 1986 after a few games with Edmonton.

At the height of his powers, with the Sabres, he was a pure scorer much more than a passer, but his quick release and deadly accurate shot made him a vital part of any success the Sabres enjoyed in the late 1970s. He was also very solid defensively and could more than hold his own when the going got tough, as it often did for a small player who had to prove himself night after night. Gare also played for Canada at both the 1976 and 1981 Canada Cup tournaments.

CEREMONY

Gare was joined on the ice for the ceremony by the entire roster of the current team, each wearing a number 18 sweater with the Gare nameplate on the back. Later, Gare signed each one and they were auctioned off, profits going to the Buffalo Sabres Foundation.

Joining Gare and the active roster were many alumni, notably the three members of the French Connection Line.

THE GAME: New York Rangers 3–Buffalo Sabres 2 (SO)
Not only did the game have historic value for Danny Gare, it was important in the annals of the NHL as well. For starters, this was the first game to go to a shootout at HSBC Arena. And second, it featured both Buffalo goalies in the penalty-shot contest. Of course, these things happened because twice the Sabres failed to hold a lead during regulation time.

After a scoreless first period, Chris Drury opened the scoring for the Sabres at 8:10 of the second, only to see Jaromir Jagr tie the game a few minutes later. In the third period, the pattern repeated itself as Jay McKee put Buffalo up 2–1, and Mikael Nylander tied it with just 4:14 left in regulation.

A scoreless five-minute overtime gave Sabres' fans their first taste of the shootout, but goalie Mika Noronen allowed a goal on the first shot by Martin Straka and then pulled himself from the game. He had injured his groin in the third period and tried to finish, but coach Lindy Ruff saw no useful purpose to this and inserted Martin Biron instead.

Incredibly, five of the six shootout shots were goals. Only the last one, by Drury, missed and decided the outcome. "I pulled my groin with eight minutes left in the third period," Noronen related. "In the shootout, I couldn't go side to side. Lindy decided to take me out, and I can't argue with that. My thing is, I didn't want Marty [Biron] to come into the game cold and face Nylander and Jagr."

That's what happened, and both Rangers players scored.

11

MARK MESSIER

NEW YORK RANGERS
JANUARY 12, 2006

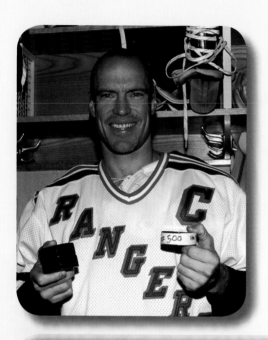

Born: Edmonton, Alberta, January 18, 1961
Position: Forward
Shoots: Left
Height: 6'1"
Weight: 205 lbs.

HONOURS
- **Stanley Cup** 1984, 1985, 1987, 1988, 1990, 1994
- **Hart Trophy** 1990, 1992
- **Lester B. Pearson Award** 1990, 1992
- **Conn Smythe Trophy** 1984
- **NHL All-Star Game** 1982, 1983, 1984, 1986, 1988, 1989, 1990, 1991, 1992, 1994, 1996, 1997, 1998, 2000, 2004
- **Hockey Hall of Fame** 2007

NHL CAREER STATS

	Regular Season					Playoffs				
Years	GP	G	A	P	Pim	GP	G	A	P	Pim
1979–2004	1,756	694	1,193	1,887	1,910	236	109	186	295	244

NEW YORK RANGERS CAREER

Mark Messier spent the first 12 seasons of his NHL career with the Edmonton Oilers, winning five Stanley Cups and recording five 100-point seasons. He was traded to the Rangers prior to the 1991–92 season for Bernie Nicholls, Steven Rice, Louie DeBrusk, and $1.5 million. "Paramount owned the Garden then," New York GM Neil Smith explained. "We had signed Adam Graves, but Stanley Jaffe of Paramount wanted us to do something bigger. Nothing was bigger than Messier, and I knew there was no way the Rangers were going to win the Stanley Cup if we didn't bring in someone who had done it before."

Messier immediately agreed to a five-year, $13 million contract, and in his first season he had 107 points, won the Hart Trophy, and took the Rangers to the second round of the playoffs. The next year, the team faltered and missed the

playoffs, despite Messier's 91 points. Although his point production dipped further in his third year with the team, 1993–94 had a magical ending.

The Rangers played the New Jersey Devils in the conference final in April 1994 and trailed 3–2 in games with the prospect of being eliminated in game six in the Meadowlands. But Messier guaranteed a victory in that game, a guarantee he signed himself with a hat trick performance in a 4–2 win.

The Rangers went home for game seven, won 2–1 on a Stephane Matteau goal in overtime, and headed to the Cup Final to face Vancouver. That series, too, went to the deciding game, and the Rangers used their boisterous home crowd to propel them to a 3–2 victory and the city's first Cup since 1940. Messier had 12 goals and 30 points in the team's 23-game playoff run.

During Messier's sweater retirement week teammate Kevin Lowe related that, "I remember him one time saying to me, 'We've got to slay the dragons. We've got to slay the demons and everything else that's gone on here for a lot of years in order to do this.'" Messier did just that.

After the Cup win, he spent three more years with the Rangers, went to the Canucks for three years, and then played the last four years of his career back on Broadway. New York didn't make the playoffs in his final stint with the team, but that didn't matter. The accomplishments and leadership in 1993–94 that brought the Cup to the team were everlasting and earned him a lifetime pass to the city.

CEREMONY

It took 77 minutes to honour Messier in a manner befitting "the captain." Incredibly, almost every member of the 1994 Stanley Cup team appeared on the red carpet to pay tribute to their leader. Only four players couldn't make it because they were either still playing (Brian Leetch, Sergei Zubov, and Alexander Karpovtsev) or coaching (Greg Gilbert, in the OHL). Leetch, Messier's longtime roommate and best friend, delivered a recorded video message, and Alexei Kovalev of the Canadiens flew in during an off day.

Among the many gifts bestowed upon Messier were a fishing chair for his yacht, rods and reels shaped like hockey sticks, a team portrait of the '94 Cup team, and, most important, a cheque for $211,000 for Messier's Tomorrows Children's Fund.

As Beethoven's Symphony No. 9 played, the number 11 was hoisted to the rafters. Messier, his dad, Doug, and son, Douglas, watched in teary-eyed awe. Only three other numbers have been retired in team history: Ed Giacomin's 1, Rod Gilbert's 7, and teammate Mike Richter's 35. "This is like every big game I ever played condensed into one night," the crying hero explained during his 14-minute speech.

THE GAME: New York Rangers 5–Edmonton Oilers 4 (OT)
Playing with number 11 patches on their shoulders, the Rangers scored a dramatic 5–4 overtime win in a back-and-forth game. The home side went ahead 1–0 in the first period, only to fall behind 3–1 midway through the second. New York rallied to go ahead 4–3 early in the third, and in the extra period Jaromir Jagr scored his 28th goal of the season just 14 seconds from the start to give his team the win.

Coincidentally, it was Jagr who also scored the game winner for Pittsburgh in Madison Square Garden the afternoon of Wayne Gretzky's final game, on April 18, 1999, a 2–1 overtime win by the Penguins.

10 RON FRANCIS

CAROLINA HURRICANES
JANUARY 28, 2006

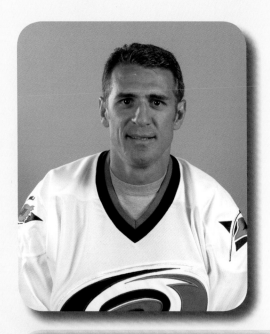

Born: Sault Ste. Marie, Ontario, March 1, 1963
Position: Centre
Shoots: Left
Height: 6'3"
Weight: 200 lbs.

HONOURS
- **Stanley Cup** 1991, 1992
- **Frank Selke Trophy** 1995
- **Lady Byng Trophy** 1995, 1998, 2002
- **King Clancy Memorial Trophy** 2002
- **Hockey Hall of Fame** 2007

NHL CAREER STATS

	Regular Season					Playoffs				
Years	GP	G	A	P	Pim	GP	G	A	P	Pim
1981–2004	1,731	549	1,249	1,798	979	171	46	97	143	95

CAREER

When Ron Francis was drafted fourth overall by the Hartford Whalers in 1981, the 18-year-old could not possibly have imagined the career that lay ahead for him. Although he played part of the next year back in junior with his hometown Sault Ste. Marie Greyhounds in the OHL, Francis played most of the 1981–82 season with the Whalers. He never looked back.

Francis was a complete player. Skilled offensively and responsible in his own end, he was physical yet gentlemanly, competitive yet respected by teammates and opponents alike. He could score goals but was better known for his passing, but perhaps his greatest asset was the most intangible—his leadership.

After nearly 10 seasons in Hartford, he was traded to Pittsburgh, a team on the cusp of greatness. During more than seven seasons with the Penguins he won the only two Stanley Cup titles of his career, in 1990–91 and 1991–92, playing

second-line centre behind the great Mario Lemieux. During his years in Pittsburgh, the Whalers relocated to Carolina and became the Hurricanes. Francis signed with Carolina in the summer of 1998 and spent most of the next six seasons there, captaining an ever-improving team.

His career numbers are staggering. In 23 seasons, he is second all-time in assists with 1,249, behind only Wayne Gretzky. His 1,731 regular-season games played trails only Gordie Howe and Mark Messier; and his 1,798 total points is fourth behind Gretzky, Messier, and Howe. He reached 100 points in a season three times, but more important than that was his consistency. He had 20 seasons of at least 20 goals and in every season but his last he had at least 54 points.

As remarkable, he was one of the classiest players of his era. He won the Lady Byng Trophy three times and averaged only 42 penalty minutes a season, and he played in the All-Star Game on four occasions. He won the Selke Trophy in 1994–95 and the King Clancy Trophy in 2002 to honour his work off the ice in the community. In 2007, he was inducted into the Hockey Hall of Fame.

CEREMONY
Francis worked with the Raleigh Youth Hockey Association during the lockout of 2004–05. When hockey returned the following year, he decided it was time to retire. Soon after, the Hurricanes announced that Francis's number 10 sweater would be hoisted to the rafters of the RBC Centre on January 28, 2006, a home game against the Atlanta Thrashers.

The tribute began during the warm-up when all Hurricanes appeared in number 10 sweaters.

"There aren't too many times in my career when I've had chills in warm-ups, but I did tonight when I stepped on the ice with that Ronnie Francis number on," defenceman Bret Hedican said. "He has represented everything in this community for hockey and he has carried the franchise on his back and kept hockey in Raleigh."

Once the lights dimmed and the ceremony began, emotions started to flow throughout the building. Francis's entourage appeared at centre ice, notably his wife, three children, brother, parents, and close friends. They watched a video tribute capture the essence of his career. The sold-out crowd looked on as Francis wore his sweater one last time, skating a final lap around the ice in full equipment before watching his number 10 float into the rafters in the Hurricanes' Ring of Honor.

"All week I wasn't sure how it was going to go and how I was going to react, and I had a lot of sleepless nights leading up to tonight but it was kind of a remarkable feeling," Francis said. "I dressed with the boys before the game and I felt a sort of calm and when I went on the ice I was able to hold it together. It was a fun night."

THE GAME: Carolina Hurricanes 4–Atlanta Thrashers 1
Once the puck dropped, the Hurricanes played an inspired game and won 4–1. Carolina jumped into an early 2–0 lead thanks to goals by Justin Williams and Erik Cole in the first period, and the team made it 3–0 on an Anton Babchuk power-play goal in the second. Although the Thrashers made it 3–1 early in the third, they could get no closer and Kevyn Adams scored into the empty net to close out the scoring.

"We wanted to win this game for him," Hedican said. "We talked about it and came out playing the game we wanted to play."

4

SCOTT STEVENS

NEW JERSEY DEVILS
FEBRUARY 3, 2006

Born: Kitchener, Ontario, April 1, 1964
Position: Defence
Shoots: Left
Height: 6'2"
Weight: 215 lbs.

HONOURS
- **Stanley Cup** 1995, 2000, 2003
- **Conn Smythe Trophy** 2000
- **NHL All-Star Game** 1985, 1989, 1991, 1992, 1993, 1994, 1996, 1997, 1998, 1999, 2000, 2001, 2003
- **NHL First All-Star Team** 1988, 1994
- **Played for Canada at Canada Cup** 1991,
- **Played for Canada at World Cup** 1996
- **Played for Canada at Olympics** 1998
- **Hockey Hall of Fame** 2007

NHL CAREER STATS

	Regular Season					Playoffs				
Years	GP	G	A	P	Pim	GP	G	A	P	Pim
1982–2004	1,635	196	712	908	2,785	233	26	92	118	402

CAREER

The most feared checker of the modern era, Scott Stevens used his shoulder and hip to punish any player who encroached on his space. While the highlight reel for other defencemen might show great rushes, lightning shots, or perfect passes, the visual summary of Stevens' career consisted of opposing players crashing to the ice.

Drafted fifth overall by Washington in 1982, he stepped into the NHL immediately on a Capitals team that was lacking in all areas. Stevens was just 18 years old, but he took on all comers in an effort to have an impact and establish himself as one tough hombre, averaging more than 200 penalty minutes a year over his first seven seasons.

New free agency rules, though, allowed him to change teams in 1990 when he was still in his prime, and Stevens decided to sign with St. Louis. The next year, the Blues signed another free agent, Brendan Shanahan, from New Jersey, and as

compensation Stevens was sent to the Devils. It was, at the time, not a move he wanted to make, but he would end up making the Meadowlands his last stop, a stop that lasted 13 seasons and three Stanley Cups.

The Devils in 1991 were nothing much to look at, but with Stevens, and soon the emergence of goalie Martin Brodeur and other young players, the team became a consistently tough team to play against. They won the Cup in 1995 and 2000, and it was in the latter year that Stevens played his best, winning the Conn Smythe Trophy in the process.

Because hitting was his forte, he never won the Norris Trophy or any other individual award (excepting the aforementioned Conn Smythe), but he was so well respected in the dressing room and around the league that he was named New Jersey captain in 1992 and kept the "C" on his sweater until he retired.

CEREMONY

Scott Stevens captured the spirit of all retired number nights when he started his speech by saying, "I think this is the first time I've ever felt intimidated on this ice surface."

His number 4 was the first sent to the rafters by the New Jersey organization in a stirring, 30-minute celebration of his fantastic career with the Devils. The evening began with a video highlight package of his career—and a package of devastating hits, for which he was most notorious.

Stevens came out to centre ice accompanied by his parents, Larry and Mary, his wife, Donna, and three children—Kaitlin, Ryan, and Kara—where they were greeted with a three-minute standing ovation. He thanked general manager Lou Lamoriello for bringing him to the team and reflected on the rise in fortunes from a sad-sack club to Cup champion. "With your support," he said, "I had the best years of my career in this arena. I feel privileged to have played on three Stanley Cup championship teams and finally help the New Jersey Devils get the respect they deserve."

Stevens received a nice selection of gifts including a vintage bow-and-arrow (to meet his hunting interests) and a new pickup truck.

"I leave this incredible game with no regrets and only amazing memories," he said in closing, amid more cheers. "Thank you from the bottom of my heart."

THE GAME: New Jersey Devils 3–Carolina Hurricanes 0

The stairs were painted with the number 4, and the players sported number 4 patches. They came ready to play after the inspiring ceremony, and Martin Brodeur recorded another shutout in a 3–0 win over Carolina, the number-one team in the overall standings at that point. It was Brodeur's 100th career shutout (regular season and playoffs combined), a feat previously accomplished by only Terry Sawchuk (115 total) and George Hainsworth (102), two of the greatest goalies in hockey history.

It took a while for either team to get going, but a slow first period gave way to an entertaining and offensive second in which the Devils scored twice. The first goal came at 2:18 from Patrik Elias, and Zach Parise followed up four and a half minutes later with the Devils' second. Brian Gionta closed out the scoring in the third.

"Whenever there's a ceremony like that, if you're home or away, you always have to be careful not to get too stale," Gionta said, after scoring his team-best 30th goal of the season. "But it sparked a lot of emotion, and that kept us going. It felt like a playoff atmosphere out there."

16

PAT LaFontaine

BUFFALO SABRES
MARCH 3, 2006

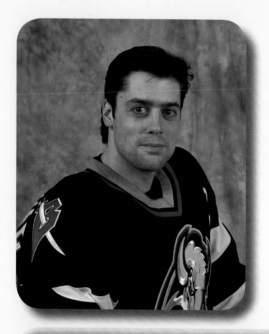

Born: St. Louis, Missouri, February 22, 1965
Position: Centre
Shoots: Right
Height: 5'10"
Weight: 182 lbs.

HONOURS
- **Bill Masterton Trophy** 1995
- **NHL All-Star Game** 1988, 1989, 1990, 1991, 1993
- **Played for United States at Olympics** 1984, 1988
- **Played for United States at Canada Cup** 1987, 1991
- **Played for United States in World Cup** 1996
- **Hockey Hall of Fame** 2003

NHL CAREER STATS

	Regular Season					Playoffs				
Years	GP	G	A	P	Pim	GP	G	A	P	Pim
1983–98	865	468	545	1,013	552	69	26	36	62	36

CAREER

A superstar scorer wherever he played, Pat LaFontaine had to retire at the ripe old age of 33 because of a series of concussions. But before he left the game, he managed to record more than 1,000 points while playing with dignity and skill.

Unlike many American-born players of the early 1980s, LaFontaine played junior hockey in Quebec rather than college hockey at home, and in one season he shattered records for goals and points that foreshadowed what he could do in the NHL. He took all of 1983–84 off to play for the U.S. National Team and at the Olympics, and then joined the Islanders right after, the team that had drafted him a flattering third overall in 1983.

LaFontaine didn't disappoint, scoring 13 goals in just 15 games at the end of the season, and the next four years saw him increase his goal production to 19, 30, 38, and 47. The Islanders were on the downswing after winning the Cup four

years in a row, but LaFontaine was a superstar who looked to usher in a new era of success for the team.

The team traded him to the Sabres, however, and it was there he had his best—and in many ways worst—years. His first season in Buffalo ended after 57 games when he suffered a broken jaw, but he recovered to have a career year in 1992–93, scoring 53 goals and 148 points. He suffered a serious anterior cruciate ligament (ACL) injury in November 1993 and was gone for nearly a year and a half. His return won him the Masterton Trophy for a truly heroic rehabilitation.

These injuries were mere child's play compared to what happened on October 17, 1996, in a game against Pittsburgh. Giant defenceman François Leroux elbowed LaFontaine to the side of the head, knocking his helmet off and sending him to the ice, where he lost consciousness.

His career seemed so thoroughly over that when he declared his intention to play the next year, the Sabres traded him because they didn't want him to risk further and more serious brain damage.

The Rangers took a chance on LaFontaine, and for a few months everything looked great. He scored a bit, felt healthy, and looked to have turned things around. Then, on March 16, 1998, he collided with a teammate at centre ice in a game against St. Louis. It wasn't ferocious contact, but it was enough to send him spiraling to the dressing room for the last time.

CEREMONY

As nice a guy as ever passed through the NHL, Pat LaFontaine had his number retired in impressive fashion at HSBC Arena. He was accompanied by his father, John, his wife, Marybeth, and their children, but even before he was introduced he made an appearance on the giant scoreboard above centre ice.

It was there fans watched a highlight pack replete with great plays as well as tributes from Mike Eruzione and Jim Craig, members of the 1980 Miracle on Ice team, as well as former teammates Curtis Brown and Matthew Barnaby.

LaFontaine runs the Companions in Courage Foundation, and several children from that charity program were introduced, followed by Danny Gare and the three members of the French Connection Line, all of whom preceded LaFontaine to the rafters.

The guest of honour chose his words carefully in speaking to the crowd: "Thank you, to the greatest fans, for your support. It inspired me whenever I played . . . It was a gift to spend my six years here."

THE GAME: Buffalo Sabres 6–Toronto Maple Leafs 2

All Sabres players came out for the warm-up wearing number 16 LaFontaine sweaters, which they replaced with their own once the game began.

Derek Roy had his first career hat trick and Maxim Afinogenov had three assists in leading the Sabres to an easy 6–2 win over the Maple Leafs. The two played on a line with Thomas Vanek and combined for four goals and seven points in all.

Roy got the opening goal early on, but Alexei Ponikarovsky tied the score at 12:48 of the first, the last time the Leafs were close in this one. Chris Drury got the only other goal of the period to stake the Sabres to a 2–1 lead after 20 minutes, and in the second it was all Buffalo as they increased the lead to 4–1.

Bryan McCabe got an early goal for Toronto in the final period, but Vanek and Roy, at 19:56, put the game well out of reach.

5

BERNIE GEOFFRION

MONTREAL CANADIENS
MARCH 11, 2006

Born: Montreal, Quebec, February 16, 1931
Died: Atlanta, Georgia, March 11, 2006
Position: Right wing
Shoots: Right
Height: 5'9"
Weight: 166 lbs.

HONOURS
- **Stanley Cup** 1953, 1956, 1957, 1958, 1959, 1960
- **Hart Trophy** 1961
- **Art Ross Trophy** 1955, 1961
- **Calder Trophy** 1952
- **NHL All-Star Game** 1952, 1953, 1954, 1955, 1956, 1958, 1959, 1960, 1961, 1962, 1963
- **Hockey Hall of Fame** 1972

NHL CAREER STATS

	Regular Season					Playoffs				
Years	GP	G	A	P	Pim	GP	G	A	P	Pim
1950–68	883	393	429	822	689	132	58	60	118	88

CAREER

Bernie Geoffrion is surely the only player in NHL history to be booed vociferously in his own arena on the night he won the scoring championship. Indeed, context is all, because he later won again to cheers and shouts of joy.

The first event took place at the end of the 1954–55 season. He and teammate Maurice Richard were neck-and-neck for the Art Ross Trophy, but late in the season Richard attacked a linesman and was suspended the rest of the season. Geoffrion then earned the extra point on the final day of the season, at the Forum, to edge Richard 75 points to 74. Fans believed that out of respect for the Rocket, Geoffrion should have not even tried to register a point to give his teammate what would have been his only Art Ross Trophy.

Flash forward to 1960–61, Richard retired and Geoffrion in mid-career form. He scored 50 goals on the season, the first since the aforementioned Richard in

1944–45, and led the league with 95 points. That year he received a standing ovation for his historic achievements.

Geoffrion joined the Canadiens toward the end of the 1950–51 season and quickly earned the nickname "Boom Boom" for his hard slapshot, a shot of which he was master at this time in league history. He was very much a pure scorer, often earning more goals than assists over the course of the season, and he was with a team that was at the very apex of its dominance.

In fact, Geoffrion's timing was so perfect he holds a record likely never to be broken. From the 1951 playoffs to the 1960 playoffs—10 years—he played in every Stanley Cup Final game on the NHL's schedule. Those 10 trips to the Final yielded six victories for "Boom Boom."

In all, he played 14 seasons for the Canadiens, but after two years of coaching he came out of retirement and played for two more years with the Rangers.

CEREMONY

It was a sombre and sad ceremony, but it was also a night to cherish and remember. Fighting a losing battle with stomach cancer and too sick to travel from his Atlanta home to attend the retiring of his number 5 in person, Geoffrion passed away the very morning his number was lifted to the rafters.

But he knew the honour was coming, and the Bell Centre was full of family and friends who represented the great scoring legend. Bernie's two sons, Danny and Bobby, were front and centre, as was his daughter, Linda, and wife, Marlene. His two daughters-in-law, son-in-law, and eight grandchildren were there, as were eight teammates—Marcel Bonin, Emile Bouchard, Phil Goyette, Andre Pronovost, Henri Richard, Dollard St. Laurent, Jean-Guy Talbot, and Dickie Moore.

Danny spoke about his dad and mom. "Our dad's first date with Mom was at a boxing match at the Montreal Forum, of all places. He told her that his number would one day join her father's [Howie Morenz] hanging above the ice at the Forum. As usual, my dad kept his promise."

The opposition, New York Rangers, also made a presentation to the Geoffrion family in honour of his brief time playing with the Blueshirts. Captain Jaromir Jagr gave them a silver platter, and Montreal Canadiens president Pierre Boivin presented them with a Michel Lapensée painting depicting the important moments in Boom Boom's career.

THE GAME: Montreal Canadiens 1–New York Rangers 0

Two appropriate events occurred in the game after Geoffrion's number 5 was raised to the rafters. First, Canadien goalie Cristobal Huet recorded his fifth shutout of the season in Montreal's narrow 1–0 win. And, that goal came courtesy of a Craig Rivet slapshot, the shot Geoffrion was most famous for. The goal came late in the first period and beat Henrik Lundqvist cleanly, and it proved the only time all night that the red light went on.

"Huey [Huet] has just been outstanding, and the confidence he's playing with is oozing into the rest of the team," Rivet said after. "We go into every game knowing that he'll come up with the big saves."

The Habs preserved the win with exceptional penalty killing to start the third period. They had to kill a 5-on-3 that lasted 1:42, with Jagr, the league's top point getter, being held off the scoresheet.

3

KEN DANEYKO

NEW JERSEY DEVILS
MARCH 24, 2006

Born: Windsor, Ontario, April 17, 1964
Position: Defence
Shoots: Left
Height: 6'1"
Weight: 215 lbs.

HONOURS
- **Stanley Cup** 1995, 2000, 2003
- **Drafted 18th overall by New Jersey in 1982**
- **Bill Masterton Trophy** 2000

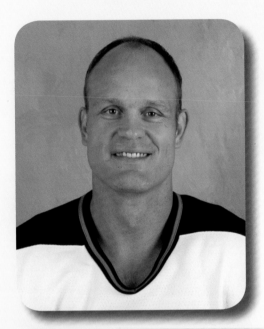

NHL CAREER STATS

	Regular Season					Playoffs				
Years	GP	G	A	P	Pim	GP	G	A	P	Pim
1983–2003	1,283	36	142	178	2,516	175	5	17	22	296

CAREER

Over 20 years and more than 1,400 NHL games (including playoffs), Ken Daneyko played for only one team—New Jersey. And over that time, he saw it all. He was with the Devils when Wayne Gretzky called it a "Mickey Mouse" team after a lopsided Edmonton Oilers' victory, and he was with it in 1995 when the Devils won their first Stanley Cup.

It took Daneyko some four years to make the team, from the spring day in 1982 when he was drafted by New Jersey, to training camp in 1986 when he became a regular on the Devil's blue line. Big and tough, he made no bones about the kind of player he was—defensive, physical, competitive. There were no end-to-end rushes in his repertoire, no glorious goals or first-star selections.

Indeed, Daneyko once went 256 games without scoring even once, but he also had an Iron Man run of 388 consecutive games played. On a team known for its

defence and lack of scoring punch, Daneyko fit into the team perfectly, worrying first and foremost about preventing goals.

No one could have predicted from those Devils teams in the 1980s that they would go on to win the Stanley Cup three times, but that's what happened during Daneyko's career. The first, in 1994–95, was a fortuitous one in that it came at the end of the short, 48-game regular season.

Daneyko was part of the Cup teams in 2000 and again in 2003, after which he retired.

CEREMONY

Before Daneyko was introduced to fans at the Continental Airlines Arena at the start of a 40-minute ceremony, the team showed a video tribute to the man of the night, highlights of which included his contributions to the team's three Stanley Cup victories. When his name was called he made his way to centre ice, where he was greeted by a four-minute standing ovation from the sellout crowd.

Daneyko was joined on the red carpet by his father and mother; brother, Peter; sisters, Leanne and Karen; wife, JonnaLyn; son, Shane; and daughter, Taylor.

Among Daneyko's guests were former New York Jets defensive lineman Joe Klecko and former heavyweight boxer Gerry Cooney. Later, he was given a beautiful piece of crystal from team owner Jeff Vanderbeek, which Daneyko almost dropped. He later commented: "That pretty well summed my career: fumbled it, but made a great recovery."

Other gifts included a golf driver from the team's trainers, a five-day holiday to Nevis in the Caribbean courtesy of the current players, a truck from team owner Jeff Vanderbeek, and his number 3 sweater framed from Martin Brodeur and Sergei Brylin.

Daneyko told the crowd about the day he was drafted, in 1982. He was in Edmonton at the time, and when he found out it was the Devils that selected him, he was confused. The team had just moved to that state from Colorado. "The problem was," he told the fans, "I looked at my mom and asked her where New Jersey was."

THE GAME: New Jersey Devils 4–Boston Bruins 2

Being the backup goalie to Martin Brodeur is never easy, but Scott Clemmensen held himself together for a win in his first start since December 29, 2005, in a key Eastern Conference game. The win put New Jersey solidly in seventh place, three points ahead of Atlanta in a fierce race for the playoffs.

The Devils used the energy from the Daneyko banner-raising to jump into an early 2–0 lead after four minutes thanks to goals from Scott Gomez and Brian Gionta. Gomez had suffered a cut below his eye in the previous game and wasn't supposed to play, but on this night he had to. "The guy has always meant a lot to me," Gomez said of Daneyko. "He was a true competitor."

The Devils made it 3–0 midway through the second courtesy of Zach Parise. Glen Murray got one back in the final minute for the visiting Bruins, but Paul Martin restored the three-goal lead in the third. Brad Isbister closed out the scoring in the final minute.

2

AL MacInnis

ST. LOUIS BLUES
APRIL 9, 2006

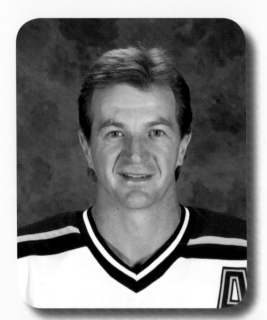

Born: Inverness, Nova Scotia, July 11, 1963
Position: Defence
Shoots: Right
Height: 6'2"
Weight: 205 lbs.

HONOURS
- **Stanley Cup** 1989
- **Conn Smythe Trophy** 1989
- **Norris Trophy** 1999
- **NHL All-Star Game** 1985, 1988, 1990, 1991, 1992, 1994, 1996, 1997, 1998, 1999, 2000, 2003
- **Won gold medal with Canada at Olympics** 2002
- **Hockey Hall of Fame** 2007

NHL CAREER STATS

	Regular Season					Playoffs				
Years	GP	G	A	P	Pim	GP	G	A	P	Pim
1981–2004	1,416	340	934	1,274	1,511	177	39	121	160	255

CAREER

There are two distinct halves to Al MacInnis's career, but no matter which half is under discussion one thing was a constant—his shot. One of the few Nova Scotians to make it to the NHL, he was drafted by Calgary in 1981 even before his 18th birthday and made it into the team's lineup for two games that season.

It wasn't until early in the 1983–84 season that he stuck with the team full time, spending 13 years in all with the Flames. The highlight of his time in Calgary was the 1988–89 season when he led the team to the Stanley Cup and was named Conn Smythe Trophy winner in the process.

Feared for his incredible shot—released throughout his career with a wood stick—MacInnis was the quarterback on the power play and one of the highest-scoring defencemen in league history. He had seven seasons of 20 goals or more and is one of a small and rare group of defencemen to reach 300 for his career.

More than half that number came from the point on the power play, his shot so dangerous that players sometimes got out of the way, knowing full well bones had been broken and careers derailed because of it.

MacInnis was traded to St. Louis in 1994 and it was there he played the last 10 years of his career. Although he never brought the Stanley Cup to Missouri, he did continue to bring his high level of play to the team. In his own end he was a force, and his leadership was an unquestioned trademark of his play. In the community, MacInnis was highly popular, and he both embraced and was embraced by the people. He continues to live in St. Louis and work with the team, so it was no surprise when it retired his number 2.

CEREMONY

One of the most popular Blues players in team history, Al MacInnis got a night to remember equal to the career he gave the team and its fans. Many alumni joined him on the red carpet, and the ceremony also featured no fewer than 10 video tributes from teammates and opponents alike, including Wayne Gretzky, Brett Hull, and Steve Yzerman.

"I wish I could skate one more shift, take one more slapshot from the blue line, for the best fans of hockey," MacInnis said. "But knowing my number 2 will forever have a home here is more than I could ask. I'm forever a St. Louis Blue."

Blues fans rallied with cheers on this night because the team was riding an atrocious 13-game losing streak and sitting near the bottom of the standings, but for one special hour they forgot the team's woes.

His was the fifth number retired by the team after Bob Gassoff (3), Barclay Plager (8), Brian Sutter (11), and Bernie Federko (24). "It was the names of these four men that reminded me why playing for the Blues is as good as it gets in the National Hockey League," MacInnis said, as he looked into the rafters.

MacInnis received gifts from the organization and players, notably a trip to Scotland and a round of golf at the hallowed grounds of St. Andrews, and a guitar autographed by country music star Tim McGraw.

THE GAME: St. Louis Blues 2–Edmonton Oilers 1
Relief as much as joy was painted on the faces of Blues players at the end of this game, as the team ended a 13-game losing streak. Jamal Myers scored early in the second period and Mark Rycroft early in the third to carry the day, and only a last-minute goal from the Oilers' Chris Pronger spoiled the shutout for third-string goalie Jason Bacashihua.

"It was a touching ceremony," Mayers said of the lengthy MacInnis honour before the game. "Having Al's jersey retired was a special day, and the guys did a great job of coming up with a solid effort."

18

SERGE SAVARD

MONTREAL CANADIENS
NOVEMBER 18, 2006

Born: Montreal, Quebec, January 22, 1946
Position: Defence
Shoots: Left
Height: 6'3"
Weight: 210 lbs.

HONOURS
- **Stanley Cup** 1968, 1969, 1971, 1973, 1976, 1977, 1978, 1979
- **Conn Smythe Trophy** 1969
- **Bill Masterton Trophy** 1979
- **NHL All-Star Game** 1970, 1973, 1977, 1978
- **Hockey Hall of Fame** 1986

NHL CAREER STATS

	Regular Season					Playoffs				
Years	GP	G	A	P	Pim	GP	G	A	P	Pim
1966–83	1,040	106	333	439	592	130	19	49	68	88

CAREER

Any player who wins the Stanley Cup eight times must be doing something right, and Serge Savard did many things right. For starters, he was part of the Montreal organization when it was at its zenith, playing two games with the team in 1966–67 and joining the Habs full time in the fall of '67. The Canadiens won the Cup in Savard's rookie season, although the big, hulking defenceman was still in the learning days of his career. A year later, he was not only holding the Cup for a second time he was also cradling the Conn Smythe Trophy after a dominant playoff performance.

Savard wasn't as able on offence as Larry Robinson came to be when he joined the Habs in 1972, but he was strong and a stabilizing force inside his own blue line nonetheless.

Just as it looked like Savard was establishing himself as one of the best defencemen in the game, however, his career was derailed not once but twice. Midway

through the 1970–71 season he broke his leg in five places and required a steel plate and three operations to ensure the leg healed properly. Next season, he played just 23 games before breaking the same leg again. He persevered, trained even harder to recover, and worked his way back into the lineup the next year, receiving the Masterton Trophy in 1979 for his two courageous—and successful—returns to the game.

Savard, Robinson, and Guy Lapointe formed the "big three" of the Montreal blue line throughout the 1970s when the team won the Cup six times. Perhaps the most important of these came in 1976 when the team knocked off Philadelphia, a team that had won the trophy the previous two years using tactics of intimidation and brawling. Montreal fought right back, and then let their vastly superior skill prevail, taking the game from its darkest days into an era of firewagon hockey with highlight-reel goals and heart-stopping plays.

Savard can boast of being the only player in the 1972 Summit Series on either side who did not play in a losing game. In five appearances of the eight games, he won four and tied one, a unique and special record in the "series of the century."

CEREMONY

Incredibly, the retiring of Serge Savard's number 18 was only the second for a defenceman in team history, the first being Doug Harvey. The ceremony was emceed by Dick Irvin in English and Richard Garneau in French, and they were accompanied by distinguished guest and former Montreal coach, Scotty Bowman. Several times they started to speak, only to be drowned out by the crowd.

"Serge was the kind of player that every coach wishes they could have had," Bowman finally said between bursts of applause.

Savard was humbled by the whole honour: "To see myself up there next to Maurice Richard is just incredible, even though I would never even dream of comparing myself to him. I don't even come up to his ankles. Retiring a jersey is always something major, but it's even more so here in Montreal."

Team captain Saku Koivu was signed by Savard, who became the Montreal Canadiens general manager after he retired. "I never expected when I signed my first NHL contract with Serge that I would still be here or get to be part of a great moment like this," Koivu admitted.

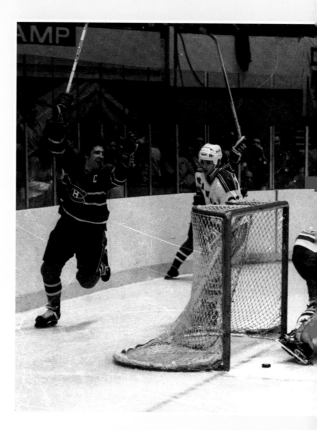

THE GAME: Montreal Canadiens 3–Atlanta Thrashers 1

Coming off a loss the previous game, 5–1 in Florida, the Canadiens did what they had done all season to date—avoid losing consecutive games. Oddly, the team also hadn't won two in a row this season, an inconsistency that they knew needed to be eradicated. Said defenceman Mike Komisarek: "We want to be one of the elite teams in the conference instead of one of those teams that's always teeter-tottering back and forth."

Michael Ryder opened the scoring midway through the first to give Montreal the early lead. Sergei Samsonov thought he had made it 2–0 in the second period, but a lengthy video review determined that the puck was under the glove of goalie Johan Hedberg but not over the goal line.

The Thrashers tied the game at 3:30 of the third on a goal by Glen Metropolit, but Alexander Perezhogin got the game winner three minutes later by swatting a loose puck out of the air and past Hedberg. Radek Bonk closed out the scoring with an empty netter.

16

BRETT HULL

ST. LOUIS BLUES
DECEMBER 5, 2006

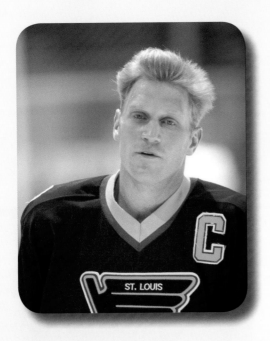

Born: Belleville, Ontario, August 9, 1964
Position: Right wing
Shoots: Right
Height: 5'11"
Weight: 203 lbs.

HONOURS
- **Stanley Cup** 1999, 2002
- **Hart Trophy** 1991
- **Lady Bying** 1990
- **Lester B. Pearson Award** 1991
- **Led NHL in goals scored** 1990, 1991, 1992
- **Won silver medal with United States at Olympics** 2002
- **Played for United States in Canada Cup** 1991
- **Played for United States in World Cup** 1996
- **Played for United States in Olympics** 1998
- **Hockey Hall of Fame** 2009

NHL CAREER STATS

	Regular Season					Playoffs				
Years	GP	G	A	P	Pim	GP	G	A	P	Pim
1985–2006	1,269	741	650	1,391	458	202	103	87	190	73

CAREER

One of the greatest pure goal scorers the game has ever seen, Brett Hull was a chip off the old block, as they say. His dad, Bobby, after all, was the highest-scoring left winger of all time when he retired, and Brett's 741 career goals put him third all-time behind only Wayne Gretzky (894) and Gordie Howe (801).

Brett's career wasn't always as promising, though, as the old man's had been. In his teens he admittedly ate everything in sight, earning the jokey nickname "Pickles" from teammates and derision from coaches who saw so much talent wasting away on poor discipline. When he was failed to be invited to play for Canada's junior team, though, the message sunk in.

It took a while, though. Hull started his career with Calgary, but his weight and unwillingness to backcheck were his tickets out of town, to St. Louis, where

he quickly became one of the most potent scorers in the game. In his first full season with the Blues he had 41 goals and then followed with seasons of 72, 86, and 70, tops in the league in all three seasons.

His forte was the one-timer shot from the off wing, so although he was a right wing on paper, he often moved to the top of the faceoff circle on the left side, waiting for a crisp pass across the ice.

In all, Hull played 10 and a half years in St. Louis, scoring most of his goals with the team but having little playoff success. He signed with Dallas as a free agent in 1998, bought into coach Ken Hitchcock's defensive system, and won his first Stanley Cup. Hull scored the winning goal, just as he had when the Americans beat Canada to win the inaugural World Cup in 1996.

Hull won his second Cup in 2002, with Detroit, and then signed with Phoenix in 2005. The move to the Coyotes was the result of two factors. One, his friend Wayne Gretzky was starting his first year as coach of the team, and two, it was with this franchise—when it was in Winnipeg—that his father played such a prominent role. The team brought Bobby's number 9 out of retirement so Brett could wear it, but after only five games Brett retired.

CEREMONY

The retiring of any number is historic, of course, but it was doubly so in the case of Brett Hull. He joined his father, Bobby, whose number 9 was retired by the Chicago Blackhawks (and, later, the Winnipeg Jets) as the only father-son pair with retired numbers in any sport.

Hull was surrounded by some 20 former teammates for the ceremony, but most important he was accompanied to centre ice by his father. Adam Oates spoke eloquently about his former teammate, finishing with, "Brett, nothing compares to the three years I got to play with you. It was the highlight of my career."

When Hull spoke, he referred to a career-changing talk he had with former teammate and then coach, Brian Sutter. Hull thought that Sutter was going to say something like, "Boy, am I lucky to be coaching you." Hull recounted, "He sat me down and had a half-hour tirade, and I was flabbergasted. I had no idea how good I was, the impact I could have on the game. Without that meeting I'm not sure I would be standing here today, and I thank Brian so much for that," Hull said.

As Hull's banner took flight, he put his arm around his dad while the loudspeaker played the Neil Young song that begins with the line, "Old man take a look at my life; I'm a lot like you."

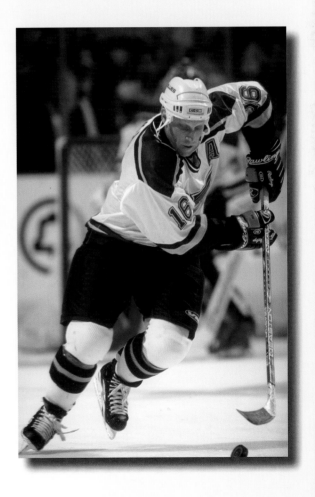

THE GAME: Detroit Red Wings 5–St. Louis Blues 1

All players wore number 16 sweaters during the pre-game skate, but once the game began the Red Wings swamped the home Blues. Both sides waited out the 45-minute ceremony, but it was Detroit, the team with which Hull won a Stanley Cup later in his career, that showed greater signs of life. The Wings scored the only three goals of the first period and built a 5–0 lead before St. Louis got a late goal, serving only to spoil Dominik Hasek's shutout bid.

Henrik Zetterberg scored first, just 2:34 into the game on a power play, and Pavel Datsyuk followed up less than two minutes later with a second score. Daniel Cleary made it 3–0. Valtteri Filppula midway through the second and Robert Lang late in the third made it a 5–0 count before defenceman Eric Brewer managed to beat Hasek at 16:36 to close out the scoring.

19

STEVE YZERMAN

DETROIT RED WINGS
JANUARY 2, 2007

Born: Cranbrook, British Columbia, May 9, 1965
Position: Centre
Shoots: Right
Height: 5'11"
Weight: 185 lbs.

HONOURS
- **Stanley Cup** 1997, 1998, 2002
- **Lester B. Pearson Award** 1989
- **Conn Smythe Trophy** 1998
- **Frank Selke Trophy** 2000
- **Bill Masterton Trophy** 2003
- **Played for Canada at Canada Cup** 1984
- **Played for Canada at World Cup** 1996
- **Played for Canada at Olympics** 1998, 2002 (won gold medal at 2002 Olympics)
- **Executive Director of Team Canada for Vancouver Olympics** 2010
- **Canada's Sports Hall of Fame** 2008
- **Hockey Hall of Fame** 2009

NHL CAREER STATS

	Regular Season					Playoffs				
Years	GP	G	A	P	Pim	GP	G	A	P	Pim
1983–2006	1,514	692	1,063	1,755	924	196	70	115	185	84

CAREER

By the time he retired in 2006, Steve Yzerman ranked among the greatest offensive players of all time. His 692 career goals placed him eighth and his 1,063 assists put him seventh on the all-time list. His 1,755 points put him sixth, and his 1,514 regular-season games in 10th. But one fact stands above all others—Yzerman played his entire 22-year career with only one team: Detroit.

In an era of increased free agency and player mobility, this is without compare Indeed, history might prove him to be the last one-team player for such an extended career. On top of that, Yzerman was the Red Wings captain for the last 19 seasons of his career, a record for leadership longevity.

Yzerman made an immediate impact at his first training camp by making the team as an 18-year-old. The rookie had 39 goals and 87 points and was runner-up to Buffalo goalie Tom Barrasso for the Calder Trophy.

Over the next several years "Stevie Y" continued to develop and lead a once-dismal team to the playoffs with annual regularity. He was named captain in 1986, and the next year he reached the two great scoring landmarks for a season—50 goals and 100 points (102 points, to be exact). This was the first of six straight 100-point seasons, all but one of which also saw him score at least 50 goals (except 1991–92 when he had 45). He peaked in 1988–89 when he had 155 points and was named Lester B. Pearson Award winner.

Despite his scoring, and despite the team's qualifying for the playoffs, the Red Wings never came particularly close to winning the Stanley Cup. However, Scotty Bowman became the coach and convinced his captain to sacrifice some offence for defence and two-way play. Yzerman obliged, and in 1995 the team went to the Cup Final, only to lose to New Jersey in four straight games.

The Red Wings added some key players, though, and they won the Cup in 1997 and again the next year. Yzerman led his team to one more Cup, in 2002, before his retirement. In addition to his NHL career, he represented Canada at every level of play, culminating in 2002 with the Olympics in Salt Lake City.

CEREMONY

Such was Yzerman's popularity that the pre-game ceremony to raise his number 19 to the rafters of the Joe Louis Arena lasted some 90 minutes. That in itself was a record. He was lavished with tributes and gifts as well as a video package of career highlights. The night was hosted by longtime friend Darren Pang and included special guests Gordie Howe, Alex Delvecchio, and Ted Lindsay, the three living members whose numbers have been previously retired by the team (the late Sid Abel and Terry Sawchuk are the others).

The current Red Wings players were called to the ice where they wore four different sweaters—Red Wings, Peterborough Petes, Team Canada, and Campbell Conference—in honour of Yzerman's career. A lengthy video retrospective followed, after which coach Scotty Bowman delivered a moving speech, calling Yzerman the most responsible player he had ever coached and admiring him for his threshold for playing in pain.

Knowing Yzerman's passion for soccer, current captain Nicklas Lidstrom, on behalf of the team, presented Yzerman with tickets for him, his wife, Lisa, and three daughters (Isabella, Maria, Sophia) to attend Euro 2008. Owner Mike Ilitch then recognized Yzerman's contribution, and then finally the man himself spoke. Yzerman thanked the Hall of Famers who were in attendance, as well as Bowman and teammates for their contributions, and then the number 19 was raised to the rafters where it came to rest beside Sawchuk's 1.

THE GAME: Detroit Red Wings 2–Anaheim Mighty Ducks 1

All members of the Red Wings wore number 19 patches on their shoulders, and although it wasn't a classic contest, the home side won the game, 2–1. All goals came in the second period. Tomas Holmstrom opened the scoring one minute into the period, but Ryan Getzlaf tied the score for the Ducks less than three minutes later. It was another Swede, Henrik Zetterberg, who got the winner near the end of the period off a nice pass in front from Holmstrom.

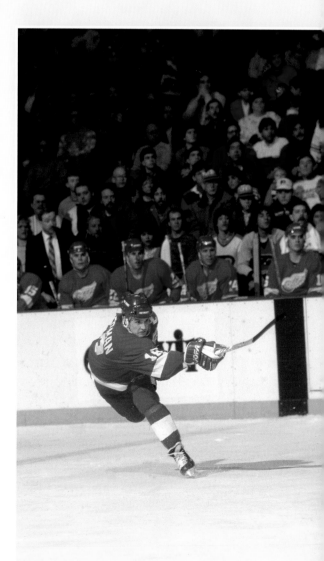

20

LUC
ROBITAILLE

LOS ANGELES KINGS
JANUARY 20, 2007

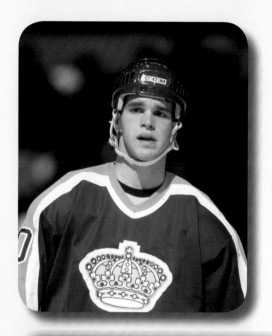

Born: Montreal, Quebec, February 17, 1966
Position: Left wing
Shoots: Left
Height: 6'1"
Weight: 215 lbs.

HONOURS
- **Stanley Cup** 2002
- **Calder Trophy** 1987
- **NHL All-Star Game** 1988, 1989, 1990, 1991, 1992, 1993, 1999, 2001
- **Highest-scoring left winger in NHL history**
- **Hockey Hall of Fame** 2009

NHL CAREER STATS

Years	Regular Season					Playoffs				
	GP	G	A	P	Pim	GP	G	A	P	Pim
1986–2006	1,431	668	726	1,394	1,177	159	58	69	127	174

CAREER

Drafted a remote 171st in 1984 by Los Angeles, Luc Robitaille was labeled a weak skater who wouldn't last long in the NHL. But, 1,431 games and 668 goals later, the laugh seems to be on the naysayers, as Robitaille retired in 2006 as the highest-scoring left winger in league history. He may have been nicknamed "Lucky" by former teammate Tiger Williams, but there was nothing lucky about Robitaille's remarkable career.

After averaging nearly a goal a game in three years of junior with the Hull Olympiques, Robitaille joined the Kings in 1986 and hammered home 45 goals as a rookie, winning the Calder Trophy in the process, the first and only Kings player to do so. In his first eight seasons, he had no fewer than 44 goals and peaked at 63 in 1992–93, the year Los Angeles advanced to the Stanley Cup Final (only to lose

to Montreal in five games). In all, he had three 50-goal seasons and four 100-point years in 19 years as a player.

In truth, Robitaille's greatest assets were his shot and instinct. He was in the right place at the right time. The puck followed him; he knew how to anticipate play; the puck was in the net. He had three separate stints of ever-shorter duration with the Kings, the first for eight years, then four, then two, before he retired.

Yet although he is most identified with Los Angeles, he won his only Stanley Cup in 2002 with Detroit when he had just four goals in 23 playoff games. Captain Steve Yzerman was judicious after accepting the Cup, handing it first to Dominik Hasek, the oldest player who hadn't yet won, who then handed it to Robitaille, next in seniority.

Robitaille's final regular-season game was memorable. First, captain Mattias Norstrom gave him the "C" for one night. At the end of the game, the sold-out crowd gave him a long standing ovation after which he gave a thank-you speech and skated a final lap around the Staples Center. He still holds all-time records for goals and points (1,394) for a left winger, and three years after his final game he was dutifully inducted into the Hockey Hall of Fame.

CEREMONY

The only number 20 retired in NHL history, Luc Robitaille's number went up to the rafters of the Staples Center to join four other Los Angeles honoured numbers: Rogie Vachon (30), Marcel Dionne (16), Dave Taylor (18), and Wayne Gretzky (99).

The ceremony clocked in at just under an hour and featured video tributes from Kobe Bryant of the L.A. Lakers and Mark Messier. Guests attending the event included 19 former teammates, including Gretzky, Larry Robinson, Jimmy Carson, Butch Goring, Bernie Nicholls, Jari Kurri, Marty McSorley, Bob Berry, Barry Melrose, and NHL commissioner Gary Bettman. Taylor and Dionne couldn't attend, but they wrote congratulatory notes that were read by the evening's emcee, the Kings' play-by-play man, Bob Miller.

"It wasn't about scoring goals; it wasn't about money; it wasn't about fame. I just wanted to play hockey and play in the NHL," Robitaille said. "I wasn't the fastest player, and I had flaws, but I was a student of the game, and every day I was grateful to live my dream. I heard your chants every time I touched the puck or took a shot."

THE GAME: Phoenix Coyotes 3–Los Angeles Kings 2

The Staples Center ice featured the number 20 behind each goal, and all Kings players skated out wearing number 20 sweaters for the warm-up. The Kings came out on fire to start the game and were ahead 2–0 after just 5:46 of play thanks to quick goals from Alexander Frolov and Anze Kopitar. Goalie Sean Burke, making his Los Angeles debut, played a solid game.

The Coyotes' Josh Gratton got one goal back late in the first, though, and after a scoreless second things started to turn against the Kings. Burke had to leave the game early in the final period because of dehydration, and Yutaka Fukufuji, the first Japanese player in NHL history, came on in relief. It was not a successful change, though, as he gave up the tying goal to Ladislav Nagy at 13:58 and then the game winner to Travis Roche with just 1:39 to play.

29

KEN
DRYDEN

MONTREAL CANADIENS
JANUARY 29, 2007

Born: Hamilton, Ontario, August 8, 1947
Position: Goalie
Catches: Left
Height: 6'4"
Weight: 205 lbs.

HONOURS
- **Stanley Cup** 1971, 1973, 1976, 1977, 1978, 1979
- **Conn Smythe Trophy** 1971
- **Calder Trophy** 1972
- **Vezina Trophy** 1973, 1976, 1977, 1978, 1979 (shared with Michel Larocque)
- **NHL All-Star Game** 1972, 1975, 1976, 1977, 1978
- **Hockey Hall of Fame** 1983

NHL CAREER STATS

Regular Season

Years	GP	W-L-T	Mins	GA	SO	GAA
1970–79	397	258-57-74	23,352	870	46	2.24

Playoffs

Years	GP	W-L-T	Mins	GA	SO	GAA
1970–79	112	80-32-0	6,846	274	10	2.40

CAREER

Not many players in the 1960s went from U.S. college hockey to the NHL, and probably only one came out of Cornell—Ken Dryden. And, despite playing only a little more than seven full seasons in the league, Dryden won an incredible six Stanley Cups. And he was inducted into the Hockey Hall of Fame in 1983 at age 36, one of the youngest so honoured.

Dryden's entrance into the NHL was arguably the most dramatic in league history. He was called up from the Montreal Voyageurs, the team's AHL affiliate, late in the 1970–71 season and won all six games he played. He instantly became the number-one goalie for the playoffs at the behest of coach Al MacNeil, and the Habs

knocked off the defending Cup champions, the Bruins, en route to a most improbable Stanley Cup win. Dryden was named winner of the Conn Smythe Trophy even before he had a chance to win the Calder Trophy, an unheard of achievement.

In his first full season, 1971–72, Dryden led the league with 39 wins, but the team didn't advance to the Cup Final as was their custom during these years. Based on this slim NHL experience, though, he was named one of two goalies for Canada at the 1972 Summit Series, and he was in goal the night of September 28, 1972, when Paul Henderson won the series in the final minute.

Dryden led the Habs to another Cup win the next year and then became embroiled in a contract dispute with general manager Sam Pollock. Pollock rarely finished second in any hockey confrontation, but this was one of those times. The goalie took a year off to work at a law firm as he dug in his heels on a new deal, and his position solidified when the team lost in the first round of the playoffs. Pollock gave Dryden a big, new contract, and the goalie was back at training camp in the fall of 1974.

The next five years were extraordinary for the goalie. He never won fewer than 30 games, but even more amazing, he never lost more than 10 games in a season. The Canadiens won four Cups in a row, 1976–79.

CEREMONY

Making his way from the Montreal dressing room to the Bell Centre ice wearing his familiar number 29 sweater and famous red, white, and blue bull's-eye mask, carrying a goal stick, it was easy for Ken Dryden to bring back memories for the sold-out crowd come to honour him this night.

Joined by his wife, Lynda; children, Michael and Sarah; brother, Dave; granddaughter, Khaya; and first coach, Al MacNeil, who famously put the untried rookie in net for the first time, Dryden was eloquent with his carefully chosen words.

"Guy Lafleur had his hair flowing in the wind; Jean Béliveau had such a presence on the ice; Maurice 'Rocket' Richard was so powerful; and as for me, the enduring image everyone has is of me leaning on my stick, not doing much, and watching the game. That was what the 1970s were all about—that and a whole lot of Stanley Cups."

More surprisingly, the man Dryden most wanted to attend was Vladislav Tretiak, his nemesis in the 1972 Summit Series and the man who shocked the nation in the first game on September 2, 1972 with a win at the Montreal Forum.

"I'm both happy and proud that Ken wanted me to be here," Tretiak said. "As soon as I got the call, I didn't hesitate one bit, even though it's a long way from Moscow to Montreal."

THE GAME: Montreal Canadiens 3–Ottawa Senators 1

Ottawa's Chris Phillips scored the first goal of the game just 55 seconds after the opening faceoff, on goalie David Aebischer. The goal gave the Senators a 1–0 lead, but the Canadiens exploded for three goals in a 2:24 span in the second period to take control and claim two points in the tight Eastern Conference standings.

The game changed on two quick plays. Chris Neil took a hooking penalty, and on the power play Sheldon Souray got a goal to make it a 1–1 game. Just 66 seconds later Mark Streit scored on a breakaway after taking a pass from Andrei Markov and making a cute deke on goalie Ray Emery. And then, to make matters worse, the Habs' Tomas Plekanec scored a short-handed goal with Souray in the box.

30

MIKE
VERNON

CALGARY FLAMES
FEBRUARY 6, 2007

Born: Calgary, Alberta, February 24, 1963
Position: Goalie
Catches: Left
Height: 5'9"
Weight: 180 lbs.

HONOURS
- **Stanley Cup** 1989, 1997
- **Jennings Trophy** 1996 (with Chris Osgood)
- **Conn Smythe Trophy** 1997
- **NHL All-Star Game** 1988, 1989, 1990, 1991, 1993

NHL CAREER STATS

Regular Season

Years	GP	W-L-T	Mins	GA	SO	GAA
1982–2002	781	385-273-92	44,449	2,206	27	2.98

Playoffs

Years	GP	W-L-T	Mins	GA	SO	GAA
1982–2002	138	77-56-0	8,214	367	6	2.68

CAREER

Mike Vernon made his first appearance with the Flames during the 1982–83 season, playing two games, and the year after he appeared in a single game during a year in which he played in the CHL. The year after he worked his way up to the AHL, and in 1985–86 he came close to making a remarkable splash with the team. That year he was called up from the minors and appeared in 18 games in the regular season, playing so well that he played nearly every minute of the playoffs. And what a run it was!

The Flames went all the way to the Cup Final before losing to Montreal and Patrick Roy, but Vernon had now made certain he was a Cup-quality goalie. Over the

next three years he played 54, 64, and 52 games, but the first two years ended with disappointing playoff losses to the great Oilers teams. Not so in 1989. That year the team went all the way again, meeting the Canadiens in a rematch of the 1986 Final.

It was a playoff run made possible by Vernon. In the opening round of the post-season, the Flames played Vancouver. The best-of-seven series went to game seven, went to overtime, and once there Stan Smyl had a breakaway for the win. Vernon flicked out his glove hand to make one of the most dramatic overtime saves in recorded history, and the Flames went on to win the game and move on.

The Final ended with a six-game win over the Canadiens. Vernon remained the starting goalie for the next six years, but the team could not replicate its miracle playoff run of 1989. Calgary traded him to Detroit in 1994, and Vernon settled in as the backup to Chris Osgood for much of the next three years.

Red Wings coach Scotty Bowman, however, chose to make Vernon the go-to goalie for the playoffs, resulting in a trip to the semi-finals in 1995 and the Final in 1997. Vernon played so well in 1997, when the team won its first Stanley Cup since 1955, that he was named winner of the Conn Smythe Trophy.

CEREMONY

Only the second Calgary number to be retired after Lanny McDonald's 9, Mike Vernon's 30 was celebrated among family, friends, teammates, and hometown fans. He was at centre ice with his wife, Jane, and four children—Amelia, Matthew, John, and Will.

Many teammates from the historic Stanley Cup win in 1989 were also with Vernon, notably McDonald as well as Joe Nieuwendyk, Al MacInnis, Joel Otto, Jamie Macoun, and Theo Fleury. General manager Cliff Fletcher was there, as was executive Al MacNeil, coach Tom Watt, and minor hockey coach Al Keebler.

"This is your day," McDonald said. "Well deserved and long overdue. You are the biggest reason we are all wearing Stanley Cup rings. When a player retires, he leaves the ice, but he never leaves the team. Mike, congratulations—and welcome to the rafters."

Vernon grew up in Calgary and lived virtually his entire life in the city that was honouring him. "Winning a Stanley Cup in Calgary was special to me because of who I am—a Calgarian," he said as the sold-out crowd erupted into cheers. "Playing in front of you was like playing in front of 20,000 friends. You were passionate, and you were demanding, which is exactly what a friend should be. Take some credit because number 30 is going to the rafters. Thank you, Calgary, my hometown."

THE GAME: Chicago Blackhawks 3–Calgary Flames 2 (SO)
Calgary held Chicago to just one shot in the first period, and then Jeff Friesen scored the opening goal late in the second for the Flames. Kristian Huselius made it 2–0 on an early power play in the third, and goalie Miikka Kiprusoff was stopping everything coming his way.

But with just 2:43 remaining, Martin Havlat drew the Hawks to within a goal on the power play, and then with goalie Nikolai Khabibulin on the bench for an extra attacker, Havlat struck again to tie the score and force overtime. Five minutes more hockey produced no goals, and in the shootout, Havlat was again the hero, scoring the winner.

11

MARK
MESSIER

EDMONTON OILERS
FEBRUARY 27, 2007

Born: Edmonton, Alberta, January 18, 1961
Position: Forward
Shoots: Left
Height: 6'1"
Weight: 205 lbs.

HONOURS

- **Stanley Cup** 1984, 1985, 1987, 1988, 1990, 1994
- **Hart Trophy** 1990, 1992
- **Lester B. Pearson Award** 1990, 1992
- **Conn Smythe Trophy** 1984
- **NHL All-Star Game** 1982, 1983, 1984, 1986, 1988, 1989, 1990, 1991, 1992, 1994, 1996, 1997, 1998, 2000, 2004
- **Hockey Hall of Fame** 2007

NHL CAREER STATS

	Regular Season					Playoffs				
Years	GP	G	A	P	Pim	GP	G	A	P	Pim
1979–2004	1,756	694	1,193	1,887	1,910	236	109	186	295	244

CAREER

One of the greatest moves Glen Sather made as coach of the incredible Edmonton Oilers came early in the 1979–80 season, the team's first in the NHL. Young Mark Messier, 18 and destined for greatness, was taking his position too lightly, so Sather dispatched him to the Houston Apollos of the Central Hockey League (CHL) for a week. Messier came back a changed player, a young man, no longer a kid.

It took a couple of years for him to blossom, but once he got going he was an integral part of the team's success. He racked up 100-point seasons with seeming ease, and when the Oilers won their first Stanley Cup in 1984 it was Messier, not Gretzky, who was named winner of the Conn Smythe Trophy.

Messier was a strong and powerful skater who liked cutting down the right wing and snapping a quick shot to the far post off his back skate. No one could pull off that deceptively fast shot better than he could. He had only one 50-goal

season, 1981–82, but recorded six seasons of 100 points or more, and by the time he retired only Gretzky had more career points than Messier's 1,887.

In some respects, though, Messier's greatest season came in 1989–90. Yes, he had won the Stanley Cup four times in five years with the Oilers between 1984 and 1988, but in August of '88 Gretzky was traded to Los Angeles and Messier was named captain. On the one hand, he felt isolated. Gretzky was gone, Paul Coffey had been traded even earlier, and now there was no hiding the fact that the fortunes of the Oilers rested on Messier's shoulders.

In the 1989 playoffs, the team got a jolt when Gretzky and the L.A. Kings took the Oilers out of the playoffs in the first round, but "Moose" made sure that wasn't going to happen again. He took the team to the Cup in 1990, a surprise victory, really, given the situation the team had been in. The win made clear in retrospect that perhaps he was more instrumental in the previous Oilers wins than he had been credited for. He was Paul McCartney to Gretzky's John Lennon, as it were.

CEREMONY

The tissues were out in full force as the Oilers welcomed home Mark Messier to retire his number 11. Many of his teammates from the glory days joined him, including Wayne Gretzky, now coach of the opposing team, the Phoenix Coyotes.

Paul Coffey, Jari Kurri, Glenn Anderson, Kevin Lowe, Al Hamilton, and Dave Semenko were among the teammates who shared the evening with Moose.

The set-up on ice was elaborate. A replica of the dressing room was created, Messier's number 11 sweater hanging from his stall, and to the right was a display with all the mini-trophies Messier had won during his career. Ron MacLean was the emcee, and after some opening remarks, the Powder Blues Band performed a cover of "The Lion Sleeps Tonight."

When Messier first appeared, he was wearing his old Oilers sweater and carrying the Stanley Cup above his head. Riotous cheers greeted his entrance to the red-carpeted ice.

Messier's father, Doug, and first coach, Glen Sather, came out to greet the hero of the night, and then Lowe and public relations man Bill Tuele told stories as videos flashed highlights of Messier's career. Colin James then performed.

Later, Jim Peplinski, longtime nemesis in Calgary, spoke about how Messier not only made the Oilers better because of his leadership but the Flames as well, because they had to compete harder to keep up. Tom Cochrane then sang two songs, and current coach Craig MacTavish spoke.

Team president Patrick LaForge and Daryl Katz also spoke and then presented a cheque for $75,000 to the Edmonton Oilers Community Foundation and Alberta Lung Association on Messier's behalf. Moose then performed "Suspicious Minds" with Tom Cochrane to cap off an entertaining retirement ceremony.

THE GAME: Phoenix Coyotes 3–Edmonton Oilers 0

The emotions were too much to carry over to the game and the Oilers went down to the Coyotes. Owen Nolan scored the only goal of the opening period for the visitors who outshot the Oilers, 10–2. In the second, a period enlivened by several fights, Yanick Lehoux and Steve Reinprecht got goals to make it 3–0. Curtis Joseph was perfect in goal for the Coyotes, stopping Marc Pouliot with a great glove save in the third to preserve the shutout.

10

DALE
HAWERCHUK

WINNIPEG JETS/
PHOENIX COYOTES
APRIL 5, 2007

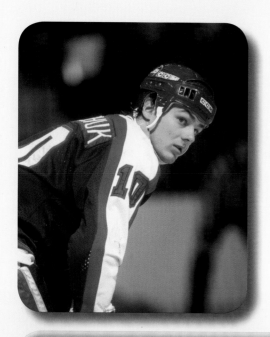

Born: Toronto, Ontario, April 4, 1963
Position: Centre
Shoots: Left
Height: 5'11"
Weight: 190 lbs.

HONOURS

• **NHL All-Star Game** 1982, 1985, 1986, 1988, 1997
• **Calder Memorial Trophy** 1982
• **Played for Canada at Canada Cup** 1987, 1991
• **Won Memorial Cup with Cornwall Royals** 1980, 1981
• **Drafted first overall by Winnipeg in** 1981
• **Hockey Hall of Fame** 2001

NHL CAREER STATS

Years	Regular Season					Playoffs				
	GP	G	A	P	Pim	GP	G	A	P	Pim
1981–97	1,188	518	891	1,409	730	97	30	69	99	67

CAREER

The 1980s was the decade of centremen. Never before—or since—have so many greats played at the same time. Wayne Gretzky and Mario Lemieux dominated, but Steve Yzerman, Peter Stastny, Bryan Trottier, and Dale Hawerchuk were there as well. This depth of talent is the only way to explain how a player with 1,409 career points didn't make the First All-Star Team even once, never won a Hart or Art Ross Trophy despite posting six 100-point seasons, and never won the Stanley Cup even once. In another time, another era, he might well have been called one of the greatest players in the game's history.

To make matters worse for Hawerchuk, he played for the Winnipeg Jets, a great team for a long time, but one that happened to be, unfortunately, in the same division as the Edmonton Oilers and Calgary Flames. Year after year the Jets would play well only to be knocked out in the first round of the playoffs by their nemeses from the West. Between 1982 and 1990, they made the playoffs every year but one, and six times out of eight they were eliminated by Edmonton. Bad luck, indeed.

Hawerchuk was a first overall draft choice (in 1981) who didn't disappoint. He joined the Jets as an 18-year-old, recorded 103 points as a rookie, won the Calder Trophy, and never looked back. His six 100-point seasons came in seven years, the lone exception a 91-point "letdown" in 1982–83.

Like the other great centres of his day, he could do it all. He was a flashy skater with a great shot, nifty stickhandler, and brilliant passer. This combination of skills was what made these players so dangerous—play him to shoot, he'll make a great pass; play him to pass, he'll drive a rocket through the back of the net or make a quick deke to leave the opponent looking at the ice.

Because of his skill, and his often early departure from the playoffs, Hawerchuk played for Canada at three World Championships. Additionally, he made the team for both the 1987 and 1991 Canada Cup tournaments, victories both years for the host country. He retired in 1997 at age 34 because of a recurring hip injury, but by that time he had 518 goals to his credit and was among the top point getters in NHL history.

CEREMONY

It was a strange honour, to say the least, but a fitting one all the same. Some new teams keep retired numbers from their older incarnations while others return the digits to circulation. For the Phoenix Coyotes, not only did they keep Dale Hawerchuk's number 10 out of the lineup, so to speak, they held a ceremony for him a decade after his last game with the old club, the Winnipeg Jets.

The Coyotes had inaugurated their "Ring of Honour" to acknowledge past greats from the organization and wanted Hawerchuk to take his rightful place therein. He was more than happy to oblige, these many years later, even though he never actually played for the Coyotes.

"When I came into the league," he said, "I wanted to prove that I could really play, but I knew I couldn't do it by myself and I needed those 20 other guys."

THE GAME:

Phoenix Coyotes 3–Los Angeles Kings 2
Two oldtimers had good nights this night. Jeremy Roenick had a goal and an assist and goaltender Curtis Joseph earned his 445th career win to move to within two of the legendary Terry Sawchuk.

Roenick scored the first goal midway through the opening period on a nice deflection that eluded goalie Sean Burke, and Bill Thomas made it 2–0 later in the period when his quick wrist shot beat Burke over the glove.

Tom Kostopoulos scored at 17:23 of the second to make it a 2–1 game, but captain Shane Doan restored the two-goal lead before the end of the period. The teams exchanged goals in the third, and Phoenix snapped a five-game losing streak with the win. It was Los Angeles' sixth loss in a row.

19

LARRY ROBINSON

MONTREAL CANADIENS
NOVEMBER 19, 2007

Born: Winchester, Ontario, June 2, 1951
Position: Defence
Shoots: Left
Height: 6'4"
Weight: 225 lbs.

HONOURS
- **Stanley Cup** 1973, 1976, 1977, 1978, 1979, 1986
- **Conn Smythe Trophy** 1978
- **Norris Trophy** 1977, 1980
- **NHL All-Star Game** 1974, 1976, 1977, 1978, 1980, 1982, 1986, 1988, 1989, 1992
- **Appeared in the playoffs a record 20 consecutive seasons**
- **Played for Canada at Canada Cup** 1976, 1981, 1984
- **Hockey Hall of Fame** 1995

NHL CAREER STATS

Years	Regular Season					Playoffs				
	GP	G	A	P	Pim	GP	G	A	P	Pim
1972–92	1,384	208	750	958	793	227	28	116	144	211

CAREER

If the measure of success is the Stanley Cup playoffs, Larry Robinson was one successful player. Indeed, he holds one of the most difficult records to equal. He played in the NHL for 20 years, and his teams made the playoffs 20 times. Such a perfect record over such a period of time exists nowhere else in the game.

Tall and gangly, Robinson was a powering force on the Montreal blue line, among the physically strongest players in the game in his own end, and a very capable threat offensively when he got his body in motion on the rush or fired a bullet slapshot from the point. He played for a year and a half in the minors with the Nova Scotia Voyageurs but was so good he was called up midway through the 1972–73 season and never went back.

Robinson was one of the "big three" of the Canadiens defence corps along with Serge Savard and Guy Lapointe. Together, the trio dominated the game for a

decade and more. Robinson won the Norris Trophy in 1976–77 and 1979–80, and in between won the Conn Smythe Trophy in 1978 for his excellent playoffs. The team won the Stanley Cup in his rookie season and then reeled off four in a row in the late 1970s, but it was his final championship that was his most cherished.

By 1984, Robinson had been in the NHL for 12 years and won the Cup five times. He felt he was skating towards the sunset of his career when Glen Sather invited him to Team Canada's camp for the 1984 Canada Cup. Surprised and flattered, he not only made the team but had a terrific tournament, and in the process he found renewed enthusiasm for the NHL game. In 1986, with most of the players from the 1970s dynasty gone, he took the Habs to a surprise Cup, backed by rookie goalie Patrick Roy.

Three years later and still enjoying the game, he signed as a free agent with Los Angeles after it became clear Montreal believed his best days were done. For the Kings, the deal signaled the buildup to a contender now that they had Wayne Gretzky, so adding an experienced future Hall of Famer to the lineup couldn't hurt. And it didn't. The Kings made the playoffs each year Robinson was there, and he retired in 1992 a contented man who could boast of having played against Bobby Orr and Gordie Howe and with Wayne Gretzky.

CEREMONY

Accompanied by his wife, Jeannette, and his grandson, Dylan, Robinson walked out to centre ice to a deafening ovation that would not let up. When he eventually spoke, he was choked with emotion.

Among those who spoke in Robinson's honour was New Jersey general manager Lou Lamoriello, a friend and colleague of Robinson's for years and an admirer of the Canadiens system for longer.

"I am certain everyone here has different memories of 'Big Bird' as he was known while helping the Canadiens win the Stanley Cup," said Lamoriello of his current assistant coach in New Jersey. "Tonight marks another moment in Larry's brilliant career. He was one-of-a-kind on the ice and one-of-a-kind off the ice, and I continue to cherish the opportunity to work with him every day."

Robinson's number 19 was painted on ice behind both goals à la Wayne Gretzky on the day of his final game, and all Montreal players wore number 19 during the pre-game skate and the ceremony itself. His was the 13th number retired by the Canadiens.

THE GAME: Ottawa Senators 4–Montreal Canadiens 2

The Senators jumped into a 2–0 lead in the first period and withstood a slight Canadiens rally in the second to hold on for the win. Dany Heatley led the way with a goal and two assists and line mate Jason Spezza had three assists.

Patrick Eaves and Chris Neil got things started early for Ottawa, making it 2–0 by the 8:57 mark of the first. Guillaume Latendresse scored a power-play goal midway through the second to halve the lead and get the fans back in the game, but less than four minutes later Heatley snuffed out the potential rally with a goal to restore the two-goal lead.

Teams exchanged goals in the third, but the Senators weren't threatened. Martin Gerber was the winning goalie for the Sens while Cristobal Huet took the loss for the Habs.

2

BRIAN
LEETCH

NEW YORK RANGERS
JANUARY 24, 2008

Born: Corpus Christi, Texas, March 3, 1968
Position: Defence
Shoots: Left
Height: 6'
Weight: 185 lbs.

HONOURS
- **Stanley Cup** 1994
- **Calder Trophy** 1989
- **Conn Smythe Trophy** 1994
- **Norris Trophy** 1992, 1997
- **Silver medal with United States at Olympics** 2002
- **Hockey Hall of Fame** 2009

NHL CAREER STATS

Years	Regular Season					Playoffs				
	GP	G	A	P	Pim	GP	G	A	P	Pim
1987–2006	1,205	247	781	1,028	571	95	28	69	97	36

CAREER

Almost certainly the finest American-born defenceman in just about anyone's books, Brian Leetch made a name for himself on Broadway and around the world. He started a life in athletics as a pitcher with a great fastball, but this early teen dream was replaced by the game of sticks and pucks.

Leetch attended Boston College, but he was so good he was there only one year. Drafted ninth overall by the Rangers in 1986, he didn't join the team until after the 1988 Olympics, by which time he had also played in two World Junior (U20) Championships and a senior World Championship.

Cut from the same cloth as Bobby Orr and Paul Coffey, Leetch liked to carry the puck up ice and drive to the net to create offence. As a full-time rookie in 1988–89, he scored 23 goals, still a record for defencemen and a sign of greater things to come. He took home the Calder Trophy for his outstanding first season and was the centre of a fine nucleus of young talent.

In 1991–92, Leetch joined exclusive company by recording 102 points, one of only a handful of defencemen to hit the century mark. He had the best year of his career in 1993–94, though, with fewer points but far greater impact. Although he had "just" 23 goals and 56 assists during the regular season, he took his game to another level during the playoffs, leading the team to its first Stanley Cup since 1940. Yes, the team had Mike Richter in goal and Mark Messier as captain, but Leetch had 23 assists and 34 points in the post season to lead all scorers.

When Messier left the team to sign with the Vancouver Canucks in 1997, it was clear the successor to his captaincy was Leetch, a position he held for the next three seasons. He won the Norris Trophy twice, only the third American after Rod Langway and Chris Chelios to be named top defenceman in the league, and he was part of the historic Team USA that won the World Cup in 1996.

CEREMONY

The 50-minute tribute was hosted by sportscaster Sam Rosen, and Leetch was introduced by none other than Mark Messier himself.

Rosen began by calling Leetch "one of the greatest defencemen ever" and followed with a video tribute on the scoreboard above centre ice. Leetch then walked from the Rangers' dressing room to the ice where the Stanley Cup sat on a table for him to admire once again, as he had done after winning in 1994.

Many important people in Leetch's life were on the red carpet, notably Brian Mullen (his first roommate), Ron Greschner, Jan Erixon, and defence partner Jeff Beukeboom. Adam Graves attended along with Harry Howell and Brad Park, and four other players who have had their sweater retired by the team: Ed Giacomin, Rod Gilbert, Mike Richter, and Messier. Finally, Leetch was accompanied by his wife and three children.

Then it was time for some gifts. Former players gave Leetch a customized Harley-Davidson motorcycle and presented a cheque for $25,000 to the John J. Murray Foundation in honour of a friend who was killed in the 9/11 attacks on the World Trade Center.

After thanking teammates and fans, acknowledging how special the city and arena had been to him, Leetch then had a surprise of his own that shocked the crowd. He announced that Graves would soon have his number 9 retired, a revelation that shook the rafters yet again on this special night.

THE GAME: New York Rangers 2–Atlanta Thrashers 1 (SO)

Playing their final game before the All-Star break, the Rangers rallied from 1–0 down to beat the Thrashers in a shootout. Brendan Shanahan was the hero, scoring the only goal of the shootout to give the Rangers two points.

"One of the things we told our guys before we went out to play was that you don't know how many of these opportunities you're going to get to see a jersey retired of a league all-star, a future Hall-of-Famer," Rangers coach Tom Renney said. "So, you want to make sure that you punctuate your contributions the right way, by playing hard and winning."

Marian Hossa got the game's first goal just 45 seconds into the middle period, on a power play, and it wasn't until midway through the third that Michal Roszival tied the score. Both goalies played well, but Lundqvist was perfect in the shootout, stopping Mark Recchi, Slava Kozlov, and Hossa for the win.

23

BOB GAINEY

MONTREAL CANADIENS
FEBRUARY 23, 2008

Born: Peterborough, Ontario, December 13, 1953
Position: Left wing
Shoots: Left
Height: 6'2"
Weight: 200 lbs.

HONOURS

• **Stanley Cup** 1976, 1977, 1978, 1979, 1986
• **Selke Trophy** 1978, 1979, 1980, 1981
• **Conn Smythe Trophy** 1979
• **Played for Canada in Canada Cup** 1976, 1981
• **Hockey Hall of Fame** 1992

NHL CAREER STATS

	Regular Season					Playoffs				
Years	GP	G	A	P	Pim	GP	G	A	P	Pim
1973–89	1,160	239	262	501	585	182	25	48	73	151

CAREER

It was Soviet coach Viktor Tikhonov who called Bob Gainey technically the best player in the world during the 1976 Canada Cup. It was a curious compliment, but once parsed came to describe Gainey's all-round ability despite being no superstar in any particular area. That is, he didn't have a bullet shot or tremendous speed. He wasn't a magnificent stickhandler, awesome goal scorer, or even pin-point passer. But he could do everything well, including all the little things that made the difference between winning and losing.

Gainey was a master of two-way play, a capable forward in the opponent's end of the ice and a superb defensive player inside his own blue line. He was an artist in the faceoff circle, tenacious in the corners, a leader by word and deed. The Montreal Canadiens, for all their superstar Lafleurs and Robinsons and Drydens, could not have won as often as they did without Gainey.

Drafted by the Habs in 1973, he made the team almost right away and spent his entire 16-year career with Montreal. He had nine seasons of 15 goals or more, modest totals to be sure, but he was a plus player in the plus-minus stats in 14 of those seasons despite playing against the top opposition line pretty much every shift, every night.

Such was his reputation for defensive play that the NHL instituted the Frank Selke Trophy for top defensive forward more or less in his honour. Indeed, he won it the first four times of its existence (1978–81), but he also won the Conn Smythe Trophy in 1979 for his outstanding playoffs and Cup win. This was the fourth in a row for the team.

Gainey was named team captain in 1981, and the first half of the decade was full of disappointment and early playoff exits. The team had lost many of the core players from the 1970s dynasty, and Gainey, now older and a step slower, seemed to be on borrowed time. But the team had one more great run, and buoyed by the goaltending of rookie Patrick Roy won a surprise Cup in 1986.

CEREMONY

Hosted by Dick Irvin in English and Richard Garneau in French, the ceremony to honour Gainey was a night to remember. It began when he stepped onto the ice in full equipment and skated several laps, acknowledging the applause.

When he took the microphone to begin his thank-yous, the roar continued. After several minutes, he finally said a few words and then invited his best friends and former teammates to join him. "Come on out here, Doug Jarvis and Guy Carbonneau," said Gainey. "Rarely was I ever on the ice without one of those two guys right by my side. I first became teammates with Doug in 1971 and we went on to win four Stanley Cups together with the Canadiens. In 1980, I met a young centreman named Guy Carbonneau and we won a Stanley Cup together in 1986. I played with the Drydens, Robinsons, and the Lafleurs," Gainey noted, "but these two are my superstars."

Gainey was accompanied by his children, Anna, Steve, and Colleen; his sister, Maureen; close family friend Christine Pickrell; and, of course, many teammates from the 1986 Canadiens by his side.

"It's tough to explain all the ways my time here has impacted my life," said Gainey. "My association with this incredible organization has filled my life with adventure and success, and that's all thanks to the Canadiens and the best city in the world, Montreal."

THE GAME: Columbus Blue Jackets 3–Montreal Canadiens 0

Pascal Leclaire made his first start at the Bell Centre, just a few kilometres from where he was born in Repentigny, and recorded his league-leading ninth shutout of the season before some 25 family and friends. He stopped 31 shots, and Rick Nash, Andrew Murray, and Manny Malhotra scored for the visiting Blue Jackets who spoiled the night for Gainey.

"That's the thing I'm upset the most about," Montreal coach Guy Carbonneau said after he himself was part of the ceremony for Gainey, having been a player on the Stanley Cup team of 1986.

"We're definitely a better team when we score the first goal, so that helped us," Nash said. "They had some jump. It was lucky for us that we kind of took their fans out of it and kept them down a little bit."

3

PIERRE
PILOTE

Born: Kenogami, Quebec, December 11, 1931
Position: Defence
Shoots: Left
Height: 5'10"
Weight: 175 lbs.

HONOURS
- **Stanley Cup** 1961
- **Norris Trophy** 1963, 1964, 1965
- **NHL All-Star Game** 1960, 1961, 1962, 1963, 1964, 1965, 1967, 1968
- **NHL First All-Star Team** 1963, 1964, 1965, 1966, 1967
- **Hockey Hall of Fame** 1975

NHL CAREER STATS

	Regular Season					Playoffs				
Years	GP	G	A	P	Pim	GP	G	A	P	Pim
1955–69	890	80	418	498	1,251	86	8	53	61	102

CAREER

When the Chicago Blackhawks decided to honour Pierre Pilote and Keith Magnuson on the same night, they united two great players who wore the same number but also two men who played in different eras and embodied different values of the game.

Pilote was an offensively capable defenceman who played tough but was durable during his career. In fact, from his first game in the league in the 1955–56 season until early in the 1961–62 season when he dislocated his shoulder, he didn't miss a game.

That run of 376 games was exceptional given that he was also trying to establish himself in the league and play tough. He led the NHL in penalty minutes with 165 in 1960–61, not coincidentally the year of the Hawks' Stanley Cup victory.

That fall, Pilote was named captain, a position he held for seven seasons until his trade to Toronto in 1968.

Once players around the league came to respect him, Pilote settled in to a game less about fighting and penalty minutes and more about defensive responsibility. His partner on the blue line was often Elmer "Moose" Vasko, and together they were among the best tandems in the league for many years. Pilote, though, won the Norris Trophy for three straight years, crediting Vasko for his success.

Perhaps the most incredible thing about Pilote is that he made the NHL at all. When the local arena burned down when he was 14, he didn't don a pair of skates for three years! And, when he did, at age 17, he played organized hockey for the first time in his life. Yet two years later he was playing in the Ontario junior leagues, after which he apprenticed in the AHL for four years.

3

KEITH
MAGNUSON

CHICAGO BLACKHAWKS
NOVEMBER 12, 2008

Born: Saskatoon, Saskatchewan, April 27, 1947
Died: Vaughan, Ontario, December 15, 2003
Position: Defence
Shoots: Right
Height: 6'
Weight: 185 lbs.

HONOURS
- NHL All-Star Game 1971, 1972
- Later coached Chicago Black Hawks after playing his whole career with the team
- NCAA Championship tournament MVP 1969 (University of Denver)

NHL CAREER STATS

	Regular Season					Playoffs				
Years	GP	G	A	P	Pim	GP	G	A	P	Pim
1969–80	589	14	125	139	1,442	68	3	9	12	164

CAREER

A stay-at-home defenceman, Magnuson wore the Black Hawks logo on his sleeve. He played every one of his 657 career games (regular season and playoffs) with the Black Hawks over an 11-season career. He had to retire at age 32 because every game he played was like two for anyone else. The reckless abandon, the emotion, the injuries, all took their toll on his body.

Anyone who remembers the Magnuson era in Chicago can recall watching him slide out to block a Brad Park slapshot with his jaw, refusing to be carted off on a stretcher despite the extreme pain. Magnuson led the NHL in penalty minutes his first two seasons and finished with 1,442 by the time he retired. Tough and physical, his forte was keeping the puck out of the net and keeping opponents away from his goal.

He and the Hawks had playoff success in 1971 when they went to the Cup

Final against Montreal, but they were no match for rookie sensation Ken Dryden and the rest of the more experienced Habs.

Magnuson was a leader on and off the ice, and such was his dedication to the team that in retirement he organized the alumni, worked in the front office, and coached the team for two seasons.

He wasn't the most skilled player to pass through the league, but if any player ever symbolized his club's values and ambitions, it was Keith Magnuson in Chicago.

CEREMONY

The Blackhawks were making up for lost time, having retired several numbers from days gone by in the preceding couple of years. This night featured two number 3s: Pierre Pilote and Keith Magnuson, players from different eras but equally devoted to the team.

In fact, Pilote's last season was Magnuson's first, and both were the first defencemen to have their numbers retired by the Hawks. All other players whose number had been retired were part of the ceremony: Bobby Hull, Stan Mikita, Tony Esposito, and Denis Savard, with the exception of goalie Glenn Hall. Chris Chelios also attended.

The late Keith Magnuson, who died in an automobile accident in 2003, was represented by his son, Kevin, who gave special thanks to two former teammates, Cliff Korroll and Dale Tallon.

Kevin addressed the crowd: "Although my dad and Pierre had different styles of play, they had one thing in common: the love of the Indian-head sweater," he said, referring to the team's logo. "My dad took tremendous pride in what the Blackhawks sweater meant to him. Our family will always look at that number in the rafters and remember how proud he was to be a Chicago Blackhawk."

Chairman Rocky Wirtz made a short speech praising both players, calling them both "leaders, winners, legends. To Pierre, the most important thing was that he brought the Stanley Cup to Chicago," Wirtz said. "Keith played with reckless abandon, passion, and heart."

Doug Wilson, a former teammate of Magnuson, still has a picture of "Maggie" in his office in San Jose, where he is the team's general manager, and often refers to Magnuson's motto: "You make a living by what you get; you make a life by what you give."

"I have received several awards and honours in my time," Pilote said, his wife, Anne, by his side, "but I am truly humbled by this one."

THE GAME: Boston Bruins 2–Chicago Blackhawks 1 (SO)

This was a goaltender's battle from the drop of the puck, with Chicago's Nikolai Khabibulin and Boston's Tim Thomas stopping almost everything that came their way. The game was scoreless for nearly two periods, but Marco Sturm put the Bruins ahead 1–0 at 19:06 of the second on a power play. Jonathan Toews tied the game for the Hawks midway through the final period, and a wild overtime resulted in great scoring chances but no goals.

Khabibulin made a glove save off Marc Savard in the OT to prevent defeat, and then Thomas stopped Patrick Sharp in a rare overtime penalty shot to force a shootout. Patrick Kane scored for the home side in the extra shots as did Blake Wheeler for the Bruins; Toews and Dave Bolland missed for Chicago and P. J. Axelsson scored the winner for the visitors.

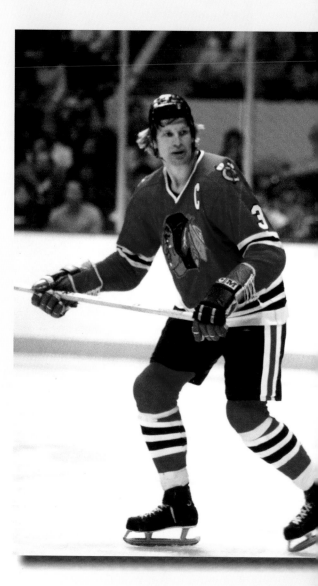

33

PATRICK
ROY

MONTREAL CANADIENS
NOVEMBER 22, 2008

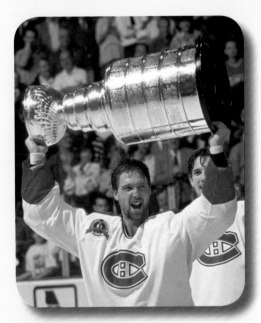

Born: Quebec City, Quebec, October 5, 1965
Position: Goalie
Catches: Left
Height: 6'2"
Weight: 185 lbs.

HONOURS
- **Stanley Cup** 1986, 1993, 1996, 2001
- **Conn Smythe Trophy** 1986, 1993, 2001
- **Jennings Trophy** 1987, 1988, 1989 (with Brian Hayward), 1992, 2002
- **Vezina Trophy** 1989, 1990, 1992
- **NHL All-Star Game** 1988, 1990, 1991, 1992, 1993, 1994, 1997, 1998, 2001, 2002, 2003
- **Hockey Hall of Fame** 2006

NHL CAREER STATS

Regular Season

Years	GP	W-L-T	Mins	GA	SO	GAA
1984–2003	1,029	551-315-131	60,235	2,546	66	2.54

Playoffs

Years	GP	W-L-T	Mins	GA	SO	GAA
1984–2003	247	151-94-0	15,209	584	23	2.30

MONTREAL CAREER

Not since Ken Dryden in 1971 had a goalie entered the league with such spectacular success as Patrick Roy during the 1985–86 season. The previous year he was being hammered to the tune of five and a half goals a game in Quebec junior with Granby, and a year later he was leading the Montreal Canadiens to the Stanley Cup. In between, it didn't hurt his reputation that he managed to lead the AHL's Sherbrooke Canadiens to the Calder Cup as well.

Roy insisted his time with Granby was the best thing for him. A goalie needs shots to learn, and Granby was a bad team that gave up a lot of shots. Roy learned all right. He had a 23–18–3 record during the regular season with the Habs, but in the playoffs he was often unbeatable, allowing just 39 goals in 20 games. He won the Conn Smythe Trophy, but the most amazing thing about this win was the team wasn't particularly good. Despite its middling regular-season record of 40–33–7, Roy earned the moniker "St. Patrick" for almost single-handedly leading the team to Stanley Cup victory.

The next decade was much the same. The team wasn't skilled offensively and didn't have a "big three" on defence as it had had in the 1970s, but Roy was sensational. He took the team to the Final again three years later, this time coming up short against Calgary, the team Roy stonewalled in the 1986 Final, and in 1993 Roy had his greatest success.

Not only did he take the team back to Cup victory, he did so in record fashion. The Habs won the required 16 games, of course, but fully 11 of those victories came in overtime. If Roy's value had been forgotten since 1986, it shot through the roof after 1993.

In all, Roy was with the Canadiens for more than 10 years, and although he departed under controversial circumstances, the fans never forgot his heroics and his number was duly retired during the team's centennial celebrations of 2008–09.

CEREMONY

The ceremonies for Patrick Roy began when he emerged from a tunnel in the stands and walked down toward the ice as fans, some still finding their seats, turned in surprise. Roy was praised by coaches Jean Perron, Pat Burns, and Jacques Demers, as well as friend and former agent, Pierre Lacroix.

"I may have left without probably saying goodbye the way I would have liked to, but I've always cherished my great memories from my time in Montreal," said Roy. "I remember those nights when we made the walls of the Forum tremble as we lit up Montreal. Tonight, I've come home."

He was accompanied by his three children, Jonathan, Frederick, and Jana; his parents, Michel and Barbara; brother, Stephane; and sister, Alexandra.

THE GAME:

Boston Bruins 3–Montreal Canadiens 2 (SO)
The Bruins improved their record for November to 9–0–1 with the overtime win and were led by goalie Tim Thomas who stopped, appropriately, 33 shots this night. Blake Wheeler scored on the Bruins' first shot in the shootout and Thomas stopped Alex Kovalev, Andrei Markov, and captain Saku Koivu in the shootout. Wheeler's was a lucky goal in that he lost control of the puck as he started to deke Carey Price, but it dribbled over the line nonetheless.

Teams exchanged goals in each of the second and third periods. Andrei Kostitsyn scored early in the second to give the home side a 1–0 lead, but rookie sensation Milan Lucic tied the game midway through and Matt Hunwick put the Bruins ahead at 9:41 of the third. It took a Tom Kostopoulos goal with just 3:05 left in the third to force the overtime, but the shootout was dominated by Boston.

16 TREVOR LINDEN

VANCOUVER CANUCKS
DECEMBER 17, 2008

Born: Medicine Hat, Alberta, April 11, 1970
Position: Centre
Shoots: Left
Height: 6'4"
Weight: 220 lbs.

HONOURS
- King Clancy Memorial Trophy 1997
- NHL All-Star Game 1991, 1992
- Played for Canada at World Cup 1996
- Played for Canada at Olympics 1998
- Captain Vancouver Canucks 1990–97

NHL CAREER STATS

Years	Regular Season					Playoffs				
	GP	G	A	P	Pim	GP	G	A	P	Pim
1988–2008	1,382	375	492	867	895	124	34	65	99	104

CAREER

Despite a five-year absence from Vancouver in the middle of his career, Trevor Linden was a Canucks leader and star in spirit for 20 years. Drafted by the team second overall in 1988, he came within a game of leading the team to the Stanley Cup. The Canucks lost game seven of the 1994 Final to the Rangers, 3–2, with Linden scoring both Vancouver goals.

Linden enjoyed a tremendous rookie season in 1988–89, scoring 30 goals and establishing himself as a big and strong presence up the middle. It was the first of six, 30-goal seasons with the team, and already by the start of his sophomore season he was one of three alternating captains with the team. The next year he was sole captain, a role he held until Mark Messier signed as a free agent more than seven years later.

Linden was a leader on and off the ice. His offensive skills drove the team, but

he also loved the city of Vancouver and became an important member of the community. But when Messier signed with the team, the Canucks were able to trade Linden to the New York Islanders without losing a great leader.

Pretty much overnight, Linden's production dropped. His heart wasn't in Long Island, or Montreal or Washington, where he played for brief stretches after, and he was traded back to Vancouver early in the 2001–02 season. Linden played five and a half more years with the team, and although he wasn't as potent offensively, he was still a leader and fan favourite.

One of the biggest moments of Linden's career came in the semi finals of the 1998 Olympics playing for Canada against the Czechs. Trailing 1–0, Canada pulled goalie Patrick Roy for the extra attacker, and with less than two minutes to go Linden scored to tie the game and send the game to overtime.

CEREMONY

"Captain Canuck" received an emotional farewell and thank you as his number 16 was lifted into the rafters of GM Place. Accompanied by his wife, Cristina; mother, Edna; and father, Lane, Linden was feted by teammates and friends, notably coach Pat Quinn; Mattias Ohlund, a current player and Linden's roommate for seven years; Stan Smyl, the only other player to have his number (12) retired by the team; Martin Gelinas; and Gino Odjick.

"There could be no finer representative not only of the NHL, but of professional athletes anywhere," Bettman acknowledged.

"To share this honour is a great thrill," Smyl said prior to Linden's introduction. "Your leadership inspired your teammates to play not only at a high level for themselves, but for each other."

Ohlund described Linden as "a perfect example on and off the ice" and called him both "a friend and mentor."

Linden thanked Quinn, his former coach, for helping him develop. "Not only did you teach me about the game, you taught me how to be a professional. Your guidance allowed me to reach my full potential."

As might be expected, he finished by thanking the fans who'd embraced him for so long. "To the fans of Vancouver and British Columbia, it's hard to express my gratitude to you," he said. "Thank you for letting me into your lives. Thanks for being incredible, passionate hockey fans."

THE GAME: Vancouver Canucks 4–Edmonton Oilers 2

Daniel Sedin came up big for his mentor, scoring two goals and adding an assist to lead the Canucks to a 4–2 win over visiting Edmonton. After a scoreless first period, the Canucks took control of the game with three goals in the second, two by Sedin and a single sandwiched in between from Ryan Kesler. But the Oilers rallied in the third to make the final minutes more dramatic than the home side would have liked.

Dustin Penner scored early in the final period to make it 3–1, and then with 1:29 remaining Sam Gagner made it a one-goal game. The Oilers pulled goalie Dwayne Roloson for the sixth attacker, but Jannick Hansen scored into the empty net to seal the win in Linden's honour.

After the game, Daniel Sedin talked about Linden's early influence: "He came in, taught us a lot, and helped us get better. He was a big help to us. We talked to him a lot. He's been a big part of our success."

11

MIKE GARTNER

WASHINGTON CAPITALS
DECEMBER 28, 2008

Born: Ottawa, Ontario, October 29, 1959
Position: Right wing
Shoots: Right
Height: 6'
Weight: 187 lbs.

HONOURS
• **NHL All-Star Game** 1981, 1985, 1986, 1988, 1990, 1993, 1996
• **Drafted fourth overall by Washington in** 1979
• **Played for Canada in Canada Cup** 1984, 1987
• **Hockey Hall of Fame** 2001

NHL CAREER STATS

	Regular Season					Playoffs				
Years	GP	G	A	P	Pim	GP	G	A	P	Pim
1979–98	1,432	708	627	1,335	1,159	122	43	50	93	125

CAREER

You can count the number of career 700-goal scorers on one hand (plus a thumb), and Mike Gartner is among that number (the thumb, or, sixth all-time) with 708. More amazingly, he scored at least 30 goals a season for 18 straight years, all but his last in the NHL, a record not even Gretzky, Howe, or Lemieux were able to match. Indeed, it was that consistency that was his trademark over a 19-year, Hockey Hall of Fame career that ended in 1998.

Drafted fourth overall by Washington in 1979, Gartner stepped into the lineup of a weak team right away and made an impact. He had 36 goals as a rookie and garnered some Calder Trophy votes, but on a team with a 27–40–13 record that had yet to make the playoffs in its eight years of existence, he didn't stand a chance.

Gartner came to the rink every day ready to skate down the right wing and let go one of his wrist shots à la Lanny McDonald. He was positionally strong, a pure

winger, and if every teammate had been as consistent and reliable, the team would have won many more games. In his nine and a half seasons with the Capitals, the team made the playoffs six times, but they made it past the first round only once. He had his best statistical year in 1984–85 when he had his only season of 50 goals and 100 points (102).

After a trade to the Minnesota North Stars for a year and a half, Gartner found life again with the New York Rangers, a team on its way to the Stanley Cup. However, at the trade deadline in March 1994, he was sent to Toronto for Glenn Anderson, and it was Anderson, not Gartner, who was part of that Cup-winning team. This was as close as he got to the Cup, and he finished his career playing two years in Phoenix. Only in his last season, when he had 12 goals in 60 games, did he fail to score at least 32 goals in a year (not counting the lockout season of 1994–95, which was reduced to 48 games).

CEREMONY

Mike Gartner became the fourth Caps player to have his number retired after Yvon Labre's 7, Rod Langway's 5, and Dale Hunter's 32. His longtime friend and business partner, Wes Jarvis, hosted the evening.

"He put us on the edge of the seats every time he swooped down that right wing and took that big slapshot," Jarvis related. "We saw his puck-handling and passing skills evolve to make him an all-star. What stood out to all of us, though, was his passion and enthusiasm for the game of hockey."

Team president Dick Patrick made a special presentation to the player: a painting from Michel Lapensée, a framed vintage Capitals number 11 sweater, and a silver puck.

Gartner was joined by his wife, Colleen; sons, Josh and Dylan; daughter, Natalie; and her husband, Adam. During the warm-up the players all wore number 11 sweaters that they and Gartner signed and auctioned off after the game, with proceeds going to World Vision.

Other guests in attendance at centre ice included former teammates Greg Adams, Bob Carpenter, Bobby Gould, Al Hangsleben, Craig Laughlin, Paul Mulvey, Larry Murphy, Errol Rausse, Gary Rissling, and Scott Stevens, as well as Labre and Langway.

Every fan at the game also received a number 11 pin in tribute to the honoured player.

THE GAME: Washington Capitals 4–Toronto Maple Leafs 1
Washington improved its record at the Verizon Centre this year to 15–1–1 with a victory over Toronto, thanks to goals from Alexander Ovechkin and Brooks Laich and some timely saves from goalie Jose Theodore. The Maple Leafs' Niklas Hagman got the only goal of the first period, but this proved to be the only score his team would get all night.

Laich got things going for the Caps in the second on a power play at 12:54, and Ovechkin put the team ahead for good with only 10 seconds left in the middle period.

The Leafs had their chances to tie the game in the third, but Theodore held the fort and Laich and Ovechkin closed out the scoring (into an empty net). Ovechkin had scored 23 goals now in his last 24 games while the Caps were now 21–1–1 in their last 23 games at home.

9 GLENN ANDERSON

EDMONTON OILERS
JANUARY 18, 2009

Born: Vancouver, British Columbia, October 2, 1960
Position: Right wing
Shoots: Left
Height: 6'1"
Weight: 190 lbs.

HONOURS

- **Stanley Cup** 1984, 1985, 1987, 1988, 1990, 1994
- **NHL All-Star Game** 1984, 1985, 1986, 1988
- **Played for Canada at Olympics** 1980
- **Played for Canada at Canada Cup** 1984, 1987
- **Hockey Hall of Fame** 2008

NHL CAREER STATS

	Regular Season					Playoffs				
Years	GP	G	A	P	Pim	GP	G	A	P	Pim
1980–96	1,129	498	601	1,099	1,120	225	93	121	214	442

CAREER

He didn't like being called "Mork" by his teammates, but it was an apt moniker in that he was out of this world, a person apart from the rest of the gang. No matter. His playing career speaks for itself. By the time Anderson retired, he had five playoff overtime goals to his credit. Only Maurice Richard, with six, had more.

Anderson and Richard had much more in common. Both played right wing and shot left, meaning they had a better angle on goal as they drove to the net. Both also had no trepidation in using their sticks on opponents to create a little extra space, and both were great scorers. Unfortunately, Anderson couldn't quite hang in there long enough to reach 500, having to settle for 498 over the course of his 16 years in the NHL.

He was also a more rounded person than most, happily delaying his entrance into the league for a chance to play for Canada's National Team, travel the world,

and play in the 1980 Olympics in Lake Placid. Ditto for the end of his career, which he also put off to play in Switzerland, Germany, Finland, and Italy.

It was the meat of his career, though, for which he is best remembered, and that means the 1980s with the Edmonton Oilers. Anderson was front and centre with Gretzky, Messier, et al, scoring at a terrific pace. He had at least 30 goals in each of his first eight seasons, peaking with 54 in both 1983–84 and 1985–86.

Of course, he also won the Cup five times during the decade, chipping in with those timely overtime goals, none more crucial than game six of the conference final for Toronto in 1993 against Los Angeles. The Leafs lost that series in seven games to Gretzky's Kings, and a year later Anderson was traded to the Rangers late in the season where he won a sixth Cup on a team loaded with Oilers from the glory days of the 1980s.

In all, his 93 playoff goals rank him fifth all-time, and his 225 playoff games played is also among the career leaders. Anderson was a rare player who excelled in the regular season but raised his game to an even higher level for the playoffs, when games were even more important.

CEREMONY

Once the Oilers and Coyotes had taken their places on the players' benches, a video tribute played above centre ice, after which Anderson hopped over the boards in full equipment and skated a celebratory lap.

Kevin Lowe, team president and former teammate, made the introductory speech, but the ice was replete with teammates from those glory days of the 1980s, including Wayne Gretzky, current coach of the opposition, Phoenix.

Anderson's thank-you speech was moving for its warmth in acknowledging his place in team history. "It's great to be back in this uniform again," he said. "Putting this jersey on is like coming home and getting into your comfy clothes.

"As a team we accomplished so much in this building. We have unforgettable moments together. And to be here on this ice with this group of people here in front of the Edmonton hockey fans makes me want to say what a remarkable journey and you guys are the greatest hockey fans in the world.

"We had the times of our lives here, and I want to thank you for this great honour," Anderson said to the standing crowd. "Part of me will always remain an Edmontonian and an even bigger part of me will always be an Oiler. Once an Oiler, always an Oiler."

After he finished, he picked up a stick while Mark Messier, dressed in a suit, dished a pass to him. Anderson streaked down the right wing and snapped a shot into the net, as he had done so many times before.

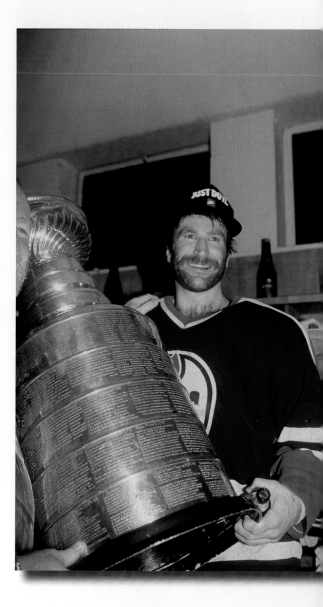

THE GAME: Edmonton Oilers 6–Phoenix Coyotes 3

The Coyotes started out as spoilers when Keith Yandle scored at 5:30 to give the visitors a 1–0 lead. But Ethan Moreau scored twice and sandwiched in between was a third goal from Ales Hemsky, and the Oilers took a 3–1 lead to the dressing room after the first period.

The Coyotes scored twice in the second to tie the score, but Dustin Penner's late goal gave the Oilers another lead, 4–3. In the third, it was all Oil, including Moreau's hat trick marker to finish the scoring into an empty net with just 0.4 seconds left on the clock.

9

ADAM
GRAVES

NEW YORK RANGERS
FEBRUARY 3, 2009

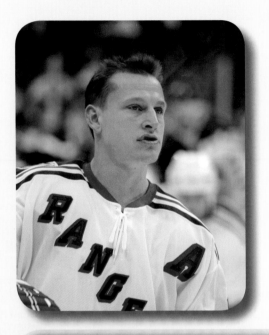

Born: Toronto, Ontario, April 12, 1968
Position: Left wing
Shoots: Left
Height: 6'
Weight: 205 lbs.

HONOURS
- **Stanley Cup** 1990, 1994
- **Bill Masterton Memorial Trophy** 2001
- **King Clancy Memorial Trophy** 1994
- **NHL All-Star Game** 1994
- **Played for Canada at World Cup** 1996

NHL CAREER STATS

	Regular Season					Playoffs				
Years	GP	G	A	P	Pim	GP	G	A	P	Pim
1987–2003	1,152	329	287	616	1,224	125	38	27	65	119

CAREER

Another example of a team giving up on a draft choice too quickly, Adam Graves started his NHL career with Detroit in 1987, only to see it reach fruition with the New York Rangers two years later. He was a tough-nosed, scoring junior with the Windsor Spitfires and played a handful of games for the Red Wings in 1987–88. He spent most of the next year at the Joe Louis Arena but in 1989 he was part of a large trade with the Oilers. Graves' timing was perfect. Although Wayne Gretzky was now playing in Los Angeles, captain Mark Messier had control of the team and took it to its fifth Stanley Cup in seven years.

Graves stayed one more year in Edmonton, and then followed Messier to the Rangers for 1991–92. The fit was again perfect. Graves started scoring as he had shown he could do in junior. He loved New York with all his heart and did community work with underprivileged children, for which he was awarded the 1994

King Clancy Memorial Trophy.

On ice, everything fell into place. He went from 26 goals in his first year with the Blueshirts to 36 and then 52 in 1993–94, an historic season for any fan of the team. The Rangers beat all comers, including the Canucks in a seven-game final, to win their first Stanley Cup since 1940. Graves added 10 more goals in the post-season, and while Messier and goalie Mike Richter received most of the credit, Graves was praised for his two-way play, timely scoring, and leadership.

CEREMONY

Dubbed "Heart of a Ranger," the ceremony to retire Adam Graves' number 9 lasted an hour, an honour not only to his play on ice but his indefatigable work with charities around the city.

Emcee Sam Rosen began, "Tonight we honour grit, we honour grace, we honour generosity." After which a video tribute highlighted Graves' career. Mike Richter, Mark Messier, and Brian Leetch all spoke, and then a series of teammates appeared: Mike Gartner, Darren Langdon, Glenn Healy, Sergei Nemchinov, Stephane Matteau, Jeff Beukeboom, and lastly Harry Howell and Andy Bathgate, both of whom would have their numbers retired later in the month.

Graves was joined at centre ice by his wife, Violet, and three children—daughters Madison and Montana, and son, Logan. Graves was showered with gifts, including a guitar autographed by Bruce Springsteen. A big fan of the TV show *The Sopranos*, Graves was stunned to see the entire cast come out and present him with a Sopranos hockey sweater.

After a few words from Messier, Graves addressed the crowd: "I stand before you humbled and incredibly appreciative because I am truly blessed. Blessed to have the talent to play in the NHL, and blessed to have the ability to share that ability for 10 years with the people of New York."

He thanked the fans of the city, the organization past and present, and then stepped aside as captain Chris Drury and assistants Scott Gomez and Markus Naslund helped unfurl the banner to be lifted into the rafters. At every chance the crowd chanted his nickname, "Gray-vee! Gray-vee!"

THE GAME: Atlanta Thrashers 2–New York Rangers 1 (SO)
The night didn't go as planned, although it had its moments. In the end, the Rangers lost for the third time in a row, in overtime, despite late-game heroics from Markus Naslund. There was no scoring in the first 40 minutes, and Thrasher Joe Motzko scored first early in the third.

It took a dramatic goal from Naslund with 10.7 seconds left in regulation to tie the game with goalie Henrik Lundqvist on the bench for a sixth attacker. Seconds earlier Ilya Kovalchuk hit the post with the net empty. Overtime settled nothing, so the teams went to penalty shots.

In the shootout, Naslund beat Kari Lehtonen with the first shot, but neither Nikolai Zherdev nor Fredrik Sjostrom could follow with a second goal. Bryan Little and Slava Kozlov both beat Lundqvist for the win, though.

"We wanted to win," Naslund said. "We had a big talk about it before the game that we wanted to make it a special night for [Adam] and for the fans. Unfortunately, we couldn't come through."

2

GLEN
WESLEY

CAROLINA HURRICANES
FEBRUARY 17, 2009

Born: Red Deer, Alberta, October 2, 1968
Position: Defence
Shoots: Left
Height: 6'1"
Weight: 205 lbs.

HONOURS
- **Stanley Cup** 2006
- **NHL All-Star Game** 1989
- **Drafted third overall by Boston in** 1987

NHL CAREER STATS

	Regular Season					Playoffs				
Years	GP	G	A	P	Pim	GP	G	A	P	Pim
1987–2008	1,457	128	409	537	1,045	169	15	38	53	141

CAREER

Although he was considered offensively gifted in junior hockey with Portland of the WHL, Glen Wesley became more defensive minded once he made it to the NHL. Certainly that was the case once he landed in Hartford. Drafted by Boston in 1987, he made the team that fall as a 19-year-old and fit into the lineup easily. He had 19 goals in his sophomore season, but this was an aberration rather than a sign of things to come.

He was more consistently known as a large and forceful presence inside his own blue line, a player who made it difficult for opponents to station themselves in the slot or crease. Wesley and the Bruins went to the Stanley Cup Final twice, only to lose both times to the Oilers, in 1988 and 1990.

In the summer of 1994 Wesley was traded to Hartford for three first-round draft choices, high praise indeed for his value. The Bruins used those choices to

select Kyle McLaren (1995), Jonathan Aitken (1996), and Sergei Samsonov (1997).

The match was made in heaven. Wesley was coming to a team where he was counted on to lead. He got plenty of ice time, took his responsibilities seriously, and thrived. Three years later, when the team moved to Carolina, Wesley made the commitment to remain with the organization for the rest of his career. Over the next decade, he played all but seven games with the Hurricanes and retired in 2008 as the longest-serving player. He spent fully half of his 20 years in the league with the Hartford/Carolina organization.

His career culminated in 2006 when the 'Canes won an unlikely Stanley Cup. Not flashy and never the subject of the nightly highlight reels, Wesley nonetheless played the game with tenacity and competitive fire every night. His 1,457 career games in the regular season ranks him among the all-time leaders in that category for defencemen, and he remained with the Hurricanes as a member of its hockey personnel after retiring.

CEREMONY

Just the second Hurricanes player to have his number retired (Ron Francis, number 10, was the first), Wesley was feted for half an hour prior to the Carolina-Boston game at the RBC Centre. He was accompanied by his wife, Barb, and children who not only supported him throughout the ceremony but actually sang the national anthem, too!

The evening began with Wesley skating onto the ice in full equipment to take a final lap. He called himself, "the skinny redhead from Red Deer," during his thank-you speech, before adding, with a smile, "little did we know we would end up in Mayberry."

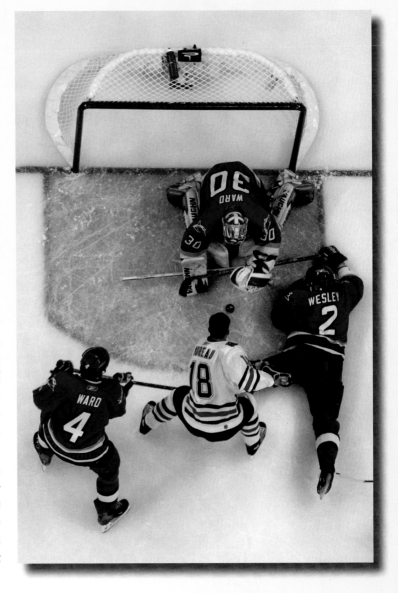

Players skated in the warm-up wearing number 2 sweaters, and during the game they all had "Wesley 2" patches on the front of their sweaters. The corners of the boards had the number 2 painted on them for this special occasion.

Among the gifts he received was a print depicting him with all his teams, with himself in a Carolina sweater hoisting the Stanley Cup.

THE GAME: Boston Bruins 5–Carolina Hurricanes 1

It wasn't the night hometown fans had hoped for as the Hurricanes were soundly beaten 5–1 by Wesley's former team. The 'Canes got the game's first goal midway through the first period courtesy of Matt Cullen, but soon after the wheels fell off. Blake Wheeler tied the game late in the period, the Bruins scored the only goal of the second, and in the third they pulled away with three unanswered markers late in the game.

"We just haven't played very well at home and it's embarrassing, it's frustrating to have your fans boo you when you leave the ice—not that it's not warranted—but it's certainly frustrating and a little bit humiliating," said Ray Whitney. "We didn't have that determination to get in front of their net as much as we should have. And then we give up breakaways. We certainly haven't finished off games at home very well lately."

3 HARRY HOWELL

NEW YORK RANGERS
FEBRUARY 22, 2009

Born: Hamilton, Ontario, December 28, 1932
Position: Defence
Shoots: Left
Height: 6'1"
Weight: 195 lbs.

HONOURS
- **Norris Trophy** 1967
- **NHL All-Star Game** 1954, 1963, 1964, 1965, 1967, 1968, 1970
- **NHL First All-Star Team** 1967
- **Hockey Hall of Fame** 1979
- **Name on Stanley Cup as a scout for Edmonton Oilers** 1990

NHL CAREER STATS

	Regular Season					Playoffs				
Years	GP	G	A	P	Pim	GP	G	A	P	Pim
1952–73	1,411	94	324	418	1,298	38	3	3	6	32

CAREER

Times sure do change. In 1949, the University of Michigan offered the teenaged Harry Howell a scholarship to play hockey there, an offer he summarily dismissed because he took his hockey seriously. Instead, he played for the Guelph Biltmores in Ontario junior and had a fine, four-year career there en route to the NHL with its sponsoring team, the New York Rangers.

In 1952, he began a 21-year career in the NHL, but despite his incredible longevity and individual skill, Howell also holds the record for most seasons and games played (1,411) without a Stanley Cup. Howell's Rangers of the 1950s were not a good team, struggling to make the playoffs at all, let alone advance to the Final. In all, he appeared in only 38 playoff games, but that doesn't diminish either his accomplishments or his contributions to the Rangers.

In 1955, about to start his fourth season, the 22-year-old Howell was named

team captain, the youngest in NHL history. A defenceman with some scoring skills, he was often the lone bright spot in the lineup, but he played every game as if it were game seven to decide the Cup.

Howell won the Norris Trophy for his outstanding play in the 1966–67 season, and upon receiving the award he promptly predicted what seemed obvious to everyone: this would be the last time anyone other than Bobby Orr would touch this trophy for many, many years. Still, Howell played in seven All-Star Games, and although the retiring of his number 3 in 2009 was a great honour, he had received an equally great one more than 40 years earlier.

On January 25, 1967, the Rangers had a Harry Howell Night to honour their longtime defenceman. It was a rare and special honour that very few Rangers had had bestowed upon them during the team's history. Nevertheless, it spoke to Howell's contributions to the team and his legacy for future generations.

9 ANDY BATHGATE

NEW YORK RANGERS
FEBRUARY 22, 2009

Born: Winnipeg, Manitoba, August 28, 1932
Position: Right wing
Shoots: Right
Height: 6'
Weight: 180 lbs.

HONOURS
- **Stanley Cup** 1964
- **Hart Trophy** 1959
- **NHL All-Star Game** 1957, 1958, 1959, 1960, 1961, 1962, 1963, 1964
- **First NHL All-Star Team** 1959, 1962
- **Hockey Hall of Fame** 1978

NHL CAREER STATS

	Regular Season					Playoffs				
Years	GP	G	A	P	Pim	GP	G	A	P	Pim
1952–71	1,069	349	624	973	624	54	21	14	35	76

CAREER

The most incredible part of Andy Bathgate's career is that he had one at all. On his first shift in junior hockey, with the Guelph Biltmores, he suffered an horrific knee injury that required a steel plate to repair and forced him to wear a brace the rest of his career. That his career lasted 17 NHL seasons is a miracle of sorts.

It was the slapshot that was Bathgate's bread and butter. He was arguably the first player to perfect its usage—well before Bobby Hull or Stan Mikita—and it was one of his shots that struck Montreal goalie Jacques Plante in the face on November 1, 1959, convincing the goalie to adopt a face mask.

Despite Bathgate's skill and shot, the Rangers were a dismal team during the 1950s and '60s and only occasionally made the playoffs. Bathgate scored 40 goals and finished third in league scoring in 1958–59. He won the Hart Trophy even though the team finished in fifth place. In 1961–62, proving he was more than just

a right winger with a big shot, he led the league in assists and points, but failed to win the Art Ross Trophy because Bobby Hull, with the same number of points, scored more goals.

A trade to Toronto near the end of the 1963–64 season proved lucky for Bathgate who then helped the Leafs win the Stanley Cup, the only one of his career.

CEREMONY

Sportscaster Sam Rosen emceed the event, and six former Rangers greats were on the Rangers-blue carpet at centre ice to honour both Howell and Bathgate: Rod Gilbert, Ed Giacomin, Mark Messier, Adam Graves, Brian Leetch, and Mike Richter.

Video tributes started the evening, after which 11 teammates of the honoured players from the 1950s and '60s were introduced: Andy Hebenton, Bill Gadsby, Bob Nevin, Vic Hadfield, Larry Popein, Earl Ingarfield, Dean Prentice, Arnie Brown, Eddie Shack, Red Sullivan, and Lou Fontinato. Then, members of other Original Six teams made an appearance: Red Kelly represented Detroit; Dick Duff for Montreal; Frank Mahovlich for Toronto; Stan Mikita for Chicago.

Lastly, the player's wives were introduced—Merle Bathgate and Marilyn Howell. Rod Gilbert, on behalf of the other retired-numbers players, gave the men watches, while Giacomin and Fontinato, on behalf of the organization, gave them cross-Canada train tours and an Alaksan cruise.

Gilbert then introduced Howell. "This night has been on my wish list for a long time," he began, before rattling off the player's lengthy and significant accomplishments. Howell then recalled Harry Howell Night all those years before when Sullivan and Fontinato drove out in a red 1967 Mercury Cougar.

Michal Roszival had been wearing the number 3 for the Rangers, but during the ceremony he removed his sweater to reveal a 33 and handed his 3 to Howell for perpetuity.

Bathgate was introduced by Adam Graves, who earlier in the month became the first number 9 to have his number retired. Graves called his elder, "the greatest player to ever wear number 9 for the New York Rangers."

Bathgate noted that 45 years ago on this day the Rangers had traded him to Toronto. "Who am I supposed to cheer for tonight?" he said. "I'm kidding." He continued: "There are two things I really dislike doing. One is backchecking, and the other is making public speaking appearances."

THE GAME: Toronto Maple Leafs 3–New York Rangers 2
The home side lost for the fifth time in six games, this in overtime to their Original Six rivals, the Maple Leafs.

The game was not particularly emotional, and the Leafs didn't score the first goal until the third period. The 1–0 lead caused fans to boo and jeer, directing much of their vitriol at coach Tom Renney and president/general manager Glen Sather.

The Rangers tied the game 1–1 on a Scott Gomez goal, but the Leafs went ahead again. Roszival earned a brief respite from the boo-birds when he tied the game with 39 seconds left in regulation to force overtime. Niklas Hagman netted the winner for the Leafs in the short overtime.

"I thought we played hard," Renney said. "We outshot this team significantly. We made a couple of mistakes in our game that we are going to continue to try to rectify. Anything drastic is outside what the needs are right now. We're going to keep playing hard, stay the course, keep working hard, go after wins."

Andy Hebenton, Andy Bathgate, Earl Ingarfield, Jack McCartain, and Vic Hadfield.

19

JOE
SAKIC

COLORADO AVALANCHE
OCTOBER 1, 2009

Born: Burnaby, British Columbia, July 7, 1969
Position: Centre
Shoots: Left
Height: 5'11"
Weight: 195 lbs.

HONOURS
- **Stanley Cup** 1996, 2001
- **Hart Trophy** 2001
- **Lady Byng Trophy** 2001
- **Lester B. Pearson Award** 2001
- **Conn Smythe Trophy** 1996
- **Won gold medal with Canada at Olympics** 2002

NHL CAREER STATS

	Regular Season					Playoffs				
Years	GP	G	A	P	Pim	GP	G	A	P	Pim
1988–2009	1,378	625	1,016	1,641	614	172	84	104	188	78

CAREER

One of the classiest players in the history of the game—with skills to match—Joe Sakic retired in 2009. This was a deep blow to the NHL for which he played exactly 20 years. He left the game near the top of the all-time lists in games played, goals, assists, and points, and played his entire career with one organization.

Sakic's life changed forever on December 30, 1986. Playing junior with Swift Current, the team bus crashed on its way home from a game, killing four teammates. If nothing else, that tragedy taught Sakic never to take anything for granted, and he didn't.

In 1988, he was drafted by Quebec and averaged nearly a point a game with a weak team. But he was its nucleus, and as he developed the team improved. He reached 100 points in three of the next four years, and the team continued to use high draft picks to select the best young talent available. In 1992, Sakic was named

and immediately after the war, first in 1944 and then two years later when many of the top players still hadn't returned to civilian life.

Bouchard was named captain in 1948, a responsibility he held until retiring in 1956. Such was the strength of the team that even though he left the game after winning the Cup for a fourth time (he also won in 1953), the team won for the next four years as well.

But it was his years with Harvey for which he is best remembered. Harvey broke into the league during the 1947–48 season and soon the two formed a perfect pair. Harvey was the brilliant puck rusher while Bouchard hung back in case of a turnover. Harvey got the glory, but Bouchard earned respect for his ability in his own end of the ice and his play without the puck. He was a prototypical defensive defenceman.

16

ELMER
LACH

MONTREAL CANADIENS
DECEMBER 10, 1975
AND DECEMBER 4, 2009

Born: Nokomis, Saskatchewan, January 22, 1918
Position: Centre
Shoots: Left
Height: 5'10"
Weight: 165 lbs.

HONOURS
- **Stanley Cup** 1944, 1946, 1953
- **Hart Trophy** 1945
- **Art Ross Trophy** 1948 (also led league in points 1945)
- **NHL All-Star game** 1948, 1952, 1953
- **Hockey Hall of Fame** 1966

NHL CAREER STATS

Years	Regular Season					Playoffs				
	GP	G	A	P	Pim	GP	G	A	P	Pim
1940–54	664	215	408	623	478	76	19	45	64	36

CAREER

The fact that 91-year-old Elmer Lach lived to see his number 16 retired is an achievement in itself, but the fact he had a career worthy of such an honour was a greater miracle. Time and again Lach suffered serious injury, only to bounce back and play better than ever.

He made his NHL debut with the Montreal Canadiens in November 1940, showing both imagination with the puck and a competitive edge few opponents could match. The first game of the next year, however, was his last for that season as he suffered a broken elbow that required almost 12 months of recuperation.

After an excellent third season, coach Dick Irvin put Lach on a line with Toe Blake and Maurice Richard. So was born the Punch Line, so called for its scoring ability. Their dangerous offence led the way to Lach's first Stanley Cup, and the next season, 1944–45, he led the league in assists (54) and points (80).

The Punch Line helped secure another Cup in 1946, but in February 1947, tragedy nearly struck. Lach fell head first to the ice after being checked, suffering a serious skull fracture and, in the estimation of doctors, ending his career then and there. Lach refused to believe as much, rallied, and came back not only to play well but win the scoring title again. More amazing, he did so on the final day of the season, scoring twice and beating the Rangers' Buddy O'Connor 61 points to 60.

The next year, a broken jaw cost him half a season, but his final great moment occurred during the 1953 playoffs. That year, in the Final, he scored at 1:22 of overtime in game five against Boston to win the Cup for the Canadiens.

CEREMONY

As part of the Montreal Canadiens' 100th anniversary celebrations, the team retired two more numbers, Emile "Butch" Bouchard's 3 and Elmer Lach's 16. The 90-year-old Bouchard used a wheelchair for the ceremony at centre ice, surrounded by many of the greatest living Habs in the red carpet ceremony, notably Yvan Cournoyer, Guy Lafleur, Bob Gainey, Ken Dryden, and Patrick Roy. Current Habs players Andrei Markov and Ryan O'Byrne helped hitch the banners to their hooks and then the new numbers were hoisted into the rafters.

O'Byrne, who had been wearing number 3 all year for the Canadiens, then took the sweater off and gave it to Bouchard, revealing a new sweater bearing the number 20 that would now be his. The sold-out crowd at the Bell Centre gave both nonagenarians a lengthy ovation in tribute to their great honour.

Lach's number was retired twice. The first time occurred on December 10, 1975, when he and Henri Richard, the other great wearer of number 16, were feted at centre ice of the Forum. It was a low-key affair, and since Richard was fresher in everyone's mind, he got the lion's share of the attention.

It was more than 55 years after his final game that the 91-year-old Lach had his number retired for a second time. At the time of the ceremony, he was the oldest living Canadiens player.

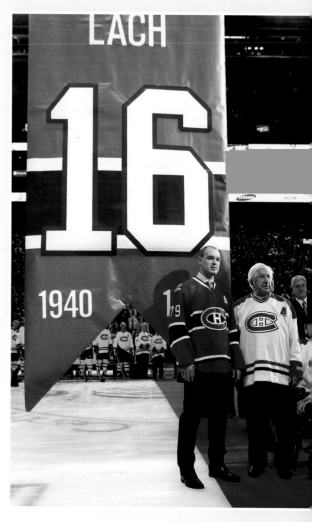

More incredibly, Lach knew nothing of the honour until the morning of the occasion. Owner Geoff Molson and team president Pierre Boivin showed up at Lach's home at 9 a.m. that Friday morning to take him to a photo shoot for the Punch Line at the Bell Centre. The plan was to drive him home after, but that he and his wife, Lise, would be needed to participate in the pre-game ceremonies to celebrate the centennial.

THE GAME: Montreal Canadiens 5–Boston Bruins 1

If there were one game in team history Montreal simply could not lose, this was it. No century celebration could end in a loss, and the players knew it. And so it was that the Canadiens got the first goal, ran up a healthy lead, and then played shutdown hockey in the final period.

Montreal's Jaroslav Spacek got the only goal of the first period, but Mike Cammalleri, a free agent signing in the off-season, rattled in three goals in the second period while Glen Metropolit added a fifth. Only a Boston goal from Vladimir Sobotka on a deflection early in the third spoiled Carey Price's shutout.

"We really wanted to win this one," Price said after. "We were pumped up watching [Lach and Bouchard] out there and chatting with vets who won championships. We wanted to win for them as well."

Andrei Markov, number 79 of the Montreal Canadiens, stands next to Elmer Lach and his retirement banner during the ceremony.

27 TEPPO NUMMINEN

WINNIPEG JETS AND PHOENIX COYOTES
JANUARY 30, 2010

Born: Tampere, Finland, July 3, 1968
Position: Defence
Shoots: Right
Height: 6'1"
Weight: 195 lbs.

HONOURS
- **NHL All-Star Game** 1999, 2000, 2001
- **Three Olympic medals**—1988 silver, 1998 bronze, 2006 silver

NHL CAREER STATS

| | Regular Season | | | | | Playoffs | | | | |
Years	GP	G	A	P	Pim	GP	G	A	P	Pim
1988–2009	1,372	117	520	637	513	82	9	14	23	28

CAREER

Drafted 29th overall by the Winnipeg Jets in 1986, Teppo Numminen went on to set a record for games played by a European in the NHL and still holds the games-played record and most points by a defenceman for Winnipeg/Phoenix. By the time he retired in the summer of 2009, he was the last active player from that '86 draft.

He remained in Finland for two years before joining the Jets in September 1988, the team for which he played all eight years before it moved to Arizona in the summer of 1996. A skilled defenceman at both ends of the ice, Numminen was known for his calm under pressure and his ability to make the right decision with or without the puck. He stayed with the Coyotes for seven more years, making it a total of 15 with the franchise. He was named captain in 2001, but in the summer of 2003 he was traded to Dallas in a one-for-one deal for Mike Sillinger.

On November 13, 2006, he played in his 1,252nd game to surpass Jari Kurri for most NHL games by a European, and his final total of 1,372 stood as a record until it was broken by Detroit defenceman Nicklas Lidstrom. The figures show that Numminen played only one game in 2007–08, with Buffalo, but that was the result of heart surgery in the summer of 2007, which kept him off ice virtually the entire season.

Numminen goes down as perhaps the finest Finnish defenceman of all time, and he is one of a small group of Finns to have won three Olympic medals in hockey. He also played at five World Championships for Suomi, both World Cup tournaments (in 1996 and 2004), and a World Junior (U20) Championship.

CEREMONY

Numminen's number 27 was officially retired by the Phoenix Coyotes on January 30, 2010, before a home game against the New York Rangers at Jobing.com Arena. Although the team was in the middle of being purchased and attendance had been weak most of the season, some 16,687 fans turned out to honour one of their favourites.

The Coyotes call their retired numbers a "Ring of Honor," and Numminen joined Bobby Hull (9), Dale Hawerchuk (10), and Thomas Steen (25). Numminen became the first player who actually played for the Coyotes to be so honoured as Hull, Hawerchuk, and Steen had their careers with the Jets. Interestingly, Numminen becomes the first number 27 to be retired in NHL history (excepting the Leafs' "honouring" of Darryl Sittler's 27).

The pre-game ceremony was hosted by the voice of Coyotes television and radio, Todd Walsh. Numminen was accompanied to centre ice by his wife, three children, and brother. The ceremony included a video tribute highlighting Numminen's career, as well as a message from Shane Doan, who succeeded Numminen as team captain. Doan ended on a light note, calling Numminen "the sexiest man in Finland."

THE GAME: Phoenix Coyotes 3–New York Rangers 2

Buoyed by the pre-game ceremonies, the Coyotes came out flying and built a 3–0 lead on Rangers goalie Chad Johnson after the first period. Johnson was subbing for Henrik Lundqvist. Goals came from captain Doan as well as Finnish newcomer Sami Lepisto (the first of his career) and Dane Mikkel Bodker. Bodker had been a surprise star with the team the previous year but had played most of the season in the minors before being recalled less than 24 hours before this game.

A scoreless second period gave way to some tense moments for the home side in the third as the Rangers rallied with two goals, one each from Marian Gaborik and Sean Avery against backup Jason LaBarbera. Late in the game Gaborik hit the post on a Phoenix power play, missing tying the game by mere inches. The Coyotes, however, held on, to solidify their playoff position in the Western Conference while the Rangers lost for the seventh time in their last 10 games.

ACKNOWLEDGEMENTS

I'D LIKE TO THANK THOSE who have helped with this book both practically and emotionally. First, to publisher Jordan Fenn for continued enthusiasm and support. Also to his assistant, the ever-patient and excellent Sheila Douglas. To editor Carol Harrison and designer Marjike Friesen. To several people who helped specifically with information about players and their retired numbers. In Montreal, Carl Lavigne, Dick Irvin, Red Fisher, and Frank Selke (okay, he's a Toronto boy!). To Nicole Bouchard in Quebec City and Murray Costello in Ottawa. In Boston, special thanks to Johnny Bucyk and Johnny MacKenzie, as well as Cole Parsons and Heidi Holland. Of course, to everybody at the now formally named Doc Seaman Hockey Hall of Fame Resource Centre not-so-far-out on Kipling Avenue, namely Miragh Bitove, Craig Campbell, Phil Pritchard, Izak Westgate, and Steve Poirier. To Paul Patskou for meticulous proofreading down the stretch. And a special thanks to Kelly Masse at HHOF for such enormous help in leading me in several directions for various pieces of information. Wow, she really was instrumental in the creation of this book. (Do I have to say any more or is that good enough for now?) To my agent Dean Cooke and his assistant, Mary Hu. To good friend Szymon Szemberg, eternal Habs fan who has come over to the light side and embraced "honouring" numbers instead of retiring them. And lastly, to my family—Liz, Ian, Zach, Emily, and my mom, for leading me to number 6, and my wife, Jane, who could care less about retired numbers (and that's okay, too).

BY THE NUMBERS
(NAMES ORDERED BY SWEATER NUMBER)

1
Bernie Parent
Terry Sawchuk
Glenn Hall
Ed Giacomin
Jacques Plante

2
Eddie Shore
Doug Harvey
Al MacInnis
Glen Wesley
Rick Ley
Tim Horton
Brian Leetch

3
Lionel Hitchman
J. C. Tremblay
Ken Daneyko
Pierre Pilote
Harry Howell
Bob Gassoff
Al Hamilton
Keith Magnuson
Emile "Butch" Bouchard

4
Jean Béliveau
Bobby Orr
Scott Stevens
Barry Ashbee
Aurèle Joliat

5
Dit Clapper
Bill Barilko
Bernie Geoffrion
Denis Potvin
Rod Langway

6
Ace Bailey

7
Howie Morenz
Yvon Labre
Phil Esposito
Rick Martin
Paul Coffey
Rod Gilbert
Bill Barber
Ted Lindsay
Neal Broten

8
Barclay Plager
Bill Goldsworthy
Cam Neely
Marc Tardif
Frank Finnigan

9
Maurice Richard
Bobby Hull
Lanny McDonald
Adam Graves
Andy Bathgate
Gordie Howe
Johnny Bucyk
Clark Gillies
Glenn Anderson

10
Guy Lafleur
Ron Francis
Alex Delvecchio
Dale Hawerchuk

11
Brian Sutter
Mark Messier
Gilbert Perreault
Mike Gartner

12
Stan Smyl
Yvan Cournoyer
Sid Abel
Dickie Moore

14
René Robert

15
Milt Schmidt

16
Henri Richard
Marcel Dionne
Pat LaFontaine
Trevor Linden
Bobby Clarke
Michel Goulet
Brett Hull
Elmer Lach

17
Jari Kurri
Rod Brind'Amour

18
Dave Taylor
Danny Gare
Denis Savard
Serge Savard

19
Bill Masterton
Bryan Trottier
Larry Robinson
Markus Naslund
John McKenzie
Steve Yzerman
Joe Sakic

20	Luc Robitaille	**31**	Billy Smith Grant Fuhr
21	Stan Mikita Michel Brière	**32**	Dale Hunter
22	Mike Bossy	**33**	Patrick Roy
23	Bob Nystrom Bob Gainey	**35**	Tony Esposito Mike Richter
24	Bernie Federko Terry O'Reilly	**66**	Mario Lemieux
25	Thomas Steen	**77**	Ray Bourque
26	Peter Stastny	**99**	Wayne Gretzky
27	Teppo Numminen		
29	Ken Dryden		
30	Rogie Vachon Mike Vernon		

BY TEAM
(ORDERED NUMERICALLY BY TEAM CONDUCTING THE CEREMONY)

BOSTON BRUINS

2	Eddie Shore
3	Lionel Hitchman
4	Bobby Orr
5	Dit Clapper
7	Phil Esposito
8	Cam Neely
9	Johnny Bucyk
15	Milt Schmidt
24	Terry O'Reilly
77	Ray Bourque

BUFFALO SABRES

2	Tim Horton
7	Rick Martin
11	Gilbert Perreault
14	René Robert
16	Pat LaFontaine
18	Danny Gare

CALGARY FLAMES

9	Lanny McDonald
30	Mike Vernon

CAROLINA HURRICANES

2	Glen Wesley
10	Ron Francis
17	Rod Brind'Amour

CHICAGO BLACKHAWKS

1	Glenn Hall
3	Keith Magnuson
3	Pierre Pilote
9	Bobby Hull
18	Denis Savard
21	Stan Mikita
35	Tony Esposito

COLORADO AVALANCHE

19	Joe Sakic
33	Patrick Roy
77	Ray Bourque

DALLAS STARS

7	Neal Broten

DETROIT RED WINGS

1	Terry Sawchuk
7	Ted Lindsay
9	Gordie Howe
10	Alex Delvecchio
12	Sid Abel
19	Steve Yzerman

EDMONTON OILERS

3	Al Hamilton
7	Paul Coffey
9	Glenn Anderson
11	Mark Messier
17	Jari Kurri
31	Grant Fuhr
99	Wayne Gretzky

HARTFORD WHALERS

2	Rick Ley
9	Gordie Howe
19	John McKenzie

LOS ANGELES KINGS

16	Marcel Dionne
18	Dave Taylor
20	Luc Robitaille
30	Rogie Vachon
99	Wayne Gretzky

MINNESOTA NORTH STARS

8	Bill Goldsworthy
19	Bill Masterton

MONTREAL CANADIENS

1	Jacques Plante
2	Doug Harvey
3	Emile "Butch" Bouchard
4	Jean Béliveau
4	Aurèle Joliat

5	Bernie Geoffrion
7	Howie Morenz
9	Maurice Richard
10	Guy Lafleur
12	Yvan Cournoyer
12	Dickie Moore
16	Henri Richard
16	Elmer Lach
18	Serge Savard
19	Larry Robinson
23	Bob Gainey
29	Ken Dryden
33	Patrick Roy

NEW JERSEY DEVILS

3	Ken Daneyko
4	Scott Stevens

NEW YORK ISLANDERS

5	Denis Potvin
9	Clark Gillies
19	Bryan Trottier
22	Mike Bossy
23	Bob Nystrom
31	Billy Smith

NEW YORK RANGERS

1	Ed Giacomin
2	Brian Leetch
3	Harry Howell
7	Rod Gilbert
9	Adam Graves
9	Andy Bathgate
11	Mark Messier
35	Mike Richter

OTTAWA SENATORS

8	Frank Finnigan

PHILADELPHIA FLYERS

1	Bernie Parent
4	Barry Ashbee
7	Bill Barber
16	Bobby Clarke

PHOENIX COYOTES

10	Dale Hawerchuk
27	Teppo Numminen

PITTSBURGH PENGUINS

19	Bobby Hull
21	Michel Brière
66	Mario Lemieux

QUEBEC NORDIQUES

3	J. C. Tremblay
8	Marc Tardif
16	Michel Goulet
26	Peter Stastny

ST. LOUIS BLUES

2	Al MacInnis
3	Bob Gassoff
8	Barclay Plager
11	Brian Sutter
16	Brett Hull
24	Bernie Federko

TORONTO MAPLE LEAFS

5	Bill Barilko
6	Ace Bailey

VANCOUVER CANUCKS

12	Stan Smyl
16	Trevor Linden
19	Markus Naslund

WASHINGTON CAPITALS

5	Rod Langway
7	Yvon Labre
11	Mike Gartner
32	Dale Hunter

WINNIPEG JETS

9	Bobby Hull
25	Thomas Steen

TORONTO MAPLE LEAFS' HONOURED NUMBERS

(Instead of retiring numbers and taking them out of circulation, the Maple Leafs "honour" numbers by raising a banner to the rafters of the Air Canada Centre with the player's name and number on it and putting a dedicatory patch on the current player who wears that number.)

1
Johnny Bower—March 11, 1995
Turk Broda—March 11, 1995

4
Clarence "Happy" Day—October 4, 2006
Red Kelly—October 4, 2006

7
Francis "King" Clancy—November 21, 1995
Miles "Tim" Horton—November 21, 1995

9
Ted Kennedy—October 3, 1993
Charlie Conacher—February 28, 1998

10
Syl Apps—October 3, 1993
George Armstrong—February 28, 1998

17
Wendel Clark—November 22, 2008

21
Borje Salming—October 4, 2006

27
Frank Mahovlich—October 3, 2001
Darryl Sittler—February 8, 2003

93
Doug Gilmour—January 31, 2009

PHOTOGRAPHY CREDITS

All photographs appear with the permission of Getty Images except those listed below.

Ace Bailey, page 12: Hockey Hall of Fame
Lionel Hitchman, page 14 and 15: Hockey Hall of Fame
Frank Finnigan, page 110: Hockey Hall of Fame
Frank Finnigan, page 111: Imperial Oil—Turofsky/Hockey Hall of Fame
Bill Barilko, page 112: Imperial Oil—Turofsky/Hockey Hall of Fame
Michel Brière, page 161: Hockey Hall of Fame